Bou...

LONG ISLAN...

ASSOCIATED FOODS

OCEANSIDE

SAND POINT CONSUMER ELECTRONICS

Beach Street

BROWER AVE VIDEO

7-11

GOOD AND PLENTY

Company Road

KENNEDY ESTATES

MEADOW PARK

BOUNDARY BAY LANES

THE CREEKSIDE

FIRST FEDERAL BANK

ad

BLUEBEARD SCRAP

THE BACK LOT

ESTES INDUSTRIAL PARK

.5 m

.8 km

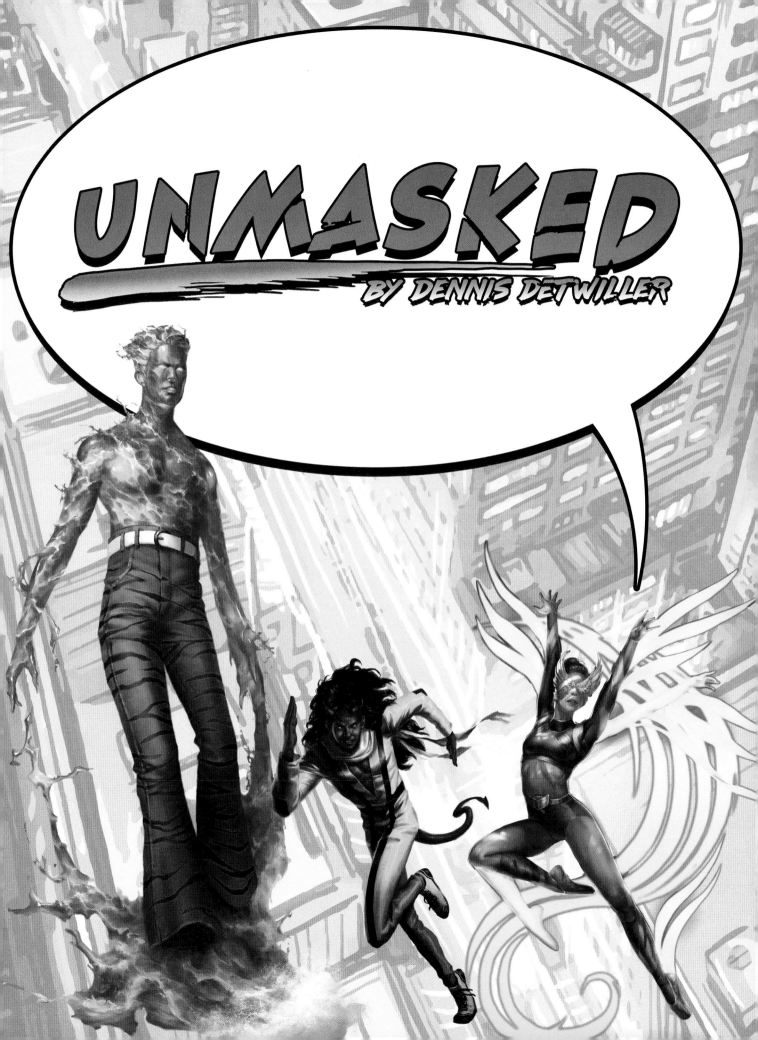

CREDITS

Writer/Designer: Dennis Detwiller
Creative Director: Monte Cook
Managing Editor: Shanna Germain
Editor: Elisa Mader
Proofreader: Adam Heine
Art Director: Bear Weiter
Graphic Designer: Zoa Smalley
Cover Artist: Guido Kuip

Artists

Jacob Atienza, Marco Caradonna, Felipe Escobar, Kurt Komoda, Brandon Leach, Raph Lomotan, Patrick McEvoy, Mirco Paganessi, Roberto Pitturru, Cory Trego-Erdner, Lie Setiawan, Joe Slucher, Shane Tyree, Cathy Wilkins

Cartographer

Hugo Solis

Monte Cook Games Editorial Board

Scott C. Bourgeois, David Wilson Brown, Eric Coates, Gareth Hodges, Mila Irek, Jeremy Land, Laura Wilkinson, Marina Wold, George Ziets

As we agree with the growing consensus that "they" can and should be used as a gender-neutral, singular English language pronoun when one is needed, we have adopted that as the style in our products. If you see this grammatical construction, it is intentional.

For Hilary, Maya, and Henry, who make my world.

MonteCook
Games

TABLE OF CONTENTS

IN THE BEGINNING WAS THE WORD (BUBBLE)

Comic books and superheroes have always been a part of my life. You might not know this, but growing up, I aspired to become a comic book artist. As a teenager, I stalked unfortunate Marvel artists around Manhattan. Eventually, I was lucky enough to have one take pity on me (they know who they are—*cough* thanks, Mr. Budiansky *cough*). It took a lot of time and a lot of practice, but I finally made it. I went to art school, and did my time inking and penciling for DC Comics, Marvel, and other comic companies back in the dim-dull days when you had to do everything by hand. There, I learned a secret, vital lesson about comic books. Are you ready? The secret is this:

In 1992, it was nearly impossible to make a living in New York City as a comic book artist.

Still, comics carried me through my teenage years. I vividly recall reading the first issue of *Watchmen* in Italian class in 1986 while Mr. Peppini conjugated at me, *ascolto, ascolti, ascolta.* I remember waiting for the delivery of the long-delayed issue of *The Dark Knight Returns* and reading it fresh out of the packing box. Picking up the masterpiece that is *Arzach* by Moebius for the first time. Seeing the culmination of the Claremont/Byrne run of the *Uncanny X-Men.* To say these experiences shaped my creative life would be a massive understatement.

When life got difficult (and it often was in New York in the 1980s), comic books were always there for me. And, amazingly, the comics appeared to change *along* with me. The switch to more serious comics with dark, "real" story lines coincided with my teenage years, and looking back, they meshed perfectly with my shift in world view.

Today, of course, it's an embarrassment of riches. Every second film is a superhero movie. Dark heroes are so old hat that they went out of style and have come back into style again. There are so many superhero films, comics, and games that I can't keep them all straight.

Unmasked is an attempt to capture the madness of my teenage life and combine it with the power fantasy of the classic superhero that helped me to get through those years. Put those two together, mix in a little horror, and you get *Unmasked.*

Unmasked is designed to take the players back to that time in their lives when anything seemed possible, and to give them the power to explore what life would be like if their characters could have reached out and shaped the world. After all, teens are violent, loving, insightful, driven, disinterested, and full of want on a level that an adult can only dream of approaching. They're fairly thrumming with energy, self-aggrandizement, and self-hate. They hope for the best possible future, and they hope for an apocalypse. I know, because I was there, too.

We all were there, once. We've all felt that power.

We've all worn a mask.

Dennis Detwiller

PART 1: ORIGINS
A KID CALLED THE END OF THE WORLD

Dude. I knew it was you. You don't recognize me. Yet. That's normal. Nothing to worry about. Sit down. I'll tell you just the same, then, when you come back here again.

Uh. That . . . must seem confusing.

Never mind. It'll make sense later.

Sit down. You may not know it yet, but we're the same. Soon, you'll be one of us. I mean, you already are, and here I go again. NOT IMPORTANT.

Since you told me to, I'll tell you the story that my mask tells me every night. Ready?

Once, there was a hole in the world. Time fell into it. Things happened, or seemed to. History. Science. Politics. The Muppet Show. People lived and died and thought and fought and did a million different things. They thought that was it. They thought that was everything.

But—

When everything had been paved and each horizon fixed with a camera, when there was nothing left inside, our brains spilled out. All that was left then was the end of the world, and it didn't come on like anyone thought. It crept. It moved through the places people couldn't see, and then, at the end of a place that everyone thought was real, finally, the hole in the world made us.

We've come to overturn it all. Or fix it. I guess it depends on how you're feeling.

The world can't be made without someone to see it, nor can it be destroyed without a witness. That's why we're here. That's why we can do what we can do. That's why the masks can talk to us.

How do you feel when you find that the world is not outside you at all? How do you adjust when you learn that everything is just the inside sent outward? That it can be retracted? That it can be overridden? Ended?

How do you feel when you know that reality is just an agreement between motes of thought floating in nothingness?

You'll see soon.

Have you made your mask yet? How do you feel now? Right now? Look inside and see it. Close your eyes. See the hole. See the nothing.

That's you.

You are the end of the world.
Welcome home, dude.

CHAPTER 1

THE WORLD OF UNMASKED

While Unmasked is a fully realized setting, you will need a copy of the Cypher System Rulebook in order to play or run the game.

Prester John, page 151

If you grew up in the 1980s as I did, or if you turned on a TV anytime in the last thirty years and watched a John Hughes film, you've seen the backdrop of *Unmasked*. The town. Disaffected teens. The mall. High school. Welcome to America, 1986.

But something else is seeping in from the edges. Normalcy and complacency are secretly being replaced by something . . . more. It always starts the same way, though the teens who are the player characters (PCs) don't know it yet. First, they begin to see things; items and places are marked as if they held some special importance. Then they have the dreams. Of a being called Prester John moving across the country, devising dark plans, and gathering followers. And finally, the teens make a mask. Each mask is different. When they wear the mask, they unleash their mask-forms and *become someone else*, someone powerful that can make impossible things happen. They can fly. Or teleport. Or lift an economy car over their head with one hand. But *only* when they wear the mask.

More importantly, the mask tells them things . . .

Even in this small town, quietly and among a select group, sides are already being drawn.

THE SECRET OF UNMASKED

In *Unmasked*, the player characters are teenagers who are somehow *different*. One day in 1986, they wake and find they can see the secret meaning hidden in everyday objects. A stop sign, a Bic pen, the clock on the wall of the gym—each seems to practically shine with power for no apparent reason. Even more fascinating, they can see other teens illuminated by the same secret light they have found within themselves.

Each teen independently feels a drive to collect items, to fashion a mask from those objects, and once that mask is finished, to

wear it. When the PC wears the mask, they become *someone else* and have amazing abilities formerly seen only in the pages of comic books. In their mask, it's almost as if they're a different person, as the mask itself appears to have a personality, drive, and even goals of its own. While the teens always have the unusual vision that allows them to sense special items and people, the teens' other powers only manifest when they become their "mask-form" while wearing their mask. If the mask is lost or destroyed, those powers may be gone forever.

These teens soon begin to realize that they are not alone in having these miraculous abilities. Others in the world hit the ground running that morning in 1986 with these newfound powers, and those forces are already in motion. Their goals and methods are, for the most part, as inscrutable as the source of these nascent powers.

BACK TO, UH . . . THE PAST?

The 1980s are everywhere. Even today, the decade creeps in through our music, our TV and movies, our clothes, and even our hairstyles. I don't think we'll ever truly escape it. Looking back on that time today, it's clear why: it was arguably the apex of Western civilization. There was a clarity of purpose, West versus East, that few could argue against.

The world was trapped in a viselike grip between the United States and the Soviet Union, each ready (if the need ever arose) to end civilization in eighteen minutes and change. America was a bastion of freedom, the Soviet Union an irresistible force. Where the Soviets pushed, we slid back, and where we overtook them, they retreated and reinforced. The Middle East and Central America were the fault points, with occasional slips that threatened to escalate until the Earth was a radioactive tomb.

The teenagers of the 1980s were caught up

in this zeitgeist like no other generation. They were inheriting a world on the brink of nuclear annihilation. A collapsing manufacturing base in North America. An explosion of weird and eclectic music pouring in from around the world. Clothes and cars and a world of *global possibilities* were suddenly present in every American town, beckoning these young people to a bigger, stranger world than their parents could ever imagine. Escape was possible on a level never before seen by any previous generation. From cable television to Japanese *manga*, the country was making its first stumbling, fledgling steps into what eventually would become the global Internet.

Didn't grow up in the 1980s? Unfamiliar with that decade? Even if it feels like you are, it's likely you're not. If you've watched *Ferris Bueller's Day Off* or MTV, you're halfway there. Below you can find lists of essential viewing and listening for *Unmasked* (note that some examples are from a little before or after 1986):

MOVIES

Back to the Future
Better Off Dead
The Breakfast Club
E.T. the Extra-Terrestrial
Fast Times at Ridgemont High
Ferris Bueller's Day Off
Fright Night
The Goonies
Gremlins
Heathers
Hiding Out
The Legend of Billie Jean

OTHER TIMES, OTHER PLACES

Unmasked is set in the 1980s for many reasons: it's a time rich in media and feeling that has been committed to thousands of films, albums, books, and comics about teens and their struggles navigating the trials of life. It was in the 1980s that the classic comic story of superpowered youth became most popular (see any of the endless X-Men comics). The 1980s were also a time when the world stared down the threat of nuclear annihilation almost with complacency, as well as a period of constant upheaval and change in the world of entertainment and communication. These concepts set the tone, but Unmasked can happen anywhere, and at any time . . . The game, after all, is the game master's to create. While nearly any time period will work, here are some specific ideas for setting Unmasked in other eras:

1920s: Prohibition, flappers, jazz, and rampant crime? This would be a perfect, violent time for the prodigies to show up and strut their stuff. You'll notice the tone is not too different from a 1980s scenario, with youth gone wild, a world on the brink of something much worse than the last world war, and huge advances in communications and media. Just add superpowers and mix.

1960s: Protests, counterculture, drugs, and music! The 1960s resembled the 1980s insomuch as the threat of nuclear war was a very real one, but differed in the response of the young people. They did not withdraw nihilistically, but instead reached out and tried to change the world. What if they could use their powers to help the cause of peace and end war?

Modern Day: A war between conservatives and liberals, a renewed threat in Russia and China, and an ever-connected, ever-commenting youth culture would make a rich setting for Unmasked. However, it should be noted that today there would be no lag for the discovery of prodigies as there would have been in previous eras. In the 1920s, 1960s, or even the 1980s, it might take months or even years before the monumental advent of the prodigies was revealed to the general public through the media (especially as prodigies strive to keep themselves a secret). In the modern day, a single appearance by a superpowered teen in public, and the world—through the magic of the internet—would know immediately. And once something appears on the internet, it's there forever.

HOW TO USE THIS BOOK

This book is broken into parts dealing with different aspects of the world of *Unmasked*.

In Part 2: Prodigies, players learn how to create their teen PCs as well as the amazing mask-forms that their teens can manifest. They build and customize powers, assign stat Pools, and pick abilities to create a teenager that can put on a mask and become an amazing super-being.

In Part 3: Welcome to 1986, the game master (GM) learns how to build the "anytown" setting for their *Unmasked* game or campaign. Just what makes a small town? How many police officers are there? How big is the fire department? What is the high school like? Where do the teens live? This section also delves more into the big-picture questions: What are the prodigies? Why are they here? Who—or what—is the threat they face?

In Part 4: Welcome to Boundary Bay, New York, we have built a ready-to-go setting for *Unmasked*. Within this section is everything you need to run a full *Unmasked* campaign. It's filled with dozens of locations, NPCs, and mask-forms, as well as tons of adventure hooks. It also defines three big threats: Prester John; its servants, the Faceless; and the federal response to oddities, the Circus.

In Part 5: GM's Toolbox, we give tips and tricks on how to best structure and run *Unmasked*—ways to keep your players on their toes, to pull the rug out from under them (in a fun way!), and to continually stoke the mystery of what their power means. We also present an adventure set in Boundary Bay, New York: Mister Monster.

Unlike many hard-and-fast settings, *Unmasked* offers a ton of options for each of these selections, and encourages you, as the GM, to choose or fashion your own with the guidelines presented. This book is a toolkit that you should feel free to take wholesale, pick piecemeal, or mix and match as needed. It is a resource to make *Unmasked* into something *you* create.

Part 2: Prodigies, page 13

Part 3: Welcome to 1986, page 65

Part 4: Welcome to Boundary Bay, New York, page 99

Part 5: GM's Toolbox, page 153

Mister Monster, page 178

CHAPTER 2

UNMASKED OVERVIEW

While this game book is jam-packed with the details of a fully realized game world, that world runs on the game engine of the Cypher System. So, you'll need the *Cypher System Rulebook* as well as this book to run an *Unmasked* game.

This book presents an entire superpowered setting for the Cypher System. It includes tons of nonplayer characters (NPCs), ideas on how to construct an *Unmasked* game and campaign, and rules for building new PCs, as well as a great grab-and-go adventure generator, a weird threat creator, and new ideas, descriptors, foci, and cyphers. It also introduces four new types for the game—the Smasher, the Thinker, the Mover, and the Changer—as well as examples and ideas on how to bend, warp, and twist the types and focus abilities from the *Cypher System Rulebook* to fit the *Unmasked* setting, along with extensive ideas on how to make your supers *unique*.

Below is a high-level summary of the roles the PCs take in the world of *Unmasked*, the nature of the masks themselves, the PCs' abilities to see *beyond*, and the importance and meaning of the items that appear to glow.

PRODIGIES

The term "prodigy" is used in this book to describe the superpowered teenagers of the *Unmasked* setting who make masks and can bend reality with amazing abilities. Masks can let their wearers fly, deflect bullets, survive terrible injuries, and do much, much more. It is important to note that in the default setting, the world is completely unaware of the existence of prodigies. As such, this term is anything the GM wants it to be—from a convenient reference term in the book, to something the teens call themselves, to a term picked up by the news when (or if) the reports of the teens' powers break worldwide.

Prodigies—who are all teenagers—can sense places of note, items of significance (which they call mementos), and most importantly, one another. Each of these sources seems to glow with an inner light that reflects in its intensity how powerful the location, object, or person is. Only the prodigies can perceive this glow. Thus, in just a few days after the prodigies "wake," they begin intermingling, questioning one another, and trying to puzzle out just what is going on.

THE MASKS

Every prodigy makes a mask. Though the prodigies each create one independently, the process they use to make the masks is always the same. First, they find themselves drawn to various mementos. Not only do these particular items flare with a light visible only to the prodigy; the items also seem to flicker, flash, and grow in power the closer the prodigy comes to them.

Throughout this book, you'll see page references to various items accompanied by this symbol. These are page references to the *Cypher System Rulebook*, where you can find additional details about that rule, ability, creature, or concept. Often, it will be necessary to look up the referenced item in the rulebook, especially if the item is a descriptor or focus ability that isn't replicated in *Unmasked*. Other times, it might not be necessary to reference the item, but doing so will provide useful information for character creation and gameplay.

Mementos, page 168

After collecting them, the prodigy fashions a mask from the individual items. When this is done, the mementos cease being individual items. Instead, the mask alone glows with that power only prodigies can see. It's almost as if these special mementos combine to create something bigger and stronger than the individual elements. This is a one-way process.

When worn, this mask transforms the teen into a being with powers and abilities beyond anything the world has ever seen before. It can even transform the wearer physically into someone who looks completely different from their normal form. The powers the masks manifest are unique, tailored to the personality that made them, but they can also prove exhausting and leave the teen feeling wiped out after each use.

Wearing a mask for too long is like running a marathon, or going for a few days without sleep. This is a hard-and-fast rule, though prodigies sometimes resist it. No one can wear their mask 24/7. Although because the PCs are teenagers, they of course all try.

Cyphers, page 340

MEMENTOS (CYPHERS)

Cyphers in *Unmasked* are called "mementos." They work like cyphers from the *Cypher System Rulebook*; they are items that allow a prodigy to activate a special ability before they cease working altogether. In *Unmasked*, normal people can't see or operate mementos—to the normals, a memento is just a mundane object.

To prodigies, these mementos are clearly lit by some secret light that only they can see. Each item can be activated to perform an amazing deed—once. For example, a snow globe of Chicago's Sears Tower might allow a prodigy to stop time in a bubble around them for one minute, or an old Seiko watch might allow a prodigy to teleport fifty feet. But once that special item is used, its power fades and vanishes from it. Mementos often have bizarre, completely random powers, and they seem to have an emotion tied into them. When activated, each memento projects a very clear *feeling* that the prodigy momentarily experiences—hence the name "memento."

When mementos are gathered together, they make an area . . . slippery. Areas with a lot of mementos tend to glow with their own light, making items and other prodigies difficult to spot in the "cloud." Some prodigies are sure that putting too many of these mementos together could be very, very bad, though they couldn't tell you why they think that. Prodigies just know that you don't carry more than a few of these objects with you at any given time.

Masks are not mementos; they're something much more powerful, and as such don't count toward this total.

SPECIAL ASPECTS OF MEMENTOS IN UNMASKED

While at their core mementos operate like normal cyphers in the Cypher System, they are special, and have their own rules in the world of *Unmasked*:

- Only prodigies can see and operate mementos.
- Prodigies can tell what a memento can do just by touching it. Until they touch it, they only know it's a memento, as well as its approximate power level.
- Mementos are always items overlooked by normal people, and the power they exhibit has nothing to do with the items' ordinary utility (a gun memento might open all doors in a mile radius, for example).
- When a prodigy first creates a mask, they *always* do so by finding special mementos which they then "assemble" into one permanently powerful mask. Once created, the mask ceases being a memento, and is instead something much more potent.
- The more mementos are collected in proximity to one another, the *stranger* the area becomes, and the more coincidental and improbable the events occurring within it.

- Areas awash in mementos inhibit the prodigies' ability to spot individual masks and mementos within the cloud from a distance, but if prodigies concentrate or go up close and check out an item, they can avoid this effect.
- When a memento is "used" by a prodigy, some sort of power is released from it that is visible to other prodigies from a distance. Therefore, this tends to draw prodigies to the location.
- Prodigies can automatically tell when another prodigy is carrying a memento, as well as get a rough idea of its power level.
- The abilities manifested by mementos are similar to the powers of the masks, but are easily distinguished from them.

PART 2: PRODIGIES
THE BOARDWALK

You know you're getting close to the boardwalk because you can smell the sea first. It's an odor I love for some reason: like a cooler full of rotting fish on ice. It's always like that this time of year—a breeze carrying in the smell from the sea. Sometimes there are gulls, and sometimes kites on the horizon, like there are now. The sky near the horizon is never blue. There is never a truly blue sky at the beach. I don't know why.

Exeter Way dies in a crumbling mess of pavement, clotted with sand and bamboo weeds, and there is a stripped Dodge Dart that has been there as long as I can remember. On Hell Night 1980, I scrawled "Cheap Trick rules" in yellow spray paint across its windshield. Since then, that window of the Dart has been smashed in. The culprit—a cinder block—lies on the destroyed, tan upholstery of the front seat

I walk up the ramp to the boardwalk. Beneath it, in the shadows, unintelligible graffiti tells stories to no one. Nobody goes under the boardwalk anymore. I mean, it used to be pretty popular for the kids to play under them, and the teenagers used to go there to fool around and drink and stuff. Then they found a human torso in a garbage bag, back in the winter of '82 or '83, I think. Now no one goes down there except the bums and every once in a while a cop or two, to kick the bums out.

It was the same year Tim Buston disappeared, just about four weeks before they found the torso. And everyone in town thinks it was his, but it was never proven. It's hard to identify just a torso.

I remember a time in the summer of '81 when me and Tim and Jody were setting rockets off under the walk, firing them down the quarter-mile stretch of the supports. Sometimes they would go wild, and once one exploded right near Tim's head, taking his glasses off and singeing him. He fell to the ground and covered his face with his hands, and I thought he was crying. But when he stood up again, gingerly touching the burn, I could see he was really laughing, silently, tears streaming down his face.

I wonder where that face is now.

I've made a new face for myself, I think, in a voice not quite my own. And I pull it out and look at it. A ski mask with "Mount Airy Lodge" sewn into it in Atari-like letters, secured with a set of crap ski goggles and an old, tangled mess of a plastic parachute army man. If I put it on right now, I could change the world.

But then I see the kid there, on the boardwalk, blazing like a spotlight. Walking. Walking away.

"Hey!" I shout, and he looks up, and I see it's a girl. And she looks at me in the same way. Confused. Excited. I run down the boardwalk, stuffing the mask in my back pocket.

"Wait up!"

CHAPTER 3
CREATING A CHARACTER IN UNMASKED

Creating Your
Character, page 14

Character Descriptor,
page 64

Character Type,
page 22

Character Focus,
page 90

Smasher, page 33

Thinker, page 38

Mover, page 42

Changer, page 46

If you've made a character for the Cypher System before, you'll be intimately familiar with making an *Unmasked* prodigy, but there are some special rules found only in the world of *Unmasked* to consider. In most Cypher System games, your character is created with a sentence like, "I am an *adjective noun* who *verbs*." The adjective is the character's descriptor, the noun is the type, and the verb is the focus.

While a PC wearing a mask *does* have all these elements—a descriptor, type, and focus—a PC not currently wearing their mask has *only a descriptor*. Their type and focus are present only when they're wearing their mask. This represents the dramatic transformation in power and appearance they undergo when they wear their mask and tap into its power. It's almost as if they were two different people.

You'll notice the *Unmasked* character sheet is unique in that it has what are essentially two characters, one built into the other. The first, smaller area is called the TEEN; it has a name, descriptor, stat Pools, recovery rolls, skills, background, and a damage track. The second, much larger area (which takes up three-quarters of the sheet) is called the MASK. This includes a name, descriptor, type, focus, the mask-form's stat Pools based on type, an ability list, skills, and a damage track (plus a lot more room for descriptions of powers).

This makes it easy to understand and play. If you're wearing your mask, you have access to the MASK sheet. If you're not, you're limited to the TEEN section. And yes, this does mean that the two characters, the TEEN and the MASK, have different damage tracks.

To build your *Unmasked* PC prodigy, begin by building the regular TEEN underneath. All prodigy PCs begin with a 6 in Speed, Might, and Intellect, and then have an additional 2 points they place in any Pool they like. After that, the player picks a descriptor. Nearly all the descriptors from the *Cypher System Rulebook* will work (such as Charming, Guarded, or Naive) in *Unmasked*, with some restrictions. Add a few skills from the suggested skill list at the GM's discretion, and the TEEN section of the character sheet is ready to go.

Then, select a type for your mask from the four new types presented in this book: Smasher, Thinker, Mover, and Changer. Each represents a style of superhero. The type gives you the base ratings for the stat Pools in the MASK section of the sheet, as well as additional points you can spend to boost your Pools. It also gives you type abilities that you customize to match the flavor of the *Unmasked* background.

Players normally choose foci from the *Cypher System Rulebook* or from the new options presented in *Unmasked* itself. New foci include Flies by Night, Wants to Be Adored, Travels Back From the Future, and Lives on the Dark Side.

CHARACTER CREATION STEPS

1. Choose your teen's name (see page 24)
2. Assign your teen's stat Pools (see page 24)
3. Pick your teen's descriptor (see page 24)
4. Pick your teen's skills (see page 27)
5. Pick your teen's background connection (see page 28)
6. Pick your mask-form's descriptor (see page 32)
7. Pick your mask-form's type (see page 32)
8. Assign your mask-form stat Pools
9. Select your type's tier abilities and modify them for *Unmasked*
10. Select your mask-form's focus (see page 52)
11. Modify your focus abilities for *Unmasked*
12. Assign your mask-form's power shifts (see page 62)

SKILLS

There is no definitive list of skills in the *Cypher System Rulebook*. With the GM's permission, PCs can have a skill in anything they like that makes sense. In addition to the list of suggested skills in the rulebook, some useful skills in *Unmasked* might include:

Arcade games
Break dancing
Comic books
Computers
Cutting class
Drinking
Gossip
Graffiti
Insults
Kissing up
Mooching
School bureaucracy
Skateboarding
Telling them what they want to hear

Skills, page 20

Power Shifts, page 270

CHAPTER 4

GMing PRODIGIES

Unmasked is a game about superpowered teens who struggle to understand their situation and keep their powers secret, so they can piece together the truth behind a threat that only they can see coming. When they use their powers, impossible things happen, and often people are put in danger. Still, the PCs are just teenagers, with the same irrational wants and dreams as any normal teenager in America in 1986. Naturally, this leads to trouble.

There are many ways to run an *Unmasked* game: either as an ongoing campaign or as a one-off adventure. But the core concept and motifs within emerge most powerfully when the PCs all begin in the same high school just after they've made their mask and some mysterious event has made them able to "see" the secret powers that are all over, as well as recognize the other PCs who glow with an inner fire.

By finding one another, revealing their powers to one another, and overcoming problems together, the players will come to bond in a way that makes their origin seem organic, filled with gameplay moments and anecdotes that will feel a million times more interesting than any written character history one player might come up with.

THE TONE OF UNMASKED

Unmasked is a classic "secret world" setting. If you've seen movies such as *Highlander*, *The Lost Boys*, or *The Terminator*, you're already familiar with the concept. Beneath the everyday world, strange forces struggle and fight and keep themselves concealed from society at large. These forces usually have access to powers and abilities far beyond the average person's, and they operate within a set of rules and structures completely unknown to the rank and file of humanity.

In *Unmasked*, of course, the prodigies represent this force: teens with secret powers accessible only when they wear a strange mask. The default force they oppose is a dream figure called "Prester John," which may or may not be real (many options are presented on how to alter or create an entirely new threat, too). The teens struggle to understand their powers, the powers' origin, and what Prester John is or what it represents, all while trying to keep from being exposed. Meanwhile, they must go to high school and live the life of (relatively) normal teenagers.

The mundane world is a touchstone for the players—they know what it's like to get a slice of pizza, go to a movie, or skip a high-school class—yet when you slip in superpowers, they feel kind of like they know what *that* is like, too. The weirdness and secrets of the prodigies work best if the PCs live in a believable, realistic world.

The normal world of *Unmasked,* barring a few small organizations, is the actual world of the '80s. As such, a GM only needs to bring up Google to find all they need to know about that far-off land of 1986.

THE NATURE OF PRODIGY POWERS

The GM is highly encouraged to begin the game from the regular, everyday world of America in 1986. From this baseline, the PC prodigies arrive and (eventually) develop the power to change everything. In this way, players will feel like a force that slowly transforms their world into something new and never before seen.

When they wear their masks, prodigies can literally do the *impossible*. They break the fundamental laws of physics and classical reality, and they make amazing things happen. For example, a PC might be able to put a full-sized 1982 Chevy

Malibu in their right front pocket and pull it out whenever they need it. Or invert the gravity inside a room so that the floor is any surface they're pointing at, with everything falling toward it accordingly.

The world at large and law enforcement will meet such "powers" with disbelief, and, in some cases, with a willful urge to ignore the impossible events, or with an attempt to frame them through personal spiritual beliefs. Eventually, given enough exposure, news of kids with amazing powers will reach the national or global consciousness. See PART 3: Welcome to 1986 for more guidelines on how to build an *Unmasked* campaign.

Part 3: Welcome to 1986, page 65

DIFFICULTY AND POWER SHIFTS IN UNMASKED

Unmasked is an unusual beast, in that it covers a spectrum of challenge and difficulty from the everyday (a teen PC needs to hop a fence while running away from bullies; difficulty 3) all the way up to superpowered shenanigans (a masked PC needs to catch a plummeting Piper Cub aircraft before it hits the ground; difficulty 13). The lower end of the difficulty spectrum is handled normally as presented in the Running the Cypher System section in the *Cypher System Rulebook*.

Running the Cypher System, page 366

Superpowered actions are handled differently, however. First off, while difficulty in the "real world" maxes out at 10 (with a target number of 30), difficulty in *Unmasked* maxes out at 15 (with a target number of 45). Difficulty 11+ tasks are *always* reserved for dealing with threats that are simply beyond human capability. A normal street cop has no hope in hell of dealing with a threat of level 13, but a prodigy in mask-form does.

Power Shifts, page 270

This is because masks have power shifts. Think of a power shift as a permanent level of Effort on a particular action or ability that is always active for the mask-form. So, if you create a mask that has three power shifts in strength, that means any strength-related task of difficulty 3 or less is routine and requires no roll (the character can smash through a door of level 3 without a roll, for instance). The power shifts are available only when the PC is wearing their mask.

During character creation, the player has three power shifts they can apply to any ability or action. Once assigned, these power shifts do not change (though advancement through the tiers by type can grant *additional* power shifts). Otherwise, only with GM permission and through great effort can the PC add more power shifts to their mask.

PRODIGY SIGHT

All prodigies can see and sense other prodigies and mementos. This is primarily a vision-based ability (though some prodigies claim they can "hear" people and objects thrumming like an electric motor when they're close to them). Mementos and other prodigies glow with an "aura" or "inner fire" with a brightness commensurate to their approximate power level. So, in game terms, a fifth-tier Mover has a greater aura in prodigy sight than a second-tier Smasher. This doesn't mean one prodigy can somehow tell what powers another prodigy possesses just by looking—they just know that the other has power.

This ability is the only prodigy ability (besides activating mementos) that works with or without the prodigy wearing their mask. It cannot be "turned off."

THE PERSONALITY OF THE MASK

All prodigies make a single mask. This item (or fetish, or charm) seems to focus the wearer's abilities in powerful ways. When the prodigy wears the mask, it's as if they become someone else and can use their powers, placing them firmly in the realm of wonders once seen only in comic books. The mask also represents the core of their psyche.

Sometimes, if the prodigy is shy and withdrawn, the personality of the mask is an extrovert, a worrywart may manifest an easygoing mask, and a prodigy terrified of the opposite sex might be a smooth talker. But not always.

The mask often has a name for itself (usually a one-off joke name, a slang term, or some shorthand for something); a prodigy who can lift 50 tons (45 t) might call herself "Tiny," for instance. Usually, the mask also appears to have needs and desires, just like the teen. Often the wants of the teenager and the mask relate somehow with one another—but again, not always.

The two forms share memories and know everything the other knows. This is, of course, because "they" are the same person.

PRODIGY MANIFESTATION, EXHAUSTION, AND RECOVERY

Putting on a mask causes the personality contained in the mask to *physically* manifest while the teen apparently vanishes to some unknown and likely unknowable location. This switch is not always self-evident. Sometimes this masked entity is physically and mentally identical to the prodigy, while sometimes it's a totally different person. A fourteen-year-old girl could put on her mask and manifest as an 8-foot tall (2 m) albino man, for example. Either way, the physical well-being and clothing of the entities are somehow separate. If the mask-form gets shot up with a dozen bullets, when the mask comes off the teen is miraculously unharmed.

Being in mask-form is exhausting. Most of this drain comes from spending stat Pool points to activate various type abilities. But a mask may attempt to recover by making a recovery roll. While the damage tracks for a teen and their mask-form are discrete, their recovery rolls are not. A mask *must* attempt a recovery roll any time a stat Pool hits 0 (a teen does not).

When any stat Pool hits 0 after the mask's last recovery roll, the mask falls off and the prodigy collapses back into their normal teen-form. Whatever rest time is needed to make that failed recovery roll is the amount of time they must wait before they can put the mask on again. During this time, they're just the teen and the mask will not allow the teen to put it on.

Example: Tina, who can transform into a first-tier Smasher, puts on her mask and becomes Tiny, a Brash Smasher who Flies by Night. Her stat Pools become Tiny's stat Pools (Tina's teen stat

Pools remain in stasis while she is in the mask). She uses all manner of Tiny's abilities, dropping her Might to 1, so she pauses for one action, takes her first recovery roll, and rolls a 5, regaining 6 points. She spends more stat Points on various actions, and when her Intellect hits 1, she takes ten minutes and tries for her second recovery roll. She rolls a 4, regaining 5 points. Again, she spends more points on actions, takes one hour, and makes her third recovery roll, regaining 4 points. When a stat hits 0 after her fourth recovery roll, she is dumped out of the mask and back to her Tina form (Tiny's stat Pools are in stasis, and she now uses Tina's stat Pools).

PRODIGY DAMAGE AND HEALING

The mask-form and the teen have different damage tracks. The teen, as a normal human, moves on the damage track precisely like in the rules presented in the *Cypher System Rulebook*. The mask-form, however, is different.

While the mask-form moves down the damage track normally, it does not move back up the damage track in the standard fashion. It does have a big advantage: it can't really reach the dead state on the damage track. Instead, when it reaches dead, the mask comes off, leaving the teen in its place. For every 24 hours from the point that the mask is *not worn*, the mask-form moves up the damage track by one.

The mask-form must at least be in the debilitated state before it can be worn again. A dead mask cannot be worn—yet.

Example: Tiny, in her punch-for-punch exchange with a shadow man, became dead. Tina—her teen-form—fled the scene, clutching her mask. Twenty-four hours later, the Tiny mask-form is at debilitated on the damage track (and the mask can be used, though Tiny would still be gravely injured). Forty-eight hours later, the Tiny mask-form is at impaired on the damage track. Seventy-two hours after Tiny's untimely "death," the Tiny mask-form is hale and ready to kick butt.

A 24-hour pause in the use of the mask has a secondary beneficial effect: all the mask-form's stat Pools are refreshed to full.

Damage Track, page 202

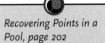

Recovering Points in a Pool, page 202

PUTTING ON AND TAKING OFF THE MASK

Masks are as easy to put on or take off as a . . . mask. A single action is enough for a prodigy to put one on or take it off. In general (barring recovery rolls and such), it requires no roll. The moment it is on, the PC has access to all the powers embedded in the mask, and can use them normally.

A prodigy struggling to take off *another* prodigy's mask must succeed at a difficulty 10 task to do so. They are very, very difficult to remove, because they don't *want* to come off. And for normal people, they are impossible to get off, because their target number is 30, well beyond what a human can achieve.

LOSING OR DESTROYING A MASK

Masks are resilient, slippery things. A normal person can't destroy a mask no matter what material it appears to be made from. It just can't happen. Throw it in an incinerator, and it appears to go in, but instead misses and drops to the ground, landing in shadow, unobserved. Carefully place it in the incinerator with a machine, and the machine breaks down or the incinerator fails to ignite. Normal people also have trouble hanging onto captured

THE PSYCHOLOGY OF THE MASK-FORM

Prodigies usually manifest in their mask-form as a being that either offsets a shortcoming they perceive in themselves, or in a way that grants them a kind of power they *wish* they had. Most mask-forms differ wildly from the teens that manifest them (this is usually reflected in the mask-form's descriptor being nearly the opposite of the teen's descriptor). GMs should readily reward those players who embrace and support this duality. In addition to offering a rich backdrop to play in, masks suggest roleplaying opportunities at every turn.

WHAT DOES MY MASK-FORM THINK OF MY TEEN-FORM?

This is an important (and fun) consideration. Since many mask-forms are directly opposed in attitude and drive to their teens, this can lead to all manner of entertaining roleplaying possibilities. Mask-forms, by default, generally won't take actions they believe will harm their teens (at least directly), but they certainly can show them "tough love" by making matters difficult for them or forcing them into awkward situations.

THE LIFE OF THE MIND

Many mask-forms believe themselves entities with a life separate from that of the teen-form they are linked to. Some claim to be from other Earths or other times, while others say they come from the stars, and still others from Hell itself. But the truth behind the curtain is they're all (somehow) from inside the human mind. Still, this does not stop the subconscious of the teen from generating fascinating stories, interrelations, and justifications for the mask-form.

Even when confronted with the fact that mask-forms depend on the teens to put on their mask before the mask-forms can manifest, the latter often just wave this truth away as inconsequential, or give some complex explanation for it which is so much malarky.

CAN MY MASK WEAR A MASK?

No. Nice try, though. When a teen dons a mask, it is usually not visible on the mask-form. Somehow, the mask-form appears as a whole new being. Attempting to put on *another* mask just plain fails.

masks, which have a tendency to get misplaced. Like a lost dog, the mask finds its way "home" to its creator, given enough time.

Only a mask can destroy a mask. First, the mask-form must get the mask off their intended target, and only then can they try to destroy it. Even so, it is a task with a difficulty rating of 15. This would require power shifts as well as the expenditure of Effort to even make it possible. When a mask is destroyed in such a manner, it has several effects:

It causes a huge disruption visible only to prodigies—like an invisible explosion.

A half dozen new mementos are created in the area, almost as if the objects were bombarded with power and absorbed some.

The teen who owned the mask shifts one step down the damage track. If the teenager was hale, they suddenly become impaired. If they were incapacitated, they die.

Whether or not a teen who has had their mask destroyed can create a new mask is up to the GM to decide. If this is possible, it is recommended that undertaking such an action requires a few sessions of gameplay that involve searching, assembling, and activating a new mask before the PC can use one again normally.

THE HIGH-LEVEL STRUCTURE OF AN UNMASKED CAMPAIGN

The nature of an *Unmasked* campaign is, of course, up to the GM to decide. Below, please find an outline of a campaign that would play to the strengths of *Unmasked*, along with some options to bake in a twist or three. (For a more detailed breakdown of *Unmasked* campaign building, please see Part 3: Welcome to 1986.)

AWAKENING

At the beginning, the GM gives a brief overview, explaining that the game is set in 1986, that the PCs are all teenagers who live in the same town, and all attend the local high school. The players make their prodigies, generating their teen, naming their mask, and picking their foci and

abilities. The PCs begin the game believing they alone have superpowers. In the very recent past, they awoke one morning feeling changed, and have since discovered how to create a mask to tap their powers. It is only when they arrive at school, and see others marked by power like they are, that they begin to suspect the truth—there's more than one mask.

Part 3: Welcome to 1986, page 65

DARK AWAKENING

Many superhero stories begin with tragedy, and *Unmasked* needn't be any different. Maybe one of the prodigies manifested to get revenge on the man who murdered their father, or used their powers and unknowingly caused an accident that harmed a child that was spying on them.

Baking in a mystery, tragedy, or setback in the awakening phase of an *Unmasked* campaign can make a story much, much richer. For example, the murderer might learn about the prodigy's powers and escape, or the injured kid could hover in a coma, ready to spill the beans about the prodigy's identity when they wake.

This can also be an opportunity to lay the groundwork for the "Big Bad™" who will threaten the PCs on a level regular folks just can't approach. The more you, as the GM, can tie these initial problems into the bigger picture of the coming threat, the better.

EXPLORATION

This phase of the game involves an exploration of the PCs' newfound powers. During this time, they can act on wishes they always hoped to turn into realities. In doing so, they will likely cross paths with other prodigies (it doesn't really matter whether these are the other PCs or an NPC with powers). It is during this time that the GM must establish and stress the importance of secrecy and keeping their powers out of the limelight.

STRANGE EXPLORATION

The weirdness of the prodigies' powers allows for exploration into *stranger* areas of thought. If a prodigy can cause any inanimate object he can see to vanish forever, can he do that to an object on television at a distance? Or just on live television? Or not at all? Teens are exploratory and apt to give something a try just to see what happens. The PC teen prodigies are no different. Let them determine the limits—and oddities—of their powers through gameplay. Often, this kind of experimentation leads to entanglements . . . and fun.

FRIENDSHIP

At some point, the PCs will develop friendships with the other PCs. Sometimes this can be baked into the story. For example, due to a background connection, they're already friends with another PC or have some other type of relationship with them defined before gameplay starts. But the best way to build relationships is to have the PCs discover one another in high school and interact naturally during the exploration phase. As they begin to compare notes, they might realize that Prester John is more than just a bad dream they keep having, and that there's safety in numbers . . .

PREDESTINED FRIENDSHIP

To raise the creepiness factor, the GM can have fate work to put the PCs together for wildly improbable reasons: They are all suddenly reassigned to the same driver's ed class after two instructors have accidents. They all have the same idea of skipping class and hanging out in the gym storage room at the exact same moment. They keep running into one another over and over again. This kind of "unseen hand" method of GM direction gives the players the feeling of being moved and directed by unknown forces.

PROBLEMS

Every teenager has ongoing problems, and prodigies are no different. They have the same hopes and dreams of any teenager, with the added oomph of superpowers. These powers don't help as much as you might think, though, and they tend to generate more problems than they fix. A group of PCs might work one week to make sure that one of their number becomes lead tuba in the marching band or gets a date, and the next week tackle much more serious issues, such as breaking up a drug ring at the school or figuring out why the janitor seems to know there's something off about their group and keeps nosing around.

SUPERNATURAL PROBLEMS

In addition to the problems in the everyday life of a teenager, the prodigies must deal with the strange, new powers at work in their world. The random discovery of mementos, what they mean and why, and what should be done with them become critical issues. What's more, there are *other* prodigies in school, and not all of them are friendly. What they're up to and why should be central in the minds of the PCs. Remember, those NPCs can see that the PCs are prodigies, too.

THE THREAT

Bigger still is the threat behind the scenes. The PCs might be pursued by reporters hot on the case of a story about a strange flying figure sighted at the school, and later, by agencies and groups hoping to locate, capture, or perhaps even *kill* a prodigy to dissect them. This threat should begin as nothing but an odd whisper at the edges of the PCs' lives, but it slowly worms its way into their world until, finally, a confrontation *must* occur.

THE IMMATERIAL THREAT

Prester John, a mysterious force somehow inextricably linked to the prodigies, should remain a looming, undefined threat that can suddenly explode into life-changing events. You can find more details on Prester John, the creature's possible origins, and its potential plans, as well as ways for a GM to customize the threat, on page 151.

REVELATIONS

All good campaigns should culminate in a revelation or two. Of course, the central question is: what are the prodigies? Where do they come from and why? And what will happen to them? A secondary question is: what is Prester John? What does this being want with the prodigies and mementos? Good GMs will make PCs work to dig their way to the center of these mysteries only over the span of many game sessions.

FINAL REVELATIONS

It is vitally important that a revelation require some sacrifice to uncover it. The PCs can't just stumble upon it randomly. For example, a prodigy might finally, after weeks of tracking leads, uncover that last summer the prodigies all went swimming in a creek connected to the Flammel Chemicals plant—and that Flammel produces psychopharmaceuticals for the army. But this discovery unleashes Flammel's black-suited hit squad on their family and friends!

OUTCOMES

What is the ultimate disposition of the world after the prodigies find out where they came from or what Prester John is? This remains up to the GM to decide, but some ideas follow, as well as a more detailed explanation of how to modify your threat to match your campaign in Part 3: Welcome to 1986.

THE "WHOLE WIDE WORLD" OUTCOME

It wasn't just the PCs' town that changed. Instead, the whole world was affected that day, and prodigies are everywhere. Who knows what powers, personalities, and knowledge exist among them throughout the world?

THE "WHY HERE?" OUTCOME

Something is special about the town where the PCs live, and the prodigies appeared only there. Perhaps the PCs now know why, and perhaps the effect is replicable (a government experiment or an accident) or persistently creeping (a natural effect, interstellar radiation, or extradimensional bleed). The PCs may want to stop it, or they may want to usher in a new era of prodigy power. Who knows?

THE "ON-THE-RUN" OUTCOME

The PCs have exposed themselves with their actions and are now on the radar of groups (government and otherwise) that want them captured or dead. As such, they're runaways, hightailing it out of town before they can be trapped and caged like animals.

Part 3: Welcome to 1986, page 65

CHAPTER 5
CREATING THE TEEN—TEEN DESCRIPTOR

The teen PC is the core of an *Unmasked* character. The PCs are regular teens who—for some unknown reason—acquire the ability to see the secret, amazing powers at work in the world, as well as the ability to put on a mask and call into being an incredible, larger-than-life superpowered being.

TEEN STATS

A teen PC's stat Pools begin as:

Stat	Pool Starting Value
Might	6
Speed	6
Intellect	6

The player may then assign 2 additional stat points to any Pool. Fill in your stats in the stat Pool boxes in the TEEN section of the character sheet. (This may seem to make the teens very similar, but you get to pick a descriptor next.)

TEEN NAME

Create a name for your teen, and write it down in the TEEN section of the character sheet.

TEEN DESCRIPTOR

Select a descriptor from the *Cypher System Rulebook* that best suits your teen character, and write it in the TEEN section under descriptor. Take a moment to mark down any special bonuses or penalties the descriptor adds to your teen in the descriptor modifications section of the TEEN section of the character sheet. This descriptor only counts when your PC is in teen-form. When in mask-form, your character is free of any such encumbrances (in this way, a Noble teen might become a duplicitous sneak when in mask-form—the mask-form has its own descriptor).

There are fifty descriptors to choose from in the *Cypher System Rulebook*, and many others in various Cypher System products.

Nearly all of them are available, with the only restriction being that since this descriptor describes the teen-form, the descriptor cannot grant the teen powers beyond those common to the everyday world. For example, Mystical—which implies the teen can cast spells—is not available. Likewise, any descriptor that grants the teen supernatural powers is not permitted.

> If you have *Expanded Worlds*, you could also choose from the following descriptors:
> Adroit
> Beneficent
> Chaotic
> Heroic
> Lawful
> Relentless
> Serene
> Young

NEW DESCRIPTORS

METAL HEAD

You live for heavy metal music, and its nihilistic view shapes your world. This goes hand in hand with a recklessness that—in less-than-perfect situations—can serve you well. You shun rules, order, and the status quo, but you often will do the minimum asked of you just to get by. After all, there's always another party to go to.

You gain the following characteristics:

Whatever, Man: +3 to your Might Pool.

Skill: You are trained in one of the following: mechanical repair, driving, or construction.

I'll Waste You: If in a tense situation, you can escalate threat to an art form. The difficulty of all your attempts to intimidate, cajole, or threaten is decreased by one step.

Inability: You always dress in the same kind of outfit: motorcycle boots and a denim jacket with a back patch of your favorite band. You've got a huge, puffed hairdo and very long hair. The difficulty on all your attempts to blend in or conceal your identity is increased by one step.

Initial Link to the Starting Adventure: From the following list of options, choose how you became involved in the first adventure:

1. You know one of the other teens knows what's what. You need to follow them until they spill the beans about the masks.

2. You know a crazy time when you see one. You've decided to follow this one to the end.

3. One of the other PCs is a goofball who opposes everything you stand for. You want to be there when they fall on their face.

4. One of the other PCs really intrigues you, but you're not sure why. You're coming along to find out more about that person.

NEW-WAVE

You are part of the new wave—artistic, individualistic, and most of all, *new*. You dress in a striking manner, and everything you do is an expression of your art. Obscure European bands, strange books and art, and a push toward experiencing the outré make you open-minded in a way not often found in your town. Sometimes you're a rebel, too, shirking responsibility.

You gain the following characteristics:

Internal World: +3 to your Intellect Pool.

Skill: You are trained in one of the following: art, literature, or music studies.

What Box? Your problem-solving skills are outside the norm. The difficulty for all mental skills that require speculative thinking is decreased by one step.

Inability: You're no good at fitting in. The difficulty for all social interaction rolls is increased by one step for you.

Initial Link to the Starting Adventure: From the following list of options, choose how you became involved in the first adventure:

1. You see something in one of the other PCs. They could be a kindred spirit. You need to find out more.

2. Something about the group of PCs says that this is your place. You don't question such feelings.

3. One of the other PCs knew you before you remade yourself in new-wave fashion, yet they don't seem to notice what you consider to be a fundamental change in you. You're going to show them why it's so important.

4. One of the other PCs really intrigues you, but you're not sure why. You're coming along to find out more about that person.

PUNK

Bring it all down! You are the embodiment of a rebuke to the order that has arisen since the end of the last World War. Music, television, art—all of it is too self-interested, too fake. You live in the moment, in a world filled with possibility, but only if you operate outside the boxes society has picked for you.

You gain the following characteristics:

That Didn't Hurt: +3 to your Might Pool.

Skill: You are trained in one of the following: skateboarding, stunt biking, or surfing.

In Your Face: You are trained in all actions that involve overcoming or ignoring the effects of fear or intimidation.

Edgy: You stink at self-control. If someone attacks, your first response is always an equivalent attack.

Initial Link to the Starting Adventure: From the following list of options, choose how you became involved in the first adventure:

1. The other PCs are freakin' annoying, but crap, they're your friends. What can you do?

2, You find one of the other PCs fascinating, though they are nothing like you. You enjoy being around them, but they must never, ever know.

3. You wandered into the PC group, and they seem to know how to have a good time. What the hell, you only live once.

4. One of the PCs is so very wrong about everything. You want to be there when they hit rock bottom.

SHOW-OFF

Anything they can do, you can do better. You feel a strong need to keep pace or outdo those around you. Sometimes this leaves you embarrassed—or, at worst, injured. Still, it's better to look like a fool in the short term than to be forgotten.

You gain the following characteristics:

Fast: +3 to your Speed Pool.

Skill: You are trained in one of the following: acrobatics, climbing, or dodging.

One-Off: Any time you attempt to imitate someone who has succeeded at an action that you've never tried before, you gain an asset on that task.

Chicken? If you are dared to do something (or otherwise socially goaded, at the GM's discretion), you must attempt the challenge.

Initial Link to the Starting Adventure: From the following list of options, choose how you became involved in the first adventure:

1. One of the PCs is always better at everything than you are. You follow them around, because someday it'll be your turn to be number one.

2. One of the PCs just decided you two were friends and began to show up everywhere you were.

3. You know one of the teen PCs is hiding something, and you really want to find out what it is.

4. You and another PC share a secret, something you never talk about. You stick near them to make sure they're not talking out of turn.

TEEN SKILLS

At the GM's discretion, you can select up to three skills for your teen character. Keep in mind, since your PC is just a kid, it's highly unlikely you have any super useful skills—except those which might make you appear cool to other teens. Thus, skills are usually things like skateboarding or break dancing. Write any skills down under the skill heading in the TEEN section of the character sheet.

TEEN BACKGROUND CONNECTION

Teens are defined by their background situation. Roll a d100 or choose from the following list to determine one fact about your background that provides a connection to the main story, or feel free to create your own fact, if you wish. Results marked with a * indicate some element tied to the prodigy phenomenon. Not only should you keep the prodigy-related result, you should also roll (or choose) again. If a result doesn't make sense due to your descriptor (for example, if your teen is Craven, but the background connection indicates they are brave), you should alter it, roll again, or pick another one.

d100	Background Connection
01	Your best friend is a jock who looks out for you.
02	Your family is loaded. Money has no meaning to you.
03	You are on track to secretly complete your first year of college credits during summer school.
04	You often get lost in thoughts that become daydreams. Sometimes they come true.*
05	You are the top student at the school, and the teachers let you get away with anything.
06	Your dreams about a weird preacher chasing you are so vivid that you're having trouble sleeping. It's beginning to affect your grades.*
07	Your best friend, who is into new wave, has just arrived in town and is shaking up your life.
08	You are in love with a student who relies on you for tutoring.
09	You got your driver's license before everyone else.
10	You work in a store and have ready access to those products a teen might want.
11	You are the favorite target of harassment by certain students. You orchestrate your entire day around not running into them.
12	You have a computer and modem, and you can hack the school schedule.
13	You tutor dozens of students and are always flush with cash.
14	Your best friend is popular, but they don't want anyone else to know about your friendship.
15	You've received an academic stipend for your fantastic grades, but you secretly spent it on a car that you have to keep hidden—you're not allowed to drive yet!
16	You'd be completely invisible in the school, except for your GPA.
17	You have a complex plan in the works to get another student to like you.
18	Your dad is in local law enforcement.
19	You are the youngest in a poor but close-knit family. Your siblings are popular where you are not, but they look out for you.
20	You carry a special memento everywhere you go. It hums with power.*
21	You are a nice person and refuse to fall in with bullies who pick on people. Everyone knows your name.
22	You have a big family, and your interest in sports is an attempt to be noticed by your parents.
23	You are terrible in school and live in constant fear of failing classes.
24	Your best friend is a geeky student who helps you get by in school.
25	You are state ranked in your sport and can get away with nearly anything.

26	You are certain something bad is coming. This anxiety is so crippling that you're beginning to underperform.*
27	You are in love with a social outcast but can't tell anyone.
28	Despite excelling in a sport, you're haunted by your failures in school.
29	You failed your driving test and can't let anyone know.
30	Your job is cool in some way (you're a lifeguard, work in a movie theater, etc.).
31	Your house has an indoor pool—it's party central.
32	Your older sibling who is off at college was the biggest sports star your high school has ever known; you struggle in their shadow.
33	You protect students from bullying in exchange for cash.
34	You are guaranteed a full ride at a big college—if you can stay out of trouble.
35	No one knows you can't read very well.
36	You hate the sport you play and would do anything not to be involved in it anymore, but you're great at it.
37	You have your eye on an unpopular student as a love interest, but you're unsure what your friends might think.
38	Your dad runs the bank in town.
39	You secretly despise your life, and you dream of running away and starting anew.
40	You have found a secret place that hums with invisible power. When you're there, you can see visions.*
41	Your best friend is a weirdo hated by the cool kids, but he doesn't care.
42	Your dad owns the town's car dealership and is a local political bigwig.
43	You are secretly in love with a geek, but you're terrified they will laugh at you if you confess your feelings.
44	Your older sibling is a well-known nerd in the school whom you do your best to avoid.
45	Your parents are never home, meaning your house is party central, but sometimes you go months without seeing them at all.
46	You dream of a grinning man all the time now. In these nightmares, he draws closer and closer to your house.*
47	A memento you found on the first morning you could "see" seems to thrum with power when you come near certain people or places.*
48	Your parents died when you were young, and you live with your religious grandparents, who have no idea about your more outré activities.
49	You've been secretly working a crap job and socking away every penny you can to afford an awesome used car.
50	You are never without some key item that everyone knows you for (a Walkman, sunglasses, a retractable keychain, boots, a trucker's cap, etc.)
51	You tried out for a sport but failed miserably, in public, and you're still recovering from it.
52	Much to your chagrin, your former love interest is the most popular person in school, and they hate you.
53	Your family name is associated with petty crime; you're the ne'er-do-wells in the town.
54	Although you look like you spend a ton of money on clothes, you're actually poor and spend every waking moment slapping together outfits from Goodwill.

55	You hate the persona you "wear" at school, but you don't know how to get off the popularity train.
56	You find yourself drawn to using your popularity to defend those who are weak or picked on.
57	Though you've never performed in front of anyone, you dream of being an actor, singer, or dancer.
58	People come to you to boost their social profile in exchange for cash.
59	You are legendary for your disdain for school authority. You mouth off all the time.
60	You keep a hate book and note all the weird or bad deeds individual students commit. If anyone ever found it, it would ruin dozens of lives.
61	You've just transferred to the school from the big city, and man, is this new school *lame*.
62	You've struck up an unlikely friendship with a jock who seems unconcerned with your weirdness.
63	When you daydream now, it always ends up with the same image: a preacher, head hung down so you can't see his face, beckoning you. It's beginning to creep you out. Like, seriously.*
64	Your house is a disaster area, and your parents are always at work.
65	You have a huge, immortal car from the 1970s that seems beyond mechanical failure—plus a permit to drive it.
66	Your family is rich, and you are the black sheep. They are sick of your shenanigans.
67	You dream of being an artist, graffiti artist, or skateboarder, but that'll never happen if you don't skip this crap town.
68	You're in love with a popular student, but you don't think they have any idea you even exist.
69	You have friends in the nearest big-city music scene, and you often end up with free tickets to sold-out concerts.
70	Your family has so many cousins and siblings that it's like you have your own gang.
71	Your family is good-natured, but secretly homeless and living out of the family van. You live in terror of anyone finding out.
72	Your love of science fiction supersedes your sense of personal embarrassment. It's all you talk about.
73	Some teachers think you are a genius, and they constantly pester you to try and do better in school.
74	Your family is career army, and you've attended as many schools as years you've been in high school.
75	You suffer from terrible acne, and you'd do anything to get rid of it.
76	Your life is all about video games. You spend every waking moment you can in front of an arcade machine.

77	A close family member died the year before, and your family struggles under the grief.
78	You are always at school because your home life sucks. Sometimes you secretly crash at the school when things are particularly bad.
79	One of your parents is a teacher in your high school.
80	You're a gearhead obsessed with cars. But you can't drive—yet.
81	You love to kitbash electronics, and you swing a decent income repairing broken radios and TVs.
82	Your oldest sibling, who once attended the high school, is your (overprotective) guardian.
83	You are all about after-school activities: band, yearbook, and chess club. You're an overachiever.
84	You've befriended a janitor who sees and hears everything at the high school.
85	Your family is devoutly religious, and they think you are, too. Only at school are you truly free.
86	Your parents are never home, and you're like a parent to your younger sibling. This takes up a lot of time, but you love them.
87	Some nights you find that your mask seems to talk to you. If you listen closely, it appears to be describing locations to you, but only you can hear it.*
88	Your mom is the town doctor.
89	You've noticed the clock tower in the middle of town glows like a memento—but only at midnight. One minute past and it's just a regular clock tower again.*
90	Your record and tape collection is as big as that of a radio station's.
91	You are a trouble magnet. Every time you open your mouth, something funny (and then bad) happens.
92	You live with your aunt or uncle, and they barely tolerate you. Your parents aren't in the picture.
93	You are the notorious graffiti artist the town is desperately searching for.
94	You've won the friendship of a nerd by taking the fall for them, and now they won't leave you alone.
95	You are never anywhere without your Walkman, boom box, or transistor radio.
96	Your whole life revolves around comic books.
97	Some people make friends. While you do have some friends, you're much better at making enemies. In fact, you enjoy it. A lot.
98	You've seen a couple of kids who seem marked with an odd kind of light. They have apparently formed a clique—but they're all dumbasses. You think they might even be dangerous.*
99	You are a night person and a well-known class screwup, because you're always falling asleep in class.
00	In the old bus station in town, you noticed a door with the sign "END OF THE LINE" that seemed lit with power, but you were too frightened to go inside.*

CHAPTER 6
CREATING THE MASK—
MASK-FORM DESCRIPTOR AND TYPE

Mover, page 42

Changer, page 46

In *Unmasked*, the mask-form has a separate descriptor from the teen. You can choose any descriptor for the mask-form (even ones such as Mystical, which aren't open to the teen-form). The descriptor should indicate the attitude of your mask-form. It's the *adjective* in the character creation sentence, "I am an *adjective noun* who *verbs*."

Type comes next. It is the core of the mask-form that the PC teen transforms into. The PC's teen-form doesn't have a type, but their superpowered mask-form sure does. It's the *noun* in the character creation sentence, "I am an *adjective noun* who *verbs*." When the teen puts on their mask, this type is the central concept of what they become (their superpowers are linked to their type abilities, but also to their focus abilities, which come after this section).

Four new types are presented here for players to choose from to create their mask-form characters: the Smasher, the Thinker,

Smasher, page 33

Thinker, page 38

the Mover, and the Changer. These types have been built out from those in the *Cypher System Rulebook* to suit a 1986 gone *weird*, and each one represents a stop along the spectrum of comic book–style characters.

Almost all the abilities in the *Cypher System Rulebook* will work for the mask-forms in *Unmasked*, so players should feel free to choose from that source as well. The new types that follow already have the abilities from the *Cypher System Rulebook* incorporated into them, so it's easy for a player to sit down with this book and quickly whip up a new character without going back and forth between the two books.

TYPE OVERVIEW

Smashers follow the old motto of walk softly and, uh . . . smash everything in sight. Their first and last thought when confronted by a threat is usually, "Can I hit it?" If the answer is yes, you'd better get out of their way.

These mask-forms are often big and brawny, but again, not always. Some Smashers are psychics and don't need muscles to get the damage done.

Thinkers live in their mind, two minutes ahead of the rest of the world. Sometimes their powers are psychic, sometimes physical, and sometimes a mix, but they are always concerned with outcomes, likely actions, and directing matters towards a desired conclusion. Most Thinker mask-forms are small, but again, there is no restriction. Their constant calculation sometimes makes them appear distant and hard to communicate with.

Movers are sure that where they are must certainly be less interesting than where they are not. As such, they're always in motion. These mask-forms tend to be small and fast, but not always. This alacrity sometimes affects more than just their movement speed or focus abilities—sometimes their mouths run a bit fast, too.

Changers change things. Whether their target is a mind or an object doesn't really matter. Some Changer mask-forms are really good-looking, others know just what to say and when, and still others can reach into the mind of a target or force the physical nature of an object to change. Changers are all about relationships—between people, places, and things. They like to smooth over disagreements and make plans work.

SMASHER

Smashers are usually bruisers, and they're not that great at considering future ramifications. They act first and ask questions later, usually when they're also licking their wounds. They think problems are best dealt with through physical action.

In general, Smashers tend to avoid situations that involve deep thought, socially embarrassing actions, and looking bad in front of others. But they can run, jump,

WHAT IS MY MASK-FORM?

When a teen prodigy puts on their mask, they become their *mask-form*. This is a unique, mighty, superpowered entity that need not be anything like the teen it manifests from. The mask-form is always the same, and it is almost like a character unto itself. Some mask-forms have a backstory that transcends their first appearance as a side effect of the mask, and *all* mask-forms have dreams and desires independent from their teen-forms'.

Mask-forms need not be human, but they need to be *people*. No matter what, their teen-forms are human, but the mask-form can appear as nearly anything. A blue-skinned alien, a ghost, or an animated, glowing pile of slime in humanoid form—all of these work. No matter what, this mask-form gains no real benefit from this cosmetic form; instead, all bonuses are conveyed only in type and focus abilities.

Selecting what your mask-form manifests as is easy and fun. Look at your teen, their descriptor, and their background information, and then try to imagine the *opposite,* or come up with a dark, hidden fantasy of the teen and build from there. Also, keep in mind that, while this duality is typical for prodigies, it is not always the case that the mask-form is the opposite of the teen. Let's create some examples:

Nancy is a Virtuous, bookish teen. Her mask-form is a huge, bloodthirsty monster that holds grudges.

Roberto is a Skeptical sports star. His mask-form is a slight, naive alien from another dimension.

Petra is a Wealthy, overweight teen. Her mask-form is a handsome, muscular man who is always everyone's friend.

Baljinder is a slight, Creative artist. His mask-form is a tall, ebony-skinned female warrior with nerves of steel.

GIVING TIER ABILITIES THE UNMASKED FEELING

Instead of rebuilding all the tier abilities from scratch to make them match the feeling of weirdness presented in *Unmasked*, we're going to show you how to take existing abilities and make them your own.

Reimagining abilities so they fit the atmosphere in *Unmasked* is simple. Mechanically, they don't need to change at all: cost, range, effect, etc. all remain the same. Instead, their *feel* changes. Sometimes this means limiting them a bit (this is mostly situational—an ability I can only use in the presence of an electrical outlet, for example). But mostly it means framing them in a new way so they *feel* different and giving them a new name. Players and GMs should feel free to come up with new ideas for any ability.

For example, let's reimagine Hedge Magic as an ability in *Unmasked*. First and foremost, it's super simple to imagine a prodigy who transforms into a classic wizard when they put on their mask, so you could just use it as is. Here's what the original ability looks like:

HEDGE MAGIC (1 INTELLECT POINT)

You can perform small tricks: temporarily change the color or basic appearance of a small object, cause small objects to float through the air, clean a small area, mend a broken object, prepare (but not create) food, and so on. You can't use hedge magic to harm another creature or object. Action.

In *Unmasked*, you could shift this description in any number of ways. Imagine something funny, strange, or weird that might produce the effects presented in the ability, or some strange side effect that makes the power feel unique. Then, go to town with it. For example, Hedge Magic might come to look like this:

LITTLE FRIENDS (1 INTELLECT POINT)
You can summon a squad of green plastic toy soldiers that can perform small tricks for you. They can temporarily change the color or basic appearance of a small object by climbing over and covering it, and they can cause small objects to move through the air by heaving it as a group. They can clean a small area, mend a broken object, prepare (but not create) food, and so on. Your little friends can't harm another creature or object. They are easily destroyed, but you never seem to run out of them. Action.

Or this:

THEY'RE HERE (1 INTELLECT POINT)
When you are in a room or area lit by a TV showing static, you can cause the screen to emit ghostly tendrils that can perform small tricks: temporarily change the color or basic appearance of a small object, cause small objects to float through the air, clean a small area, mend a broken object, prepare (but not create) food, and so on. These tendrils can't harm a creature or object. Action.

The most important thing to remember when making your abilities fit the world of *Unmasked* is that they don't need to make sense. The prodigies break the laws of physics, and their beliefs, drives, and dreams power their abilities. Therefore, any explanation is possible—even nonsense.

dodge, and fight in a way that suggests they were born for it. When they talk, they are easily distracted and sometimes have a hard time making a point. To most Smashers, this is unimportant. All they need to say they can say with their fists.

Individual Role: Smashers know how to follow the rules, and do so readily in certain situations. But they also know when they can get away with things. Still, they're not very subtle and are easily outthought. Smashers tend to leap into trouble, and it is only then that they acknowledge their lack of forward thinking. By then, they have no choice but to fight their way out. They never seem to learn this lesson.

Group Role: Smashers are sometimes leaders, and when they are, they tend to be the strong, silent type, leading by example more than by oratory. They're protective of their friends, and spend a lot of time rescuing them from bad situations (no doubt many of which were created by the Smasher in the first place, by accident). When confronting a threat, Smashers are almost always near the front of the group.

Prodigy Abilities and Foci: Smasher mask-forms tend to develop physical abilities, though there is no hard and fast restriction against psychic powers. The teens that Smashers manifest from tend to be weak or uncoordinated.

Power Shift Placement: Smashers should place power shifts into strength, attacks, resistance, Armor, or similar if they wish to be superhumanly resistant and strong.

Advancement of Smashers: As Smashers advance, so do their skills in brawling, athletics, and the like. They tend to become bigger, badder, and more resilient.

Mask-form abilities, page 50

Mask-form power shifts, page 62

SMASHER STATS
Smasher Stat Pools

Stat	Pool Starting Value
Might	12
Speed	9
Intellect	7

You get 6 additional points to divide among your stat Pools however you wish.

BUILDING A SMASHER

The core of the Smasher type in *Unmasked* is a tweaked version of the Warrior from the *Cypher System Rulebook*. As such, players playing a Smasher get to pick from the Warrior ability choices (as well as some special abilities defined below). Once a Warrior ability is selected, the player should give it a "feeling" so it fits in the weird world of *Unmasked*, where nearly anything is possible—at least for the prodigies.

Smashers can always choose an ability from a lower tier instead of adding one from their current tier, and they can replace one lower-tier ability with a different one from a lower tier.

The full text of *Cypher System Rulebook* abilities is not replicated here. Please refer to the *Cypher System Rulebook* for details on your ability and equipment choices. Below is a breakdown of what abilities are preselected or available at each tier.

FIRST-TIER SMASHER

You gain the abilities noted for a first-tier Warrior.

Mask-Form Abilities: When you select a new first-tier ability, you can instead select a first-tier mask-form ability. All prodigies have access to these special mask-form abilities.

Prodigy Sight: You can see people and places that are of special significance, as well as identify, collect, and use mementos. You can identify another prodigy on sight, even if they're not wearing their mask. This ability is *always* active and cannot be turned off, even when you're just a teen.

FIRST-TIER SMASHER ABILITIES

Choose 4 abilities + Prodigy Sight + Practiced With All Weapons

Bash (1 Might point)

Control the Field (1 Might point)

Extra Edge

No Need for Weapons

Overwatch (1 Intellect point)

Physical Skills: Pick two of the following: balancing, climbing, jumping, running, or swimming. You can select this ability multiple times.

Pierce (1 Speed point)

Practiced in Armor

Quick Draw (2 Speed points)

Swipe (1 Speed point)

Thrust (1 Might point)

Trained Without Armor

Example Selection and Customization: *Dana is making a first-tier Smasher she calls "Monster Masher." She decides her mask-form is an inhumanly large, purple Neanderthal-looking creature—while her teen-form is a willowy, bookish type. The Smasher's costume is barely present—it* always looks like it's just stepped out of a battlefield undergoing active bombardment. She selects a huge sledgehammer she calls "Percy" (heavy weapon) and a ball-and-chain shot put she calls "the bean" (heavy weapon) for equipment. Monster Masher gets the Prodigy Sight and Practiced With All Weapons abilities automatically, and Dana selects Bash, Control the Field, No Need for Weapons, and Overwatch for her Smasher's four abilities. She customizes these by saying her mask-form announces its moves before it does it: "SMASH IT!" for Bash, "MOVE IT!" for Control the Field, "PUNCH IT!" for No Need for Weapons, and "THROW IT!" for Overwatch. If somehow it can't say it, it can't do it and just stands there, goggling.

SECOND-TIER SMASHER

You gain the abilities noted for a second-tier Warrior. In addition, you can replace one of your lower-tier abilities with a different one from a lower tier.

Mask-Form Abilities: When you select a new second-tier ability, you can instead select a second-tier mask-form ability. All prodigies have access to these special mask-form abilities.

SECOND-TIER SMASHER ABILITIES

Choose 2 abilities + additional power shift to resilience

Additional Power Shift to Resilience: Might defense rolls and Armor are naturally increased or you have a permanent +1 in Armor. This can be added to previously power-shifted resilience.

Chop (2 Might points)

Crush (2 Might points)

Mighty Blow (2 Might points)

Reload (1 Speed point)

Skill With Attacks

Skill With Defense

Successive Attack (2 Speed points)

Example Selection and Customization:
Dana's Smasher hits second tier, and Dana selects Crush ("BATTER UP!") and Mighty Blow ("EAT IT!") as her Smasher's new

abilities. Again, the mask-form must announce what it is doing in advance. The mask-form also gains a power shift to resilience, which makes it harder to injure.

THIRD-TIER SMASHER

You gain the abilities noted for a third-tier Warrior. In addition, you can replace one of your lower-tier abilities with a different one from a lower tier.

Mask-Form Abilities: When you select a new third-tier ability, you can instead select a third-tier mask-form ability. All prodigies have access to these special mask-form abilities.

THIRD-TIER SMASHER ABILITIES

Choose 3 abilities

Deadly Aim (3 Speed points)

Experienced With Armor

Expert Memento Use

Fury (3 Might points)

Lunge (2 Might points)

Reaction

Seize the Moment (4+ Speed points)

Slice (2 Speed points)

Spray (2 Speed points)

Trick Shot (2 Speed points)

Example Selection and Customization:
Dana's Smasher hits third tier, and Dana selects Fury ("ENOUGH!"), Lunge ("SHUT UP!"), and Trick Shot ("SURPRISE!") as her Smasher's new abilities. Again, the mask-form must announce what it is doing in advance to use the abilities.

FOURTH-TIER SMASHER

You gain the abilities noted for a fourth-tier Warrior. In addition, you can replace one of your lower-tier abilities with a different one from a lower tier.

Mask-Form Abilities: When you select a new fourth-tier ability, you can instead select a fourth-tier mask-form ability. All prodigies have access to these special mask-form abilities.

Expert Memento Use is the same as Expert Cypher Use.

FOURTH-TIER SMASHER ABILITIES

Choose 2 abilities + power shift (+3 damage for a specific attack)

Power Shift (+3 Damage for a Specific Attack): Apply a permanent power shift to a particular attack not previously boosted by a power shift, adding +3 points of damage to it.

Capable Warrior

Experienced Defender

Feint (2 Speed points)

Minor to Major

Momentum

Opening Gambit (4 Might points)

Snipe (2 Speed points)

Tough As Nails

Example Selection and Customization:
Dana's Smasher hits fourth tier, and Dana selects Momentum ("HEADS UP!") and Tough As Nails ("THAT'S ALL YOU'VE GOT?") as her Smasher's new abilities. Again, the mask-form must announce what it is doing in advance to use the abilities.

FIFTH-TIER SMASHER

You gain the abilities noted for a fifth-tier Warrior. In addition, you can replace one of your lower-tier abilities with a different one from a lower tier.

Mask-Form Abilities: When you select a new fifth-tier ability, you can instead select a fifth-tier mask-form ability. All prodigies have access to these special mask-form abilities.

FIFTH-TIER SMASHER ABILITIES

Choose 3 abilities

Adroit Memento Use

Arc Spray (3 Speed points)

Greater Skill With Attacks

Improved Success

Jump Attack (5 Might points)

Mastery With Armor

Mastery With Defense

Parry (5 Speed points)

Example Selection and Customization:
Dana's Smasher hits fifth tier, and Dana selects Greater Skill With Attacks ("WATCH THIS!"), Minor to Major ("THIS IS GONNA HURT!"). and Jump Attack ("YOO-HOO!") as her Smasher's new abilities. Again, the mask-form must announce what it is doing in advance to use the abilities.

SIXTH-TIER SMASHER

You gain the abilities noted for a sixth-tier Warrior. In addition, you can replace one of your lower-tier abilities with a different one from a lower tier.

Mask-Form Abilities: When you select a new sixth-tier ability, you can instead select a sixth-tier mask-form ability. All prodigies have access to these special mask-form abilities.

SIXTH-TIER SMASHER ABILITIES

Choose two abilities

Finishing Blow (5 Might points)

Magnificent Moment

Shooting Gallery (5 Speed points)

Slayer (3 Might points)

Spin Attack (5 Speed points)

Weapon and Body (5 Speed points)

Example Selection and Customization:
Dana's Smasher hits sixth tier, and Dana selects Finishing Blow ("HI THERE!") and Slayer ("ENOUGH OUTTA YOU!") as her Smasher's new abilities. Again, the mask-form must announce what it is doing in advance to use the abilities.

THINKER

Because the world of social interaction and physicality is hard on them, Thinkers live mostly in their minds. They love books, puzzles, games, art, and other things that speak to their inner selves. They tend to avoid social situations, feats of physical strength, and other types of interaction that will call out their shortcomings. But their thoughts are deep, their understanding of life complex, and their suppositions rich with meaning and insight. Because they tend to be quiet, when they do speak, their words are surprisingly full of import.

Individual Role: Thinkers often try to work within existing restrictions and think their way through problems. They will play games and manipulate others in a very subtle way to make matters go their way. They're patient and tend not just to plan a few moves ahead, but to have multiple game boards going on at once in their mind.

Group Role: Thinkers tend to avoid confrontation or roles of leadership (they are often too distant to show the empathy necessary to be a great leader), but they're the voice of reason and planning in the group. They protect others by seeing the problems ahead and steering their compatriots out of the way long before they run into negative situations. Usually, the others in the group never even know such a threat exists.

Prodigy Abilities and Foci: Thinker mask-forms tend to manifest psychic abilities, though this is not a hard and fast restriction against physical powers. The teens that Thinkers manifest from tend to be . . . less than smart.

Power Shift Placement: Thinkers should place power shifts into intelligence, problem-solving skills, science, or foci or type abilities if they wish to be superhumanly brilliant.

Advancement of Thinkers: As a Thinker advances, their mastery of the world of academia, manipulation of bureaucratic systems, and general knowledge increase. They become learning machines, capable of tackling problems far beyond what the average human mind can handle.

BUILDING A THINKER

The core of the Thinker type in *Unmasked* is the Adept from the *Cypher System Rulebook*. As such, players playing a Thinker get to pick from the Adept ability choices (as well as some special abilities defined below). Once an Adept ability is selected, the player should give it a "feeling" so it fits in the weird world of *Unmasked*.

Thinkers can always choose an ability from a lower tier instead of adding one from their current tier, and they can replace one lower-tier ability with a different one from a lower tier.

The full text of *Cypher System Rulebook* abilities is not replicated here. Please refer to the *Cypher System Rulebook* for details on your ability and equipment choices. Below is a breakdown of what abilities are preselected or available at each tier.

FIRST-TIER THINKER

You gain the abilities noted for a first-tier Adept.

Mask-Form Abilities: When you select a new first-tier ability, you can instead select a first-tier mask-form ability. All prodigies have access to these special mask-form abilities.

Prodigy Sight: You can see people and places that are of special significance, as well as identify, collect, and use mementos. You can identify another prodigy on sight, even if they're not wearing their mask. This ability is *always* active and cannot be turned off, even when you're just a teen.

FIRST-TIER THINKER ABILITIES

Choose 4 abilities + Prodigy Sight + Practiced With Light Weapons

Distortion (2 Intellect points)
Erase Memories (3 Intellect points)
Far Step (2 Intellect points)
Hedge Magic (1 Intellect point)
Magic Training
Onslaught (1 Intellect point)
Push (2 Intellect points)
Resonance Field (1 Intellect point)
Scan (2 Intellect points)
Sculpt Flesh (2 Intellect points)
Shatter (2 Intellect points)
Ward

THINKER STATS

Thinker Stat Pools

Stat	Pool Starting Value
Might	7
Speed	9
Intellect	12

You get 6 additional points to divide among your stat Pools however you wish.

Example Selection and Customization: Mark is making a first-tier Thinker he calls "Duality." He decides his mask-form is a tall, thin, bald man—totally different than his character's short, squat teen-form. The Thinker's costume is made of mirror fragments to match his odd, glass-covered mask. Mark selects a mirror katana (medium weapon) and a mirror knife (light weapon) for his Thinker's equipment. Duality gets the Prodigy Sight and Practiced With Light Weapons abilities automatically, and Mark selects Distortion, Far Step, Shatter, and Ward for his Thinker's four abilities. He customizes these by saying they all work only in proximity to (any) glass surface (such as his suit!). Using Distortion, he can hide a willing creature by swirling mirror fragments from his suit around it. Using Far Step, he can leap into mirrors (even tiny ones) and emerge from any other reflective surface within a certain distance. Using Shatter, he can cause items to shatter into mirror fragments). And using Ward, he can form a swirling shield of glass to deflect incoming attacks. How does this work? He says his mask can "speak to glass." Duh.

SECOND-TIER THINKER

You gain the abilities noted for a second-tier Adept. In addition, you can replace one of your lower-tier abilities with a different one from a lower tier.

Mask-Form Abilities: When you select a new second-tier ability, you can instead select a second-tier mask-form ability. All prodigies have access to these special mask-form abilities.

SECOND-TIER THINKER ABILITIES

Choose 1 ability

Adaptation (2+ Intellect points)
Cutting Light (2 Intellect points)
Flash (4 Intellect points)
Hover (2 Intellect points)
Mind Reading (4 Intellect points)
Retrieve Memories (3 Intellect points)
Reveal (2+ Intellect points)
Stasis (3 Intellect points)

Example Selection and Customization: Mark's Thinker hits second tier, and Mark selects Stasis as his Thinker's new ability. He customizes it to fit the established feeling by saying that it's like an extension of Duality's Ward ability. With Stasis, the Thinker surrounds a target with a swirling mass of glass that nothing can pass through. Anything caught inside is impervious to harm and cannot escape.

THIRD-TIER THINKER

You gain the abilities noted for a third-tier Adept. In addition, you can replace one of your lower-tier abilities with a different one from a lower tier.

Mask-Form Abilities: When you select a new third-tier ability, you can instead select a third-tier mask-form ability. All prodigies have access to these special mask-form abilities.

THIRD-TIER THINKER ABILITIES

Choose 2 abilities + additional power shift (+3 damage for a specific attack)

Additional Power Shift (+3 Damage for a Specific Attack): Apply a permanent power shift to a particular attack not previously boosted by a power shift, adding +3 points of damage to it.
Adroit Memento Use
Barrier (3+ Intellect points)
Countermeasures (4 Intellect points)
Energy Protection (3+ Intellect points)
Fire and Ice (4 Intellect points)
Sensor (4 Intellect points)
Targeting Eye

Example Selection and Customization: Mark's Thinker hits third tier, and Mark selects Energy Protection and Sensor as his Thinker's new abilities. He customizes it to fit the established feeling by saying that Energy Protection causes the energy to become embedded in the glass fragments he controls, discoloring them so electricity trapped in the glass would be visible, as would light. The Sensor ability allows Duality to "place" a peephole on any reflective surface that he can look through—no matter the distance—with a moment's concentration. Mark adds the power shift to his Thinker's Shatter attack, meaning it inflicts 4 points of damage per detonation.

FOURTH-TIER THINKER

You gain the abilities noted for a fourth-tier Adept. In addition, you can replace one of your lower-tier abilities with a different one from a lower tier.

Mask-Form Abilities: When you select a new fourth-tier ability, you can instead select a fourth-tier mask-form ability. All prodigies have access to these special mask-form abilities.

FOURTH-TIER THINKER ABILITIES

Choose 1 ability

Exile (5 Intellect points)

Invisibility (4 Intellect points)

Matter Cloud (5 Intellect points)

Mind Control (6+ Intellect points)

Projection (4 Intellect points)

Rapid Processing (6 Intellect points)

Regeneration (6 Intellect points)

Reshape (5 Intellect points)

Slay (6 Intellect points)

Wormhole (6 Intellect points)

Example Selection and Customization:
Mark's Thinker hits fourth tier, and Mark selects Exile as his Thinker's new ability. He customizes it to fit the established feeling by saying Duality can move a target to the other side of the glass—so the target is inside the reflection. While there, the victim struggles and screams, but no sound can be heard. At the end of the duration, the target reappears, unharmed.

FIFTH-TIER THINKER

You gain the abilities noted for a fifth-tier Adept. In addition, you can replace one of your lower-tier abilities with a different one from a lower tier.

Mask-Form Abilities: When you select a new fifth-tier ability, you can instead select a fifth-tier mask-form ability. All prodigies have access to these special mask-form abilities.

FIFTH-TIER THINKER ABILITIES

Choose 2 abilities + additional power shift to intelligence

Additional Power Shift to Intelligence:
This works like a permanent level of Effort on Intellect defense rolls, as well as on knowledge, science, and crafting tasks.

Absorb Energy (7 Intellect points)

Concussion (7 Intellect points)

Conjuration (7 Intellect points)

Create (7 Intellect points)

Divide Your Mind (7 Intellect points)

Dust to Dust (7 Intellect points)

Knowing the Unknown (6 Intellect points)

Master Memento Use

Teleportation (6+ Intellect points)

True Senses

Example Selection and Customization: Mark's Thinker hits fifth tier, and Mark selects Create and Divide Your Mind as his Thinker's new abilities. He customizes it to fit the established feeling by saying that, with Create, Duality actually reaches into a reflection to somewhere else, from which he pulls the created object (whether or not it is from the real world is unknown). Using Divide Your Mind, the Thinker and his reflection can each take an action for one minute. Duality gains an additional power shift to all intelligence tasks, reducing the difficulty of all Intellect-based activities permanently by one step.

SIXTH-TIER THINKER

You gain the abilities noted for a sixth-tier Adept. In addition, you can replace one of your lower-tier abilities with a different one from a lower tier.

Mask-Form Abilities: When you select a new sixth-tier ability, you can instead select a sixth-tier mask-form ability. All prodigies have access to these special mask-form abilities.

SIXTH-TIER THINKER ABILITIES

Choose 1 ability

Control Weather (10 Intellect points)

Earthquake (10 Intellect points)

Move Mountains (9 Intellect points)

Traverse the Worlds (8+ Intellect points)

Usurp Memento: You destroy one memento that you bear and gain its power, which then functions for you continuously. The memento must have an effect that is not instantaneous. You can choose a memento when you gain this ability, or you can wait and make the choice later. However, once you usurp a memento's power, you cannot later switch to a different memento—the ability works only once. Action to initiate.

Example Selection and Customization: Mark's Thinker hits sixth tier, and Mark selects Move Mountains as his Thinker's new ability. In the world of glass, the Thinker is seen moving, reshaping, or destroying huge objects, and shortly thereafter, a similar force acts upon the real world, though it appears to occur without a source.

MOVER

No one knows what to make of Movers—mostly because they're hard to pin down—both physically and mentally. They're always on the move. They dress, act, and act out in unpredictable and wild ways. Even so, they're not *all* outgoing. Some are quiet and withdrawn. But all of them have one thing in common: they just don't care what anyone thinks. Even if they are sometimes quiet, Movers say what needs to be said—even if no one else will. In fact, to those who know them, this fact more than anything else makes them a valuable ally.

Individual Role: Movers are often on the outside looking in on *everything*. Not that they care. They're clever and quick-witted, capable of making split-second decisions that would cause others to freeze up. And their weird social standing makes it possible for them to be friends with nearly anyone, anywhere.

Group Role: Movers sometimes lead, but they will just as soon shirk their responsibilities if some distraction catches their fancy. They're often fiercely loyal and will do nearly anything to protect their friends. They often value the future of others over their own and gladly take the fall for them.

Prodigy Abilities and Foci: Mover mask-forms tend to manifest movement abilities (duh), though this is not a hard and fast restriction against other powers. The teens that Movers manifest from tend to be quiet, withdrawn, or uncoordinated.

Power Shift Placement: Movers should place power shifts into dexterity, speed, running, dodging, or similar if they wish to be superhumanly fast.

Advanced Movers: As Movers advance, so do their powers in movement, control, and physical abilities. Movers become faster, fly higher, or teleport farther the more advanced they become.

BUILDING A MOVER

The core of the Mover type in *Unmasked* is a slightly tweaked Explorer from the *Cypher System Rulebook*. As such, players playing a Mover get to pick from the Explorer ability choices (as well as from some special abilities defined below). Once an Explorer ability is selected, the player should give it a "feeling" so it fits in the weird world of *Unmasked*, where nearly anything is possible—at least for the prodigies.

Movers can always choose an ability from a lower tier instead of adding one from their current tier, and they can replace one lower-tier ability with a different one from a lower tier.

The full text of *Cypher System Rulebook* abilities is not replicated here. Please refer to the *Cypher System Rulebook* for details on your ability and equipment choices. Below is a breakdown of what abilities are preselected or available at each tier.

MOVER STATS

Mover Stat Pools

Stat	Pool Starting Value
Might	8
Speed	12
Intellect	8

You get 6 additional points to divide among your stat Pools however you wish.

FIRST-TIER MOVER

You gain the abilities noted for a first-tier Explorer, with the following changes.

Mask-Form Abilities: When you select a new first-tier ability, you can instead select a first-tier mask-form ability. All prodigies have access to these special mask-form abilities.

Prodigy Sight: You can see people and places that are of special significance, as well as identify, collect, and use mementos. You can identify another prodigy on sight, even if they're not wearing their mask. This ability is *always* active and cannot be turned off, even when you're just a teen.

FIRST-TIER MOVER ABILITIES

Choose 4 abilities + Prodigy Sight + Practiced With Light and Medium Weapons

Block (3 Speed points)

Danger Sense (1 Speed point)

Decipher (1 Intellect point)

Endurance

Extra Edge

Fleet of Foot

Knowledge Skills

Muscles of Iron (2 Might points)

No Need for Weapons

Physical Skills

Practiced in Armor

Practiced With All Weapons

Surging Confidence (1 Might point)

Trained Without Armor

Example Selection and Customization:
Michael is making a first-tier Mover he calls "The Streaker." He decides his mask-form is a gaunt runner, while his teen-form is slightly overweight and slow. The Streaker wears a breakaway track suit, which can pop off with a single tug. Michael selects Danger Sense, Extra Edge, Fleet of Foot, and Surging Confidence for his Mover's four abilities. He customizes these by saying his character needs to be . . . uh . . . naked to use them. Something about wind resistance. Luckily, when naked, the Streaker is always a blur, so no need to worry about modesty. After each significant use of his power (at the GM's discretion), the Streaker must "carb up" and eat a ton of food.

SECOND-TIER MOVER

You gain the abilities noted for a second-tier Explorer. In addition, you can replace one of your lower-tier abilities with a different one from a lower tier.

Mask-Form Abilities: When you select a new second-tier ability, you can instead select a second-tier mask-form ability. All prodigies have access to these special mask-form abilities.

First-Tier Explorer, page 39

Block, page 39

Danger Sense, page 39

Decipher, page 39

Endurance, page 39

Extra Edge, page 40

Fleet of Foot, page 40

Knowledge Skills, page 40

Muscles of Iron, page 40

No Need for Weapons, page 40

Physical Skills, page 40

Practiced in Armor, page 40

Practiced With All Weapons, page 40

Surging Confidence, page 40

Trained Without Armor, page 40

Second-Tier Explorer, page 41

SECOND-TIER MOVER ABILITIES

Choose 4 abilities + additional power shift to dexterity

Additional Power Shift to Dexterity: The difficulty for all movement, acrobatics, initiative, and Speed defense tasks is reduced by one step. This can be added to previously power-shifted dexterity.

Enable Others

Escape (2 Speed points)

Eye for Detail (2 Intellect points)

Hand to Eye (2 Speed points)

Investigative Skills

Quick Recovery

Range Increase

Skill With Defense

Stand Watch (2 Intellect points)

Travel Skills

Wreck

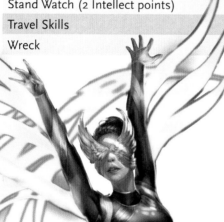

Example Selection and Customization:
Michael's Mover hits second tier, and Michael selects Escape, Quick Recovery, Range Increase, and Stand Watch. Again, these are linked to the Streaker being clothed or not. Escape is a side effect of the Streaker's high-speed stuttering movement. Quick Recovery is a by-product of the Streaker's superhuman metabolism (only when moving at high speed, of course). Range Increase again allows the Streaker to move faster and farther than most. Stand Watch is more "running watch," as the Streaker uses his superior speed to circuit an area looking for trouble. The Streaker also gains a power shift to dexterity, decreasing the difficulty of all dexterity-related tasks by one step.

THIRD-TIER MOVER

You gain the abilities noted for a third-tier Explorer. In addition, you can replace one of your lower-tier abilities with a different one from a lower tier.

Mask-Form Abilities: When you select a new third-tier ability, you can instead select a third-tier mask-form ability. All prodigies have access to these special mask-form abilities.

THIRD-TIER MOVER ABILITIES

Choose 3 abilities

Controlled Fall

Experienced With Armor

Expert Memento Use

Ignore the Pain

Resilience

Run and Fight (4 Might points)

Seize Opportunity (4 Speed points)

Skill With Attacks

Stone Breaker

Think Your Way Out

Wrest From Chance

Example Selection and Customization:
Michael's Mover hits third tier, and Michael selects Controlled Fall, Run and Fight, and Seize Opportunity. With Controlled Fall, the Streaker can vibrate so fast that he can slow his descent, making a fall less damaging. With Run and Fight, the Streaker can both move and attack, seeming to zip point to point over

short distances at such speed it appears he is teleporting. With Seize Opportunity, the Streaker can gain the upper hand while being attacked and then immediately attack his attacker—by seeming to jump short distances and land hits. Of course, all these speed abilities require the Streaker to, uh, streak to use them.

FOURTH-TIER MOVER

You gain the abilities noted for a fourth-tier Explorer. In addition, you can replace one of your lower-tier abilities with a different one from a lower tier.

Mask-Form Abilities: When you select a new fourth-tier ability, you can instead select a fourth-tier mask-form ability. All prodigies have access to these special mask-form abilities.

FOURTH-TIER MOVER ABILITIES

Choose 2 abilities + additional power shift to any ability

Additional Power Shift to Any Ability: This works like a permanent level of Effort on any ability. This permanently reduces the difficulty of actions covered by the ability with the power shift by one step per power shift.

Capable Warrior

Expert

Increased Effects

Read the Signs (4 Intellect points)

Runner

Tough As Nails

Example Selection and Customization:
Michael's Mover hits fourth tier, and Michael selects Runner (duh) and Stone Breaker as his Mover's two abilities. The Runner ability is self-evident. Stone Breaker represents the Streaker's ability to hold an object in his blurry hands and shake it to pieces. The Streaker now can boost any ability with one power shift as well, reducing the difficulty of all tasks covered in that category by one step.

FIFTH-TIER MOVER

You gain the abilities noted for a fifth-tier Explorer. In addition, you can replace one of your lower-tier abilities with a different one from a lower tier.

Mask-Form Abilities: When you select a new fifth-tier ability, you can instead select a fifth-tier mask-form ability. All prodigies have access to these special mask-form abilities.

FIFTH-TIER MOVER ABILITIES

Choose 3 abilities

Adroit Memento Use

Jump Attack (5 Might points)

Mastery With Defense

Parry (5 Speed points)

Physically Gifted

Take Command (3 Intellect points)

Vigilant (5 Might points)

Example Selection and Customization:
Michael's Mover hits fifth tier, and Michael selects Jump Attack, Parry, and Vigilant. The Jump Attack launches the Streaker into the air at a high speed and lets him deliver a flurry of punches and strikes as he lands on a target. Parry represents the Streaker's ability to see attacks coming and deflect them harmlessly before they can hit. Vigilant is just the Streaker's high-speed metabolism at work; it allows him to shrug off daze or stun attacks.

SIXTH-TIER MOVER

You gain the abilities noted for a sixth-tier Explorer. In addition, you can replace one of your lower-tier abilities with a different one from a lower tier.

Mask-Form Abilities: When you select a new sixth-tier ability, you can instead select a sixth-tier mask-form ability. All prodigies have access to these special mask-form abilities.

SIXTH-TIER MOVER ABILITIES

Choose 3 abilities

Again and Again (8 Speed points)

Greater Skill With Attacks

Mastery With Armor

Spin Attack (5 Speed points)

Wild Vitality (4 Intellect points)

Adroit Memento Use is the same as Adroit Cypher Use.

Fourth-Tier Explorer, page 42

Capable Warrior, page 42

Expert, page 42

Increased Effects, page 42

Read the Signs, page 42

Runner, page 42

Tough As Nails, page 42

Fifth-Tier Explorer, page 42

Adroit Cypher Use, page 42

Jump Attack, page 42

Mastery With Defense, page 42

Parry, page 42

Physically Gifted, page 42

Take Command, page 42

Vigilant, page 43

Sixth-Tier Explorer, page 43

Again and Again, page 43

Greater Skill With Attacks, page 43

Mastery With Armor, page 43

Spin Attack, page 43

Wild Vitality, page 43

Mask-form abilities, page 50

Mask-form power shifts, page 62

Speaker, page 44

First-Tier Speaker, page 45

Example Selection and Customization:
Michael's Mover hits sixth tier, and Michael
selects Again and Again, Spin Attack, and Wild
Vitality for his Mover's three abilities. Again
and Again is just a side effect of being so fast; it
allows an extra action. Spin Attack represents
the Streaker's ability to hit up to five foes in
reach in one action due to his superhuman
speed. Finally, Wild Vitality allows the Streaker
to tap into the energy that powers life—which
is apparently the core of his powers—and use
that force to gain various effects.

CHANGER

Changers usually know what to say and
when to say it. They see the ways people
interact—who likes whom, who is jealous
of whom, and what the newest cliques and
gangs in school are, or will be. This doesn't
mean that they're automatically shallow;
some think and feel very deeply. They just
seem *made* for the social life.

Individual Role: Changers are all about
relationships. One on one, they can talk
anyone into anything, and they often do, to
get what they want. Sometimes these choices
have a negative impact on the people whose
ears the Changers are bending, but Changers
often make up for it later.

Group Role: Changers are the movers
and shakers in a group. They go and talk
and question and keep the group abreast
of the various personalities that haunt the
standard high school. Since they know
everyone, it's likely a Changer will have a
better idea of who might be a prodigy than
anyone else in the group.

Prodigy Abilities and Foci: Changer mask-
forms tend to manifest abilities that help
them with people—either psychic powers
or talents related to physical transformation
and disguises, though this is not a hard and
fast restriction. The teens that Changers
manifest from tend to be on the less
popular end of the spectrum.

Power Shift Placement: Changers should
place power shifts into their foci or type
abilities, or on skills such as positive or
negative social actions, if they wish to be
superhumanly charming and transformative.

Advancement of Changers: As Changers
advance, they become even smoother,
cleverer, and cooler (usually).

BUILDING A CHANGER

The core of the Changer type in *Unmasked*
is the Speaker from the *Cypher System*
Rulebook. As such, players playing a
Changer get to pick from the Speaker ability
choices (as well as some special abilities
defined below). Once a Speaker ability is
selected, the player should give it a "feeling"
so it fits in the weird world of *Unmasked.*

Changers can always choose an ability
from a lower tier instead of adding one from
their current tier, and they can replace one
lower-tier ability with a different one from a
lower tier.

The full text of *Cypher System Rulebook*
abilities is not replicated here. Please refer
to the *Cypher System Rulebook* for details
on your ability and equipment choices.
Below is a breakdown of what abilities are
preselected or available at each tier.

CHANGER STATS
Changer Stat Pools

Stat	Pool Starting Value
Might	9
Speed	10
Intellect	9

You get 6 additional points to divide
among your stat Pools however you
wish.

FIRST-TIER CHANGER

You gain the abilities noted for a first-tier
Speaker.

Mask-Form Abilities: When you select a
new first-tier ability for your prodigy, you can
instead select a first-tier mask-form ability.
All prodigies have access to these special
mask-form abilities.

Prodigy Sight: You can see people and
places that are of special significance, as
well as identify, collect, and use mementos.

Mask-form abilities, page 50

Mask-form power shifts, page 62

You can identify another prodigy on sight, even if they're not wearing their mask. This ability is *always* active and cannot be turned off, even when you're just a teen.

FIRST-TIER CHANGER ABILITIES

Choose 4 abilities + Memento Use + Prodigy Sight + Practiced With Light Weapons

Aggression (2 Intellect points)

Encouragement (1 Intellect point)

Enthrall (1 Intellect point)

Erase Memories (3 Intellect points)

Fast Talk (1 Intellect point)

Interaction Skills: Pick two of the following: deceiving, persuading, public speaking, seeing through deception, or intimidating. You can select this ability multiple times.

Practiced With Light and Medium Weapons

Spin Identity (2+ Intellect points)

Terrifying Presence (2+ Intellect points)

Understanding (2 Intellect points)

Example Selection and Customization: Dee is making a first-tier Changer she calls "That Guy." She decides the mask-form is just a guy (or a gal), you know? That Guy has a form that's really difficult to describe but rarely looks out of place anywhere—totally different from the character's tall, gawky teen-form with curly red hair who can't help but stand out. The Changer's costume is difficult to pin down; it seems to change with them as they move about. Dee selects a Rambo knife (light weapon) for her mask-form's equipment. That Guy gets the Memento Use, Prodigy Sight, and Practiced With Light Weapons abilities automatically, and Dee selects Erase Memories, Fast Talk, Spin Identity, and Understanding for her Changer's four abilities. She customizes these by saying that as long as her mask-form doesn't say ANY PERSON'S NAME, they can work all their abilities and appear as a completely nondescript guy/girl whose presence people never question. While using their powers, That Guy also has to end each sentence with "dude." The moment a name is required, asked, or spoken, or if the Changer fails to say, "dude," That Guy is revealed as a mask.

SECOND-TIER CHANGER

You gain the abilities noted for a second-tier Speaker. In addition, you can replace one of your lower-tier abilities with a different one from a lower tier.

   Mask-Form Abilities: When you select a new second-tier ability, you can instead select a second-tier mask-form ability. All prodigies have access to these special mask-form abilities.

SECOND-TIER CHANGER ABILITIES

Choose 2 abilities + additional power shift to positive social interactions

Additional Power Shift to Positive Social Interactions: This works like a permanent level of Effort on positive social interaction rolls.

Babel

Impart Ideal (3 Intellect points)

Practiced in Armor

Skills

Speed Recovery (3 Intellect points)

Unexpected Betrayal

Example Selection and Customization:
Dee's Changer hits second tier, and Dee selects
Impart Ideal and Unexpected Betrayal. Impart
Ideal will be tough, since That Guy's power
restriction forces them to avoid names ("Hey,
uh, you want to hit the, uh . . . brown-haired
guy, dude?"). Unexpected Betrayal works
normally. That Guy also gains a permanent
power shift to positive social interactions.

THIRD-TIER CHANGER

You gain the abilities noted for a third-tier
Speaker. In addition, you can replace one of
your lower-tier abilities with a different one
from a lower tier.

Mask-Form Abilities: When you select a
new third-tier ability, you can instead select a
third-tier mask-form ability. All prodigies have
access to these special mask-form abilities.

THIRD-TIER CHANGER ABILITIES

Choose 3 abilities

Accelerate (4+ Intellect points)
Blend In (4 Intellect points)
Discerning Mind
Expert Memento Use
Grand Deception (3 Intellect points)
Mind Reading (4 Intellect points)
Oratory (4 Intellect points)
Telling (2 Intellect points)

Example Selection and Customization:
Dee's Changer hits third tier, and Dee selects
Expert Memento Use, Grand Deception, and
Oratory. This means her teen (and mask-form)
can carry three mementos. Grand Deception
follows That Guy's normal mask-power
restrictions. Oratory works as normal, but it's
hard for the Changer to direct people to do
anything really useful without using names . . .

FOURTH-TIER CHANGER

You gain the abilities noted for a fourth-tier
Speaker. In addition, you can replace one of
your lower-tier abilities with a different one
from a lower tier.

Mask-Form Abilities: When you select a
new fourth-tier ability, you can instead select
a fourth-tier mask-form ability. All prodigies
have access to these special mask-form
abilities.

FOURTH-TIER CHANGER ABILITIES

Choose 2 abilities + additional power shift to any ability

Additional Power Shift to Any Ability: This works like a permanent level of Effort on any ability. This permanently reduces the difficulty of actions covered by the ability with the power shift by one step per power shift.

Anticipate Attack (4 Intellect points)

Confounding Banter (4 Intellect points)

Feint (2 Speed points)

Heightened Skills

Psychosis (4 Intellect points)

Quick Wits

Read the Signs (4 Intellect points)

Suggestion (4 Intellect points)

Example Selection and Customization:
Dee's Changer hits fourth tier, and Dee selects Confounding Banter and Suggestion for her Changer's new abilities. Confounding Banter requires That Guy to say "Dude! Hey, dude!" over and over again. If That Guy can't speak, they can't use the ability. Suggestion is similar, but That Guy instead narrates what the controlled being in question is doing while they are doing it ("First, he hit the guy in the silver pants. Then, he took his keys..."). Again, no speaking, no ability. And finally, Dee applies a permanent power shift to recovery (this grants her one extra immediate recovery roll).

FIFTH-TIER CHANGER

You gain the abilities noted for a fifth-tier Speaker. In addition, you can replace one of your lower-tier abilities with a different one from a lower tier.

   Mask-Form Abilities: When you select a new fifth-tier ability, you can instead select a fifth-tier mask-form ability. All prodigies have access to these special mask-form abilities.

FIFTH-TIER CHANGER ABILITIES

Choose 3 abilities

Adroit Memento Use

Experienced With Armor

Flee (6 Intellect points)

Font of Inspiration

Foul Aura (5+ Intellect points)

Skill With Attacks

Stimulate (6 Intellect points)

Example Selection and Customization: *Dee's Changer hits fifth tier, and Dee selects Adroit Memento Use (this allows the character to carry four mementos), Flee, and Foul Aura for her Changer's new abilities. She customizes the feeling of these in the following manner. Flee requires That Guy to make a big deal about some "bad dude" coming by describing what awful things the unnamed being will inflict on those present. If the targets can't hear That Guy, they are unaffected. Foul Aura requires That Guy to swear continuously at a location, filling it with a bad aura that forces people to stay away.*

SIXTH-TIER CHANGER

You gain the abilities noted for a sixth-tier Speaker. In addition, you can replace one of your lower-tier abilities with a different one from a lower tier.

   Mask-Form Abilities: When you select a new sixth-tier ability, you can instead select a sixth-tier mask-form ability. All prodigies have access to these special mask-form abilities.

SIXTH-TIER CHANGER ABILITIES

Choose 2 abilities

Battle Management (4 Intellect points)

Inspiring Success (6 Intellect points)

Shatter Mind (7+ Intellect points)

True Senses

Word of Command (6 Intellect points + level 6 memento)

Adroit Memento Use is the same as Adroit Cypher Use.

Anticipate Attack, page 48

Confounding Banter, page 48

Feint, page 48

Heightened Skills, page 48

Psychosis, page 48

Quick Wits, page 48

Read the Signs, page 49

Suggestion, page 49

Fifth-Tier Speaker, page 49

Adroit Cypher Use, page 49

Experienced With Armor, page 49

Flee, page 49

Font of Inspiration, page 49

Foul Aura, page 49

Skill With Attacks, page 49

Stimulate, page 49

Sixth-Tier Speaker, page 49

Battle Management, page 49

Inspiring Success, page 49

Shatter Mind, page 49

True Senses, page 49

Word of Command, page 50

Mask-form abilities, page 50

Mask-form power shifts, page 62

Example Selection and Customization:
Dee's Changer hits sixth tier, and Dee selects Shatter Mind and Word of Command for her Changer's new abilities. She customizes the feeling of these in the following manner. To use Shatter Mind, That Guy must whisper in the target's ear, "What's your damage, dude?" And Word of Command (which dictates the sacrifice of a level 6 memento) requires That Guy to tell the target what to do in haiku. Five syllables, seven syllables, five syllables. Otherwise, it doesn't operate.

MASK-FORM ABILITIES

Characters of any type may choose from the following mask-form abilities at the appropriate tier, in lieu of selecting any of their type abilities. These are general abilities found throughout the prodigy population.

FIRST-TIER MASK-FORM ABILITIES

The following abilities are designed to suit any mask-forms in *Unmasked*.

Liberace (1 Intellect point): Every time your mask-form manifests, you have a different costume—though it is always built around a single thematic element. For example, your mask-form's costume might always be purple, but if they manifest near the ocean, it might be purple scuba gear. In a police station, it might be a weird purple uniform. Work with the GM to determine its final form. This outfit remains until the character goes from mask-form to teen-form. Enabler.

Seek Them Out (1 Intellect point): By searching within long range, you can see the telltale signs of any mask-form that has traveled in that area within the last 24 hours, leaving a trail of power behind like exhaust from a vehicle. If you know the mask-form, you can tell whether it was them. Action.

Where Did THAT Come From? (2 Might points): You can conceal a single heavy weapon or an inanimate object weighing up to 1 ton (1 t) on your person in an undiscoverable location immune to search. In fact, even if your character is stripped, the hidden item cannot be found until you choose to show it. Enabler.

SECOND-TIER MASK-FORM ABILITIES

Backstory (2 Intellect points): You can suddenly and significantly have a history with another mask-form—even one you have not "met" before. This revelation should be a single sentence such as, "We fought each other in Paris." The target mask-form *remembers this event as well and it shapes their thinking.* The statement can only include a shared event, not a result. For example, you could say you fought them, but not who won the fight. Enabler.

No Pictures (3 Intellect points): When you wish, your mask-form does not cooperate with cameras; all photos or video of the mask-form simply show an unidentifiable blur for the next 24 hours. Enabler.

THIRD-TIER MASK-FORM ABILITIES

Flesh Wound (3 Intellect points): When damaged, your mask-form moves up the damage track in six hours, instead of 24 hours.

Teenage Disguise (4 Intellect points): For up to five minutes outside of combat when you choose, your mask-form can appear to anyone observing it to look and sound like your teen-form. If you are attacked or attack, the illusion vanishes instantly. Action.

FOURTH-TIER MASK-FORM ABILITIES

Shrug It Off (5 Might points): You must activate this ability *before* your mask-form suffers any damage. After that, any attack that inflicts 6 or more points of damage, or that moves your mask-form down the damage track, may be "shrugged off" as if it never happened—once. To all present, the attack appears to hit and inflict damage, but you're fine. Once you remove your mask or "shrug off" the damage, the power must be reactivated normally. Action.

Suppression (5 Intellect points): You can stifle your mask-form's natural emanation of power, making it more difficult for other prodigies to see you for what you are. You still emit the power, but it's in much, much smaller amounts than for most prodigies. Instead of just seeing you, any prodigy looking at you must make an Intellect defense roll with an increase in difficulty of one step. This effect lasts for 24 hours. Action.

FIFTH-TIER MASK-FORM ABILITIES

Dancing Between the Rain Drops (7 Intellect points): Your mask-form can cross an area of great danger to a specific target in sight range and ignore all damage or attacks in the interim. For example, if the mask-form needs to cross an area of toxic waste to get to a little kid, they could do so—appearing to leap and dodge in a super specific manner to avoid the puddles. This also applies to fire, bullets, explosions, and nearly anything else. Once the mask-form arrives at the target, the effect ends. Action.

Not It (6 Intellect points): Your mask-form can cause a single target to ignore them completely for five minutes, no matter the circumstances (whether they're stealing a safe or punching a wall of living stone, or if their hair is on fire). The affected target does not clearly remember what happened, only that they ran into someone "unimportant." Action.

SIXTH-TIER MASK-FORM ABILITIES

No Can Do (10 Intellect points): You can prevent the activation of all mementos within 20 feet (6 m) of you for 24 hours. This does not destroy the mementos or prevent them from broadcasting their power; it only stops them from being used. Action.

Second Wind (10 Intellect points): When activated, this power allows the mask-form to "reset" to hale and full stat Pools until the end of the current combat engagement (what constitutes an engagement remains up to the GM to decide). At the end of the engagement, the mask-form returns to their previous damage track rating and stat Pools, and their mask comes off, returning them to teen-form, exhausted. Action.

NEXT STEP

Once you create your teen and select their mask-form type, move on to selecting your mask-form focus in the following chapter.

CHAPTER 7
CREATING THE MASK—
MASK-FORM FOCUS

In *Unmasked*, while type is the core of the mask-form that the PC teen *transforms into*, the focus is the main power that mask-form possesses. It's the *verb* in the character creation sentence, "I am an *adjective noun* who *verbs*." When the teen puts on their mask, this is their big power. They may have a ton of type abilities related to this power, but the focus—that's their main power, or the source of their power. (And remember, when not wearing their mask, they're just a teen and have no type or focus.)

CHOOSING A FOCUS

It is best for the game if PCs do not share the same focus. It's supposed to represent something unique and cool about the mask-form and shouldn't be just another run-of-the-mill ability. Luckily, due to the impossible nature of the *Unmasked* prodigies, nearly all foci (from any genre)

are available for the players to choose from, even ones that might seem—at first blush—not to be appropriate.

NEW FOCI FOR UNMASKED

The following four new foci are presented here in *Unmasked* for the first time, but they can easily be used in any appropriate Cypher System setting.

FLIES BY NIGHT

Your mask-form thrives in darkness. While you can exist in light, all rolls when your mask-form is exposed to any bright light count as one step more difficult. In the darkness—even just in shadow—you thrive. It's like a medium you swim in, drink in, and subsist on. You usually strike a terrifying figure to those who wander into your darkness.

Connection: Choose one of the following.
1. Pick Pick one other PC's mask-form.

You know them, and they know you—as if you and they had interacted for a long time—but where and when you met, and how they feel toward one another remains up to you to decide.

2. Pick one other PC's teen-form. You really dislike them. Nearly any problem can be traced back to them.

3. Pick one other PC (both forms). One of your forms is in love with one of their forms. Whether this love is unrequited or unknown is up to you to decide.

4. Pick one other PC's teen-form. This person seems to be able to see through your posturing and can always tell when you're bluffing.

Additional Equipment: You love cloaks. Riding boots and black lace shirts, too. It's likely you have several goth outfits to match your dire outlook on life in the shadows.

Minor Effect Suggestion: Your foe fails to notice you and needs a moment to turn their attention toward you again, losing an action.

Major Effect Suggestion: Your foe is terrified of supernatural beasties—and you are their worst nightmare. The difficulty of all defense rolls against them is reduced by one step.

Tier 1: Freaks Come Out at Night (1 Intellect point). You can summon small creatures that persist in darkness or shadow (nocturnal animals) to serve as your emissaries and servants. This ability functions only in an area known to be inhabited by such creatures (so, if you're in a jet aircraft, it's unlikely you can call up a rat, roach, or raccoon). The animals can be dispatched on complex tasks that do not involve violence, and they will flee normally if attacked. Otherwise, they will do their best to avoid detection while completing their charge. For example, you could instruct a brood of rats to chew through the ropes on a winch or to form a perfect circle around a person. Action.

Flies by Night GM Intrusions: *You remove your mask due to exhaustion, and some affected creatures of the night come calling when you can't control them. You remove your mask due to exhaustion while in night form or in shadow form, and you drop to the ground roughly, suffering 3 points of Might damage to your teen-form.*

The Manner of All Beasts. Nocturnal animals speak to you. The smaller the animal, the simpler the "report," and all information is channeled through the intellect of the particular beast. A roach might call a house a "woodwoodwood," while a rat might call it "a human-nest," for example. Their language is understandable only to you.

Tier 2: Ghost Dance (2 Intellect points). Living beings cut paths through shadow that only you can see, like a wake left behind a vehicle moving through water. This "dark wake" persists for an hour after a being moves through the shadow, and you can see the basic trail where it traveled in the area, as well as the wormlike trail of its body as it moved through space. In so examining the wake, you can deduce the meaning of the actions they undertook. This trail vanishes in light. Action.

Tier 3: The Killing Moon (3 Might points). Depending on the phase of the moon, you gain an additional Pool of points you can move to any mask-form Pool at any time until the next moon rises. The GM determines what phase the moon is in.

Full Moon. You gain 6 points to place in any stat Pool. When this Pool hits 0, it remains empty until the moon rises again.

Half Moon. You gain 5 points to place in any stat Pool. When this Pool hits 0, it remains empty until the moon rises again.

Quarter-Moon. You gain 4 points to place in any stat Pool. When this Pool hits 0, it remains empty until the moon rises again.

New Moon. GM's choice.

Mask-form power shifts, page 62

Mask-form abilities, page 50

I CAN'T FIND THE POWER I WANT IN MY FOCUS OR TYPE AT TIER 1!

Don't worry if you can't find precisely the power you want at tier 1 for your type or focus. Later in the process, you will be given three power shifts to assign to your mask-form. A power shift permanently lowers the difficulty of all actions covered by the ability it is assigned to by one step and does not count toward maximum Effort use. This means, if you assigned all three power shifts to strength, any strength-related task of level 3 or lower would need no roll to succeed. You could just kick in a door of level 3 without a roll. A power shift can be assigned to nearly anything.

Secondarily, if you don't see an ability at tier 1 by type or focus that interests you, remember you can always select a mask-form ability in the equivalent tier.

DEALING WITH WEIRD IMPLICATIONS IN CERTAIN FOCI

Some foci *appear* to deal with "out-of-genre" situations, such as Pilots Starcraft or Slays Monsters. Slays Monsters, of course, implies there are monsters to slay. How is that possible on Earth in 1986 without some giant retcon? Well, it's actually pretty easy. The *mask* creates the monsters (though by default, the PC doesn't know this and might never learn it). Masks tap the psyche of the user, taking everything—the good and the bad—to remake the world in a limited way. Put on the mask, and you may run into monsters gunning for you.

Other foci have much bigger implications, like Pilots Starcraft. It's unlikely a mask-form can have a starship (but you never know), so is that off the table? Well, the answer is: kind of. The abilities associated with the focus would offer little to a planet-bound mask, so there's little reason to choose it. Still, someone could choose to do so. How would this be handled? Well, for one, the mask-form might be a misplaced starship captain stuck on a desolate little backwater called Earth (or some such nonsense), and all their focus abilities that applied to the "starship" could also cover the basics of normal, earthly vehicles—since they're so damn primitive. "Of course I can fly a hell-o-copter—I came here in a Rhodassian generation ship, you trumped-up monkey!"

Tier 4: Night Moves (4 Intellect points).
If you pause and concentrate, you can expand your senses to encompass any living creature in shadow or darkness within 1 mile (2 km). This ability operates for as long as you remain still (and free from attack). When the ability is broadened to all creatures in the radius, it decreases the difficulty of all actions to do with searching, spying, sneaking, and climbing within that radius by one step, for one hour. On a successful Intellect roll, you can find a specific creature known to you and spy with its senses (hearing, sight, touch, taste, smell). This is not limited to nocturnal animals, only animals currently in shadow. It does not include humans. Action.

Tier 5: Night Shift (5 Might points). You can fold your body into a dimensionless shape that defies reason and then squeeze through absurdly small spaces, such as a crack in a door jamb or a keyhole. If air can move through it, so can you, in one swift movement. On the far side of the obstacle, you resume normal shape. If that space on the far side is not sufficient for your body to fit in, your body suffers serious damage as it tries to expand in the new, smaller space. Treat this as dropping one step on the damage track. Action.

Tier 6: Shadows of the Night (6 Intellect points). You can become a disembodied, flowing shadow of up to 20 feet (6 m) in length that can move across surfaces (even defying normal light sources by crossing lit areas), for up to ten minutes at a time. You can even float into the air (and up). In this form, you can move anywhere light can move—no matter how small the opening. Glass is as good as an open door to you. In night form, you are immune to physical damage, but likewise, you cannot attack (with physical or mental powers) until you choose to change back to your normal mask-form. Even in open light, you can maintain your night form (for a time). Action.

Lives on the Dark Side GM Intrusions: *You remove your mask due to exhaustion, and your power seems to attract the attention of enemies to your teen-form. You remove your mask due to exhaustion and drop it to the ground, out of reach.*

LIVES ON THE DARK SIDE

You see the spiritual landscape of the universe unfolding before you, moment to moment. By focusing your energies, you can change the outcome of events, see the future, and alter the minds of the weak, but these changes cause disturbances and ripples that only you can sense. These abilities allow you to know things before others do, to alter situations to suit your needs, and even to shift the outcome of life-changing events. It is an immense burden, as well as an endless boon, when used *wisely*.

You tend to be withdrawn, observant, and, above all, decisive—some might even say cruel. But then again, few understand the access to limitless power you possess.

Connection: Choose one of the following.

1. Pick one other PC's mask-form. They are buddies with your mask-form—with a long history of adventures together.

2. Pick one other PC's teen-form. Your abilities are super effective against them: all such rolls are treated as one step less difficult.

3. Pick one other PC's mask-form. It has taken a shine to your teen-form and does its best to protect and help them.

4. Pick another PC's mask-form. When it comes in contact with your teen-form, all its abilities inflict 1 point more damage.

Additional Equipment: Your mask-form tends to either be concealed beneath a cloak, or to wear an ascetic's robes and simple, monk-like attire.

Minor Effect Suggestion: Your foe is affected by the power in an unpredictable way, and they lash out, cause a problem, or destroy something—just not you or anything you possess.

Major Effect Suggestion: Your foe is somehow protected by the very force you wield, for reasons you don't understand. All attempts to use your focus abilities against them automatically fail. This effect lasts 24 hours.

Tier 1: Wax On, Wax Off (2 Speed points). When you activate this ability, you must hold your hand up in front of you. All projectile weapons targeted at you hit your hand instead and inflict 0 points of damage for as long as you keep your hand raised. To take any other action besides walking and using this ability, you must lower your hand. Action.

Tier 2: Phone Home (3 Intellect points).

You can see, sense, and feel the current situation of targets and, to a certain degree, their near future. Choose from one of effects below. Action.

Person to Person. As long as you suffer no damage, you can see, hear, and feel anything a single friendly target does, over any distance. You do not have access to their thoughts, and the ability does not operate on enemies. The target is aware of your presence. You and the target remain in contact until the connection is severed when you take damage or activate any other power or ability.

Future Proof. You see the near future of a friendly target. These visions are vague, but have revelatory clues embedded in them. Often, they are symbolic. The final disposition of the vision and its meaning are up to the GM.

Thoughts and Schemes. You can open yourself to the psyches of your enemies. You can ask one yes/no question about their plans and receive an answer. For example, you could ask, "Does the army know my identity?" and receive a truthful "yes" or "no" answer. But you couldn't ask, "Where is the army base?"

Tier 3: Fool, Pity the (4 Intellect points).

You suddenly appear to cut a terrifying figure for up to one minute. People shrink at your voice, posture, and appearance, though how you look and what you say doesn't even matter. This activates and deactivates as suddenly as a light switch flipping. The difficulty of all negative social interactions (such as threatening, bluffing, or commanding) is reduced by two steps while this power is active. If those affected by this ability are engaged in combat with you, you gain an asset on initiative tasks and the difficulty of all attacks against affected targets is reduced by one step. The ability is not selective and works on allies as well as enemies. Action.

Tier 4: Need for Speed (5+ Speed points).

For each Speed point spent above 5, you can move to any point within long range as if it were a single step. Each additional "speed run" past the first costs 1 Speed point. To those watching, you appear to blur and nearly teleport from point to point (though you still have to cross the intervening space). You can act normally for one action at the conclusion of each "speed run," but the speed run effect ends if you do not choose to "speed run" again at the end of that action, and you must pay the whole cost again to reactivate the power. Action.

Tier 5: Get Over Here! (5 Intellect points).

You can cause any person up to twice your size or any object up to 500 pounds (230 kg) to float through the air and jump to your hand or land on the ground in front of you, in a single round. This is useful for grabbing enemies at a distance, rapidly dropping some cover in front of your position, or snatching an object, gun, or other weapon. If anybody is between you and the object being pulled to you, and the object is of significant size (such as an air conditioner or a person), they suffer 2 points of damage as the object smashes past them. Action.

Tier 6: Most Impressive! (7 Speed points)

You can choose one of the following effects:

Missed Me. You can shrug off any attack that just happened in the last round, removing all of its damage and ill effects (even restoring you on the damage track, unpoisoning you, etc.). To all present, it looks as if you were hit or affected, but suddenly and inexplicably sidestepped it.

Perfect Dodge. For the next six turns, no attack (mental or physical) can hit you as long as you do not attack any target. The moment you attack, or at the end of six rounds, this effect ends. You appear to move in a preternatural way, sidestepping, jumping, and dodging with ease, as if you could see each attack coming before it lands.

Out and Over. In a single action, you leap to the lowest vertical surface that you can hang on to (such as the lip of a building), no matter the height difference. If this distance is greater than a single story, the effect looks preternatural.

Travels Back From the Future GM Intrusions: *Your mask-form blinks out of existence for a split second to fulfill some need in the past or future, causing your action to fail. Your mask-form blinks out of existence to fulfill some need in the past or future, and when you return, you're injured, knocked one step down the damage track.*

TRAVELS BACK FROM THE FUTURE

Your mask-form jumps back from a future time stream to warn you, help you, or just plain make your life better. Each time you do this, you claim, you must go back to close the loop at some future date—but who knows? It might all happen on a Wednesday in 2022, or not at all. Sometimes your future duplicate seems strange, as if they're from some alternate timeline.

Connection: Choose one of the following.

1. Pick one other PC's mask-form. They know a terrible secret about your mask-form, and you know they know.

2. Pick one other PC's teen-form. They are invisible to your abilities.

3. Pick one other PC's mask-form. You used your abilities on them, and now they don't trust you.

4. Pick one other PC's mask-form. They seem to boost your focus. When they are touching your mask-form, all rolls are treated as one step lower in difficulty.

Additional Equipment: You or your time duplicates may be dressed in bizarre, futuristic, or random clothing from any number of alternate dimensions. For example, when you summon a time duplicate, they might be wearing a spacesuit, an electrician's jumpsuit, or holding a stop sign. The standard GM response when the time duplicate is asked about their odd outfit is, "You'll see," or "Don't ask."

Minor Effect Suggestion: Your foe focuses on the time duplicate instead of you—the source of the time duplicates. When your duplicate leaves, the foe goes after you.

Major Effect Suggestion: Your foe is stunned by a time duplicate's sudden appearance or disappearance, and loses a round goggling at it.

Tier 1: That's Heavy (3 Might points). A time duplicate of yourself appears anywhere in sight range and tackles a person or lands on a target as if appearing from thin air above them. While the time duplicate encumbers them, all attacks against a tackled target are reduced in difficulty by one step. This time duplicate can't attack, but they can perform simple actions at your command, like flipping a switch, throwing a gun away, or removing someone's glasses. The duplicate has all your skills and knowledge. If the duplicate takes any damage, they vanish into the time stream. Action.

Tier 2: Time After Time (3 Might points). A time duplicate of yourself appears within 1 mile (2 km) and can act normally under your control for an hour—as long as they suffer no damage, do not see you, and do not move farther than 5 miles (8 km) from your location. The duplicate can attack normally and use all your skills. They know everything you know. The moment the duplicate takes damage or sees you, they vanish instantly into the time stream. Action.

Tier 3: Future Shock (4 Might points). Your next successful physical attack on a target is treated as three such attacks and successes (inflicting the damage three times as well). To anyone watching, it appears that time duplicates suddenly manifest in a haze, land all manner of attacks on the target, and then instantly vanish. Action.

Tier 4: Backup (5 Might points). If any of your stat Pools are below maximum, you can swap bodies with a time duplicate, restoring your stat Pools to full for the next ten minutes, whereupon you're dumped back into your old, damaged form in the current time stream. The Might cost comes out of the form you are *leaving,* but eventually you always have to pay the piper. This appears to witnesses as if you are suddenly restored to a pristine, undamaged form. If you have moved down the damage track, this *does* mean you move up the damage track to hale, instantly. Action.

Tier 5: I Already Did It (6 Intellect points). You can set any item, mechanical device, or piece of furniture in a single enclosed area into any position you want and have it fall, drop, open, light up, or turn on or off at a particular moment in time. You know this is done by going back in time and moving things around in a rapid-fire series of preselected movements, but no one else knows it. You vanish for a split second (so fast that it's hardly noticeable) and go back in time to move and rearrange the room in any manner you like. No one present realizes it, because to them, the room was *always* like this. This adjustment can provide one of the options that follow. Action.

Ouch! You set up a chain reaction of items that increases the damage of any attack you make by +3 points. For example, you tilt a bookshelf so that just tapping it causes it to smash down on a foe.

What Was That? You set up an item to fall out of sight, causing a significant enough distraction that the difficulty of all sneaking and stealth tasks is decreased by one step as attention is drawn elsewhere. For example, you place a broom on a wall around the corner, knowing it will slide and slam on the floor.

I'm Psychic! You know what's going to happen next (for example, a broom is going to drop and cause a door to slam) and can use this foreknowledge to try and bluff people in the area. The difficulty of all such bluffing actions is reduced by one step for a short time. For example, you claim to see the future, and describe how the chandelier will fall in 15 seconds, and then it *does*.

Tier 6: How Soon Is Now? (9 Might points). You can call up a time duplicate whom you control and who will fight beside you for the length of a single combat engagement (what constitutes a single engagement is up to the GM). During this time, you control the time duplicate as if it were a second character with identical powers, abilities, and skills. However, this duplicate *cannot* call another time duplicate. Action.

WANTS TO BE ADORED

Your mask-form is seductive in look, action, or speech, and sometimes all three. People like you. Those attracted to forms like yours *love* you. You wield this charm like a weapon, cutting through relationships and rules like a samurai cuts through enemies.

Connection: Choose one of the following.

1. Pick one other PC's mask-form. You intensely dislike them for unexplainable reasons.

2. Pick one other PC's teen-form. You want to help them—whether they want that help or not.

Wants to Be Adored GM Intrusions: *You remove your mask due to exhaustion, and former false allies immediately take it out on your teen-form. You remove your mask due to exhaustion, and someone begins to piece together that your powers are responsible for various oddities in the town.*

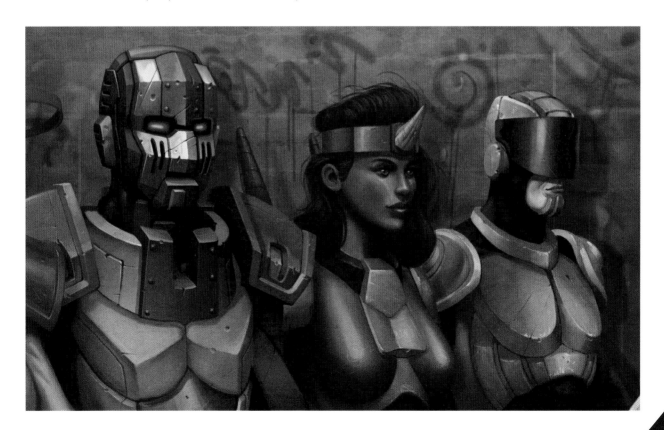

3. Pick one other PC (both forms). Something about them draws you close, but that attraction is always tinged with a feeling of impending danger.

4. Pick another PC's mask-form. They are always in your way. When you are in a fight together, the difficulty of all your physical actions is increased by one step.

Additional Equipment: You usually dress well, or at least with enough fashion sense that you can bully others into admiring such bold choices. Assume you're always dressed in some amazing fashion (this need not be attractive, but it's always striking).

Minor Effect Suggestion: Your foe, once free of your abilities, hates you and will do their best to ruin your day.

Major Effect Suggestion: Your foe becomes obsessed with you (in a good or bad way) and will do their best to track you down and enact their plans.

Tier 1: Stink Eye (1 Intellect point). You can fix a person in proximity to you with a look that has one of several effects. Action.

I Wasn't Talking to You. The target is made so uncomfortable by your glance that they disengage and step away. They don't really leave—they're just not in the conversation anymore.

That Was Dumb. The target is sure the last thing they said was a bad idea, and they won't reexamine it for at least an hour (even if it *was* a really great idea).

Hush Your Mouth. Whatever the target is saying, your look shuts them up immediately. They don't speak again in this conversation until invited to do so by you.

Tier 2: End of Line (4 Intellect points). With a single word, you can remove the ability of a person to speak except for the last word they uttered, over and over again. For example, if someone shouted, "Look out!" and was hit by this ability, they would be able to say only, "Out! Out! Out!" This effect can be removed by you with a single word, or it naturally expires in 24 hours.

Tier 3: I'll Be Back (6 Intellect points). You ingratiate yourself to one person with small talk, and convince them that no matter what you're doing (and *just* you), it's important and completely legal, and you'll be back to fix things up shortly. The target believes this wholeheartedly until they are attacked, or until you attack someone else in their presence or are out of their presence for more than an hour. Otherwise, no matter how strange it seems, you and your actions are just A-OK with the target. You're an amazing person. Action.

Tier 4: Just Do It (5 Intellect points). By shouting a single word of command directly at a person of level 4 or below, you can cause them to take a single, brief action without thinking about it. This *does* include injuring themselves or allies, but not prolonged violence. For instance, you could cause a guard to shoot himself in the foot, but not attack everyone in the room. Action.

Tier 5: EVERYBODY! (6 Intellect points). You can shout in such a manner that it gains the attention of all the people you wish it to within 1,000 feet (300 m). All who hear the shout lose an action, goggling at the speaker. For the next five rounds, the difficulty of all attacks against them is reduced by one step as they shake off the distraction. Action.

Tier 6: My Buddy (10 Intellect points). Through small talk, you form a bond with a single person. While the bond lasts, they believe they are your best friend. If given good reasons by you, they will perform nearly any action for you, including an act of violence, but you must provide the GM an explanation of how you attempt to convince them to do so. If they are predisposed to such actions, it takes less cajoling to get them to do it. This effect lasts until they lose sight of you, suffer 3 or more points of damage (or move down the damage track), or suffer any significant trauma. The ability can never convince them to physically harm loved ones, though it may make them lie, cheat, or steal from them. Action.

NEXT STEP

Once you create your teen and select the focus for their mask-form type, you can move on to assigning power shifts.

CHAPTER 8
CREATING THE MASK—
MASK-FORM POWER SHIFTS

In *Unmasked*, mask-forms can perform amazing actions that place them well beyond the everyday world, and not all of these abilities come from type or foci. Prodigies do this by using power shifts. *A power shift permanently lowers the difficulty of all actions covered by the ability it is assigned to by one step and does not count toward maximum Effort use.* This means that if you assigned all three power shifts to strength, any strength-related task of level 3 or lower would need no roll to succeed. You could just kick in a door of level 3 without a roll.

During character creation, a player may assign three power shifts to any of their mask-form's abilities. Once assigned to a particular ability, these power shifts do not change. During character advancement, as the PC rises in tiers, an additional two power shifts are unlocked for each type (some may be assigned anywhere, and others are prescribed based on type). This means that the most powerful mask-form possible has five power shifts.

Usually, these power shifts are distributed among various powers, abilities, or skills. Other times, they are clustered in a single category, to lift a super smart, resilient, or effective mask-form to an order of skill that a normal person could never match.

POWER SHIFT CATEGORIES

Players should feel free to be creative with the three power shifts they can place on abilities in their new mask-form. There is no definitive list, because power shifts can be used on nearly anything. GMs should work with their players to establish what does and does not make sense for a power shift. Players, of course, will be driven to find a way to have the power shift affect the most rolls possible, and it is the GM's job to curtail their very natural urge to gain power. Here are some helpful guidelines. Power shifts should be:

Clear: The name of the power shift should clearly establish what it is, and at least imply

what it affects. For example, "Aquatic!" goes a long way in suggesting what kinds of rolls it influences (all rolls dealing with swimming, water, holding your breath, etc.), but "Stuff" does not. What does that even mean? Jot down a note next to the power shift to make sure its meaning is clear, at least to you and your GM.

Restricted in scope: All power shifts should be attached to a power, ability, or situation. For example, you couldn't just have a "me" power shift which allowed your PC a power shift for *any* roll they made. Instead, it would work better to specify that your ionic blast ability had +3 points of damage for its single power shift, your flight had a regular power shift, and your dexterity was boosted with a power shift. You can also state that the power shift is linked to an event (for example, nightfall) or even a ritual ("I drink some blood!"). How? Just establish the limit and talk to your GM.

Indicative of the PC they are attached to: The power shifts should not stand out as odd when viewed in relationship to the mask-form. For example, a slight, brainy psychic might *need* a healing or resilience power shift, but *why* should they have it?

Some examples are provided below to give you a head start (these are by no means the only power shifts):

1. Accuracy. Your mask-form has a hard time missing. You get a boost to all attack rolls.

2. Dexterity. Your mask-form is preternaturally fast. You get a boost to all movement, acrobatics, dexterity, and Speed defense tasks.

3. Empathic. Your mask-form can sense thoughts and emotions, giving it an advantage when dealing with bargaining, negotiating, or interpersonal understanding.

4. Healing. Your mask-form gains one additional recovery roll per shift (each is one action and comes before other normal recovery rolls).

5. Intelligence. Your mask-form is brilliant, gaining a boost to all Intellect defense rolls and all knowledge, science, and crafting skills.

6. Night Ranger. At night, all your mask-form's rolls gain a power shift.

7. Perfect Organism. This power shift enhances all healing and resistance to poisons, suffocation, drowning, or biologicals while in mask-form.

8. Power. The mask-form has reduced difficulty in the use of a specific power or is granted +3 additional points of damage to the power per shift (does not affect attack rolls).

9. Psychic Power. Your mask-form gains a power shift for Intellect defense and attack rolls when using psychic powers.

10. Psycho Killer. Your mask-form's psychic attacks are boosted by +3 points of damage per shift.

11. Reaction Speed. Your mask-form has a boost on initiative and Speed defense rolls.

12. Resilience. Your mask-form knows how to take a hit, all Might defense rolls are boosted, or you gain +1 Armor per shift.

13. Run and Gun. Any attack rolls your mask-form makes while using your movement power (besides the movement power itself) are boosted with a power shift.

14. Social. This power shift boosts any positive social interactions with your mask-form.

15. Speed Freak. This power shift boosts all movement, running, jumping, or climbing in mask-form.

16. Weird Science. Any science you touch becomes *super science*. Using this weird power, you bend, break, and change the fundamentals of science, creating fascinating hybrid futuristic machines.

WRAPPING IT UP

Once you assign the power shifts, fill in your mask-form's name. Look for any outstanding info you've missed on your character sheet. If you're finished, you're ready to enter the world of *Unmasked*.

NPC PRODIGIES AND POWER SHIFTS

Of course, NPC prodigy mask-forms *also* have power shifts. These are applied as a level boost when the category of their power shift comes into play. For example, let's say the level 5 mask-form Lucifuge has two power shifts in strength. For all feats of strength, Lucifuge would count as level 7.

PUSHING IT

Prodigy mask-forms can do impossible things, often just by believing they can. The GM may allow players to *push their power shifts* in a life-or-death situation. This optional rule allows a player to move a power shift rank from one category into another *for one round* at the cost of 2 XP per shift. This can occur only if the situation is particularly dire; you can't just trigger it, and it can occur only once per game session per character. Also, the player must come up with a reasonable explanation that fits the situation, their powers, and the outcome.

Example: Doug, in his mask-form as Emerald Herald, looks up to see Igor casually throwing a school bus at him. Doug asks whether he can push his power shifts, and the GM agrees that for the Emerald Herald (a slight psychic who moves pretty slowly), being crushed by a school bus might be considered "life-threatening." The player describes the Emerald Herald as focusing psychic energy on his feet in glowing green points of light, and he spends 4 XP to move two power shifts from his intelligence to dexterity. Doug makes the Speed defense roll (with the difficulty reduced by two steps) and handily gets out of the way. The Emerald Herald claims he used his telekinesis to speed up his muscle movement. The next round, his power shifts return to intelligence.

PART 3: WELCOME TO 1986
TRUE COLORS

When the guy came in, it was like, yeah, I knew it . . . He. Him. Whatever. He shot through the door to the gym, and the doors just, like . . . exploded, man. Metal fire doors. They bounced and tumbled and slid on the rubber floor, making those big gashes. You see them?

The guy? He looked like some sort of pro wrestler. Hulk Hogan? But like, not natural. Bigger. Like, too big, man. Scary big.

That didn't stop him. He said, "Hey, lady!" What? No. That's all he said.

The other, the woman, was more like a cutout. Like those old scrape slates from kindergarten, you remember those? You draw on the plastic, and when you lift the film, the picture disappears. Yeah, well. Ah, screw it. Yeah. She looked like that. Not like she was wearing that—she WAS that. Yeah, I know how it sounds.

Why the hell would I make something like that up?

Okay? So. The guy picks up the bleacher. I mean, like, rips it out. The whole thing. What does something like that weigh? A bunch of kids go tumbling. He dumped them off before throwing it—like you'd, uh, shake off some peas from a spoon or something?—so that's good, I guess.

He threw it like, you know, it was a bit heavy even for him. But he still threw it a good 10 yards. It landed ON the lady, but it seemed to split as it fell on her. I could, like, see little bits of sparkly black around her when it hit. Like whatever she was made of was cutting through the wood. It was weird. Like, really weird.

She had these, like, uh . . . tentacles that came out of her head then. First they ripped the bleacher in half and chucked it aside. That's when Angelina, uh . . . Jaspers was hit. Is she okay? I saw her moving afterwards, but then the ambulance came.

What?

That? That's just a thing I made for art class. It's stupid. It's just a mask. Dumb. We all had to make one.

Can I, uh . . . go now?

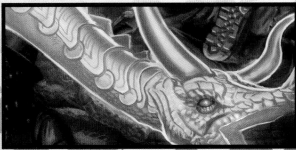

CHAPTER 9

THE EIGHTIES

The 1980s were a time of upheaval, renewal, and technological advancement in the United States. Recovering from the gas crisis and recession of the late 1970s, the first stumbling steps into the 1980s were fraught with further crises in the forms of rising inflation and interest rates, shifting leadership on a national level, and the growth in power of religious conservatism. By the mid-1980s, the country had found its footing. The recession eased, the economy rose, and the United States once again enjoyed economic growth.

To most in the nation, the American dream was still alive, and they could achieve it through hard work, education, and persistence. As the decade (and the next) dragged on, however, it became clear that the high point of the promise that America offered— decent wages and endless upward mobility to those who persevered—crested in 1986 and from there, tracked downward.

THE WORLD

The world of international relations in 1986 is one of boredom, interspersed by moments of tense alert. America and its NATO allies faced off in a constant contest of wills with the Soviet Union and the Warsaw Pact nations—communist satellites captured at the end of World War II. At any moment, a stockpile of nearly 60,000 nuclear weapons between the two countries were either deployed and ready to fire as a deterrent, or prepared for retaliatory strike. If even a fraction of these were launched, it would effectively mean the end the world.

Occasional international incidents occurred, but by 1986, the new Soviet party chief, Mikhail Gorbachev, had been actively pursuing a policy of *perestroika* ("openness") with the distrustful West for more than a year. Not all in the world were prepared to believe the Soviets were *truly* eager to end the Cold War. Others believed they had no choice, with their internal economy in ruins

and their military adventurism in Afghanistan costing them billions annually.

The youth of all nations, of course, embraced this concept wholeheartedly, and by the second half of the decade, a near-global embrace of reconciliation to end the Cold War had become an almost unstoppable force. In 1986, however, to the military forces of the world, such an outcome was hard to see coming.

COMMUNICATIONS

The 1980s were when computers—and especially personal computers, first introduced in the mid-1970s—came into their own. The promise of the home computer revolution in the 1970s rose to new, dizzying heights in the 1980s. Telephone technology also advanced dramatically. Leaps in communication such as cellular telephones (in the more urban areas), call-waiting, and group calls became

commonplace. Finally, and possibly most dramatically, cable television changed the landscape of both movies and television, bringing dozens and then hundreds of channels into the average American home.

COMPUTERS, MODEMS, AND BBS

By 1986, companies such as Atari, RadioShack, Commodore International, IBM, and Apple Computer, Inc. had infiltrated many homes across the United States.

While all of these companies made systems for playing games, many released simple terminals, which required a basic knowledge of programming to use. There were some exceptions; the Apple Macintosh was an early mass-market attempt at a graphical user interface, which would later come to rule computing, but the machine was so expensive that despite rave reviews, it never really took off. The rest of the machines offered only a command prompt.

An avid underground of companies, programmers, and fans surrounded each system's ecosystem, trading information through the mail, in monthly periodicals such as *Byte*, and online in limited forums known as Bulletin Board Systems (BBSs).

These BBSs were the precursor to the Usenet and later the full-blown internet. Each BBS could accept only a certain number of connections over modem, and as such, at peak hours, almost all were full. You would dial in on your modem, using one of a dozen numbers for the BBS, and hope for the best. If you were lucky, the "home page" would load.

There was very little art on such "pages" (though some had ASCII art), but users could post info that others could see, and they could perform other simple tasks, such as check out a book or download some text. Still, at the time, it was amazing—a harbinger of the internet to come.

ENTERTAINMENT

Kids went to the movies, watched cable TV, and collected books, comic books, and playing cards of their favorite films and examples of pop culture. The landscape of entertainment also went through a dramatic shift in the 1980s. The proliferation of video technology and special effects led directly to the boom in "music television," pressuring music stars to be attractive as well as talented. The need for cable TV content spawned a huge surge in low-budget film production, and with it, new genres to obsess about (horror and science fiction *each* supported nearly half a dozen magazines).

COMIC BOOKS

By the mid-1980s, comic books were enjoying an unexpected renaissance, and the fledgling "graphic novel" format, which had been thriving in Japan for decades in long-form comics called *manga,* had finally arrived in the United States.

Books such as *Watchmen, Batman: The Dark Knight Returns,* Frank Miller's *Ronin, V for Vendetta,* and *X-Men: God Loves, Man Kills* changed what comics meant and could

do, elevating the art form into something more violent, dark, and adult.

Still, the phenomenon was not long-lived. Comic companies, long starved of good sales, quickly escalated their publishing schedules to unsustainable levels. Soon after, by the later 1980s, the market had corrected yet again.

RECORDS, TAPES AND CDS

In 1986, the compact disc was the hot new thing in musical recording technology. Still, it was common to buy items on both cassette tapes and vinyl records. CD tech was prohibitively expensive for many, and it would take a few years before CD players became portable like cassette players. But still, the rich and the musically obsessed were drawn to CDs because of their supposed fidelity, as well as the ability to skip tracks instantly.

Top Recording Artists
Bon Jovi
Phil Collins
Peter Gabriel
Whitney Houston
Michael Jackson
Billy Joel
Madonna
The Police
Prince
Bruce Springsteen
U2
Van Halen

THE WALKMAN

Few pieces of personal technology changed the world as much as the Walkman. Though it was developed in the late 1970s in Japan, it did not "arrive" in the United States until 1984. When it did, it quickly spread everywhere. Before this technology, music was something you enjoyed at home or in the car; after its arrival, you could enjoy music nearly anywhere.

By 1986, "Walkman" was in the Oxford English Dictionary. Walk down any street in America and count to sixty, and you'd probably see a Walkman on someone's hip.

CABLE TELEVISION

Cable television opened a world of the new, cheesy, and strange to the youth of America. Many cable stations could not afford top-flight content, but their channels still had to run 24/7, so they turned to the next best thing—whatever third-rate movies they could buy. In this way, hundreds of films that would have just run in a half dozen theaters and closed (if they opened at all) found millions of viewers. Soon, the cable companies began producing their own content, once again, heralding a sea change that would fully arrive in the form of Netflix thirty years later.

MUSIC TELEVISION

If cable television hit entertainment like a bomb, Music Television (MTV) was a *nuke*. With its arrival in limited cable markets in 1981, it soon rose to prominence and power, subsuming everything musical in its path. It upended the music production company as the main public relations machine for the artist. For the first time, someone with a catchy tune, good looks, and a video camera could become famous without the backing of record producers. Even worse for the old guard, popular artists could steer their own career with outlandish and clever appearances on the channel.

MTV showed blocks of songs, each accompanied by a "music video." In the beginning these videos were usually the band lip-synching to the track. Later, with the advent of stars such as Prince, Michael Jackson, and Peter Gabriel, they were short *movies* with large budgets. For most of the 1980s, MTV was the social hub of those obsessed with modern music.

MOVIES, VIDEOTAPES, AND LASER DISCS

Movies still had a huge draw in the 1980s. Most small towns had a movie theater (or two), and on the weekends, such places were packed with visitors. Before the mall rose to full prominence, the movie theater was a place for youth to meet, hang out, and interact outside of school. A swath of huge "spectacle" movies—called blockbusters—began to arrive in the later '70s and early '80s, drawing huge numbers of viewers to the theaters. But even as this explosion of blockbuster movies was happening, another force was undermining them—VHS and laser disc technology.

By 1985, many had a videocassette recorder in their home. Not only could this device play movies, it could also *record* them from the television. With the advent of cable television and VHS tapes, this perfect storm led to the "bootlegging" movement, with people collecting, replaying, and watching their favorite movies over and over again—without buying the tape from a store.

Laser discs were higher-end technology. They were not recordable, but they offered the ability to generate still frames without distortion, skip sections instantly, listen to behind-the-scenes commentary, and see additional footage in a way that VHS did not offer. Still, by the mid-1980s, VHS emerged the clear winner.

Top Movies
Back to the Future
E.T. the Extra-Terrestrial
Ferris Bueller's Day Off
Ghostbusters
The Goonies
Sixteen Candles
Stand by Me
Star Wars: Episode V - The Empire Strikes Back
Star Wars: Episode VI - Return of the Jedi
The Terminator
Top Gun

THE WAITING IS THE HARDEST PART

Although communications enjoyed a leap forward in the 1980s due to the adoption of computer technology, both at home and by the telecom companies, trading information with others beyond a phone call was slow. If you wanted to call a friend out of state, your home phone number would rack up long-distance charges—and these could pile up high very quickly. Most people wrote letters to those they hoped to converse with if they were overseas or on the other side of the country. And if you think making a phone call to coordinate plans is slow, wait until you write a letter with a two-week turnaround time back and forth.

Discovery of new songs, movies, and other forms of entertainment was limited to catching a commercial on television, seeing an ad in a magazine, or some other archaic method. There was no real internet to disseminate pop culture, though some local BBS sites (which would eventually evolve into the Usenet) discussed fandom or science fiction, horror, and music.

CHAPTER 10

THE TOWN

The place that your PC prodigies call home can be a township, a town, or even a city (though it shouldn't be too large). The following information is presented to give you an overview of the main elements of an interesting backdrop for *Unmasked*. If you're looking for inspiration, look up any number of small towns in Google Maps, or mix and match elements to build your own. When it's done right, the town (or township, or city) will function like a character the PCs can interact with and feel a part of.

TOWNSHIP, TOWN, OR CITY

America is dominated by three main structures in local governance: the township, the town, and the city. The numbers vary on population and type, but for the purposes of *Unmasked*, they will be defined in the following manner:

Township: A largish area contained within a county (an assemblage of townships,

towns, and cities) with local government—usually selectmen or council members in the area. A township usually has a sheriff's department, a few fire stations, and some clustered population centers, but populations are generally sparse and small. They tend to rely on the county for water, power, sanitation, and maintenance. A township's population is usually less than 25,000 people, or if greater, spread over a wider area.

Town: A town is a single, clustered population center. It usually has a mayor and city council. Towns often have a police force, or share a police force and sheriff's department. They also tend to have local power generation, sanitation, and maintenance crews. A town's population is usually from 12,000 to 50,000 people.

City: A city is a large, single, clustered population center. It usually has a mayor, city council, selectmen from surrounding areas, a judicial system, and a jail. Cities

often have multiple precincts and fire stations all over the city, as well as multiple power stations, sanitation, sewer and water workers, and their own dedicated maintenance crews. A city's population is usually larger than 50,000 people.

The three types each generate a particular *feeling*.

Townships tend to have an agricultural feel, or seem removed from the rest of the surrounding area. If you want your players to tip cows, race cars on back roads, or explore the woods, choose a township as your backdrop.

Towns are neither here nor there. They are generally on the way to the "big city" but only a step above "Podunk." If you want your players to go into the city for a wild night and to feel the pull of urban problems without having the standard isolation of the country, choose a town as your backdrop.

Cities are urban and bring in urban problems, such as guns, drugs and gangs.

Still, it's likely such a small city still looks up to Chicago, New York, or Los Angeles as "real" cities. If you want your players exposed to the urban blight of rising crime, drug use, and more, choose a city as your backdrop.

HOME

Each teen PC, of course, has a home. What that home is depends a lot on the type of town they live in, who their teen character is, and what the GM wants their background to be. Players should work with their GM to come up with at least a basic idea of the place their teen calls home. The following are the most common types of home situations:

Homeless: Homelessness was a huge, newly visible problem in the 1980s. A stigma of failure was associated with it, but with massive layoffs in agriculture and manufacturing, it was an all-too-common outcome. If your teen PC is homeless, it is likely they're living out of a car or some other vehicle.

Mobile Home: Many poorer people lived in mobile homes in that time period. Clustered in undesirable areas, mobile home parks were seen as low class by most Americans. Still, financial realities made mobile homes the only viable choice for many. If your teen PC lives in a trailer, it is likely they come from the "wrong side of the tracks," and they may wish to hide their home address from their peers.

Apartment: In the 1980s, many Americans dwelled in apartments, found most often in towns or cities. Few owned those units; most rented them. In some areas, apartments were seen as low class (for

example, in smaller towns or townships), while in others, they were viewed simply as the status quo (cities). If your teen PC lives in an apartment, it's likely they spend a lot of time out and about, to avoid the long periods spent in close quarters associated with apartments.

House: A stand-alone structure, likely housing a family or extended family. Houses were found in cities, but the more urban the environment, the rarer they were. If your teen PC lives in a house, it can mean a lot of different things depending on the house, its location, and its size. In a city, a large, nicely appointed house is a sign of obscene wealth, while in a township, it just means you're likely well-to-do.

THE WRONG SIDE OF THE TRACKS

Almost all towns have areas they deem tumbledown, poor, or dangerous. Teen PCs from these neighborhoods are usually ill kept, misunderstood, or worse, actual criminals. Sometimes, a town's golden boy will come from that part of town and succeed despite the strong social stigma.

In either case, such areas are avoided as a matter of course. Everyone knows to do so, though few can articulate why exactly these neighborhoods are shunned. Only the locals, the police, and emergency services regularly go in or out.

THE HOSPITAL, TRAIN STATION, OR BUS TERMINAL

More often than not, the municipal hospital, train station, or bus terminal is located on the bad side of town. Property values around such places tend to drop due to the disturbances, riffraff, and trouble always found there. It's also the spot where runaways flock to, or end up in. Homeless people, drifters, and out-of-town criminals tend to end up around these areas, doing what they can (legal or illegal) to get by.

GANGS OR CRIMINAL TERRITORY

There's the wrong side of the tracks, and then there are gangland zones. Everyone in town knows where these criminal territories are and what routes to take to avoid the gang members that patrol the area. Gangs became a prominent problem in the 1980s in many suburban areas for the first time as the "war on drugs" heated up.

Such territories tend to be even more run down than the less desirable areas, and even the police are not a common sight. Sometimes, these high-crime areas are adjacent to a highway, or they draw traffic in from surrounding cities, but few in the town itself go there—except the unlucky ones who call it home.

Those who live in a gang area might be members of the gang or have family in the gang. Other residents might be left to their own devices because they are so poor that the gang has no use for them, or they might have a delicate truce with the gang due to a special status or role they have in the community. No one in gang areas is foolish enough to cross the gang without a very, very good reason, however.

Gang member,
typical: level 3; Armor 1

THE POLICE, FIRE DEPARTMENT, AND AMBULANCE SERVICE

The locale usually dictates the size and abilities of emergency responders.

The township often has a sheriff's department that patrols a too-large area, plus a volunteer fire department. Most townships are lucky to put their hands to a dozen or so first responders all told (double that if they go "all in"). Ambulances and higher-level rescuers, including SWAT teams, would have to be requested and called in from the county. In general, a township is ill-prepared for a serious disaster, and it will take time for the county and state to respond.

The town often has a police force, or both a police force and a sheriff's department. Towns also usually have a fire department with full-time employees and an ambulance service, since local tax revenues support such endeavors. All in all, an average town might field twenty to thirty first responders (double that if they go "all in"). A town has contingencies to deal with a disaster, but past a certain scale, that response will fail, and municipal authorities will have to request county and state support.

The city often has fire, police, and ambulance services, as well as multiple power stations and other resources. Sometimes,

RADIO DISPATCH

By 1986, many police departments across the United States had full radio dispatch, allowing their cars to call in, communicate with one another, and coordinate their response to criminal activities. Even so, this technology—especially in more rural areas—was not always terribly reliable.

The radio dispatch car made response times drop to minutes in more urban areas. It allowed police officers who were in trouble to easily and reliably call for backup. And most importantly, it allowed the police to report license plates and perpetrator descriptions across the entire police network.

given its size, a city may have a SWAT team and more specialized police responders (negotiators, snipers, etc.). A small-to-medium city might field fifty or more first responders (double that if they go "all in"). Cities have multiple contingencies to deal with a disaster, along with likely extensive plans to cooperate with county and state officials if they feel they need the assistance.

STORES

While malls had existed for some time, they took off in the later 1970s and early 1980s. A common mall consisted of an enclosed structure housing dozens of stores and usually a food court, as well as other amenities such as a movie theater, a skating rink, and other facilities for leisure activities. Having an active mall was a sign of local prosperity, and many towns and cities had a mall or two.

In townships, sometimes a single huge mall would draw people in from the surrounding areas. Such "mega malls" were built in the middle of nowhere to exploit the cheap land, low taxes, and interstate highway access.

The mall was the social hub of any 1980s town. On the weekends, it was the place where all the kids went to hang out, play in the arcade, or see a movie.

Of course, normal stores and businesses existed as well. Most towns had multiple supermarkets. The bigger the locale, the more likely it was to have a national chain store, such as Kmart, Pathmark, A&P, or Piggly Wiggly. Other popular shops included liquor stores, fast-food chains (McDonald's being the most common), ice cream parlors, diners, videotape rental places, drug stores, dry cleaners, bars, pubs, and 24-hour shops such as 7-Eleven.

COLLEGES AND OTHER SCHOOLS

Many cities and towns either encompass or abut a college, university, or trade or technical school. In your game, if such a campus exists inside the "town" proper, it is likely either a large portion or the main driver of the local economy. These college towns often all but shut down when the students are on break, and many of the local businesses sell most of their goods (if not all) to the students. College towns are usually marked by a higher level of prosperity (as money pours in through the students), as well as increased local safety and security services. Police and fire departments in such towns are usually larger and utilize cutting-edge equipment, subsidized by the needs of the college.

GAS STATIONS, JUNKYARDS, AND GARAGES

America is obsessed with automobiles. Nearly every township, town, and city has *at least* a few gas stations. Many also have junkyards, garages, car lots, and used car dealerships. Lots of teens obsess over cars, and many spend their afternoons and evenings fixing one they have, building one from scratch, or working at a gas station, junkyard, or garage.

For the gearhead teen PCs, such places are their hangouts.

ARMY, AIR FORCE, OR NAVY FACILITIES

Many towns and cities are near military facilities such as United States Air Force bases, naval shipyards, or army bases filled with soldiers, sailors, marines, or air force personnel. Those municipalities tend to cater to the service members who frequent the area, and whose families likely live nearby (if not on the base). Neighborhoods near larger military facilities often count them as a large portion—if not the lion's share—of their local economy, and the residents accordingly have a very strong sense of "supporting the troops."

Teen PCs might be "military brats" who live with their families in base housing, attending the local high school. Such teens usually cut one of two dramatic shapes— the screwup or the overachiever—but players should feel free to establish their own path.

EXAMPLE TOWN: EMORYVILLE, VERMONT

By looking around Google Maps for a few minutes and jotting down names that catch your eye, you could assemble a town like the following example town. You should feel free to mix and match your own (there are literally millions of examples on Google Maps), or use Emoryville, Vermont, for

yourself. All the elements below were snagged from slightly altered real-world examples.

Emoryville, Vermont, is an old city in Cook County bordering the Lipscomb River, near the Greenvale Ski Resort. It is also home to Cook County College, a small nursing school. Its total populace is 22,550 in the off-season. During the winter, its population balloons to 35,000 as out-of-towners rent property in town to visit the ski resort. The sheriff has four cruisers and ten full-time staff members. The fire department is volunteer only.

The city has a main downtown core with the following:

Broome's Fine Clothing Store
Green Apple Grocery
Sears department store
7-Eleven
Taggart's Sporting Goods and Supply
Woolworth's
Cook County Sheriff's Office
A volunteer fire station

This area is surrounded by low, rolling hills covered in pine trees and cut with narrow, curvy streets, each set with small houses and big lots. Past this core to the west is a secondary area called "the rust belt," or "Craptown"—the bad area of town. It contains the following:

Gas n' Sip
Moncton Apartments
A steel mill
A tin punch factory
Yarrow's Wreck Yard and Towing

On the highway into town are the following:

Cook County Municipal Hospital
Lamplighter Apartments
McDonald's
Shell Gasoline
Spotted Spruce Apartments

Just past town are the following:

Lipscomb Valley Mall
Greenvale Ski Resort
Final Straw Bar

CHAPTER 11

THE SCHOOL

The place that your PC prodigies go to high school can be a public high school, a consolidated public high school, a parochial school, or a private school. The following information is presented to give you an overview of the main elements of an interesting school backdrop for *Unmasked*. If you're looking for inspiration, there are thousands of TV shows, books, and comic books set in high schools that can serve as great resources for finding elements to mix and match to create your own high school setting.

THE HIGH SCHOOL

There are four major types of high school. A high school generally takes students from eighth to twelfth grade (or sometimes from seventh or ninth grade onward, depending on whether the district has a middle school). The GM should, of course, feel free to make up their own school and modify as needed.

Public High School: A standard public high school administered by the Department of Education and local government. These schools tend to be in a town or city, and the largest of them can have up to a thousand students.

Consolidated Public High School: Administered as above, these high schools are built in a central area between population centers and shared by multiple townships, towns, or cities. These schools tend to be larger and more modern, and they enjoy a more generous budget since many municipalities share the costs of the school. They can have up to several thousand students.

Parochial School: Private religious schools that cater to (but are not restricted to) a particular religion. Catholic, Presbyterian, and Jewish schools are all common. Usually, such schools have fewer than a thousand students, require a tuition, and are administered by a school board.

Private School: Nonreligious academies for teaching high schoolers. Usually, such schools require expensive tuition to attend, but they offer a better chance at academic success (due to the intensive nature of their courses compared to public school classes). Usually, such schools have fewer than a thousand students, and they are run by a full-time administration.

The four types each generate a particular *feeling.*

Public high schools tend to be smaller and usually just a little bit run down, though most in the town are proud of the school and what it represents. Everyone knows everyone else's business.

Consolidated public high schools are big and often well funded, thanks to multiple towns and townships kicking in taxes to pay for them. Since many more students attend consolidated schools and live spread over a much larger area, you often meet people you might not have met otherwise. Consolidated schools sometimes feel cookie cutter.

Parochial schools focus on religion. Even if they don't restrict attendance by religion, most of the school is at least draped in the appearance of religious activity. Students are required to have religious instruction or go to chapel. Parochial schools often feel stiff and vaguely authoritarian.

Private schools vary wildly in size. Since the student body pays a tuition to attend, the facilities are usually top notch. There is usually an unstated sense of pride in attending such a school, since it costs money to do so.

LOCATION

Public high schools and private schools are usually located in or very near to a population center. Municipal schools and some larger private schools have campuses. Usually this means that they are outside of town and have acreage to themselves where the main building is quite large.

Such municipal schools or academies also usually have outbuildings such as a stadium, pool, or even dorms for students who live on campus.

NAME AND MASCOT

School names and mascots are important to building up the school as a *character* in your game. The name should be memorable and roll off the tongue. Often, the name is that of a famous figure in American history or a local celebrity (for example, John Adams High School or John Wayne High School). Or, it's the area name, city name, or something older, such as a Native American name (for example, Everett High, Montgomery High School, or Greatview High School).

The mascot usually has to do with the name. For instance, John Wayne High's teams might be the Gunslingers, with a cowboy mascot, while a high school in Everett, Washington, famous for its Boeing factory, might call its teams the Jets and have an airplane mascot.

STRUCTURES

Many high schools consist simply of one large building with many rooms. Private and consolidated schools tend to be larger and have multiple structures on a campus. However, a general rule is that the larger the city the high school is located in, the smaller the structure.

CLASSROOMS

In general, most high school classrooms hold thirty or so students, though some labs and other facilities are split down the middle by a retractable wall, allowing up to sixty students in a "single" room. Sometimes teachers remain in one classroom all day, and in other schools, they move from room to room many times throughout the day as their class schedule changes. Teachers with a specialty (for example, gym, lab, or typing) tend to stay in one classroom due to the equipment required for their classes.

GYMNASIUMS, STADIUMS, AND POOLS

Consolidated and private schools tend to have more lavish sports facilities. Many even have a separate stadium for the local sports obsession (usually football or baseball). Such large facilities are usually contingent either on the wealth of the local district or the acumen of the sports team. The larger the facilities, the more locals attend and pay attention to games. In municipal schools with a stadium, a sports game is a town affair, with *everyone* going to the event, whether they have children at the school or not.

Regular high schools are often forced to make their gyms do double-duty as a gathering hall and sometimes fulfill still other functions. Many have a pool concealed beneath a closing wooden floor, allowing the whole gym to open to reveal an Olympic-size pool beneath. Others also have an elevated running ring suspended above the gym, allowing track-and-field athletes to practice.

HIDEOUTS, SMOKING LOUNGES, AND BUM ZONES

All high schools have spots known as gathering places for smokers, bad students, and "bums." Most schools restrict smoking to well-defined areas, such as an interior courtyard or a staircase at the back of the building. Some restrict it entirely. Often, these smoking areas are patrolled by teachers who "bust" students and send them back to class.

Sometimes, these zones are not known to the staff: an out-of-the-way corridor, an unused office, or a dead end at the bottom of a stairwell. Even if the teachers don't know it's there, word soon gets around to the students that such a place exists.

TEACHERS AND STAFF

Obviously, the larger the school, the greater the total staff. Smaller schools tend to force teachers to pull double or triple duty, teaching multiple subjects. The total number of teachers in a school is usually the total number of students divided by thirty or so. Some private schools have smaller classes and thus a smaller ratio of students to teachers.

Being a teacher in most high schools goes much further than a simple eight-to-three job. Teachers are often expected to stay after hours, tutor, run after-school events or special programs, or take on other duties. Many teachers don't leave until well after 6 p.m. every day.

Teachers are a useful tool for the GM to force some sort of compliance from a teen PC. Mouthing off to a teacher usually means detention or a reprimand at the very least. Violence against a teacher almost always means expulsion.

Teachers can serve as friends, mentors, and even enemies. But above all, they are *people*. Their ideals, goals, and methodologies vary wildly from one teacher to the next. As such, PCs should learn the landscape of teachers in their school. As a GM, an easy way to shorthand such people is to write down the teachers' names, give them each a descriptor as a high-level summary of their personality, and note their subject. For example, Mrs. Randazzo is a Vengeful English teacher. From there, her uses in the game seem pretty self-evident.

Teachers offer endless adventure hooks. Perhaps a favorite teacher appears to be in trouble, turning up at work late with a black eye. Another might seem suspicious, subtly indicating that they know something about the prodigies. Another still might unknowingly gather mementos into their office, causing all manner of trouble.

SECURITY

Some larger and more urban schools have professional security. Sometimes, these people are off-duty police officers from the town. Other schools use full-time employees who have no real training to serve as "hall monitors." Still others allow junior and senior students to be hall monitors.

Only the largest or most urban schools occasionally have *real* police officers. Usually such officers don't enter the school proper without some sort of justification. Instead, they stand at the entrances, tracking who is coming and going. Sometimes they search students, especially if there have been drugs or weapon violations.

An adventure hook might be that a family member becomes on-site security for the school and begins noticing odd occurrences after hours . . .

HOURS AND LOCKING UP

Most schools are open, in some form or another, most of the day and some of the night. The larger the school, the more sectional its shutdown might be. A single town high school might be locked up all night after 6 p.m., while a consolidated high school might lock down only its pool, the classrooms, and the cafeteria after dark.

Even after lights-out, a janitor or security guard is often on the premises. The larger the school, the more people are likely to be in it. Many larger high schools have more than one janitor, and their work—mopping, polishing the floors, cleaning the toilets—often begins only after the students go home.

It is rare for most school facilities to have alarms (though some private schools do). Keys are usually plentiful, and each teacher likely has a set that allows them access to nearly anywhere in the school. A great adventure hook might involve clever students finding a way to copy these keys without being discovered.

THE FEELING OF HIGH SCHOOL

Even without the weirdness of the prodigies, high school is scary. Everyone coming into it feels uncertain, eager, ready to change, and just plain frightened on some level. Emulating this feeling is the key to a good *Unmasked* campaign. Even the brightest student or most accomplished athlete should never feel like they have it all figured out, precisely. Being a teen is about feeling *uncertain*.

This puts a burden on the GM. To teens, good relationships, the social pecking order, and the need to become skilled at something are all extremely important (sometimes all three at once). While some students may focus on schoolwork, in truth, almost all of them long to be part of a strong social network of friends. After all, everyone wants to be liked and admired. The temptation of using their mask-forms to gain such praise—especially for a teen—will be overwhelming. The GM must keep in mind this web of relationships and use them to push or pull the PC in different directions. No teen should be without a desire and a fear (at least one of each), and it is up to the GM to make certain they never, ever forget them.

TESTS AND HOMEWORK

Part 5: GM's Toolbox, page 153

More on this subject is presented in Part 5: GM's Toolbox. Teen PC advancement and XP rewards are linked to fitting in and not being discovered. Those who manage to keep their mask-form a secret and who do well enough in school (or come up with some other method) to stay under the radar are, at the end of every game session, rewarded with 1 XP point. This XP can be used to advance the mask-form.

DEALING WITH TEACHERS

Students can't go for very long in school without a teacher coming along to supervise them. In most high schools, teachers are everywhere. It's their job to poke their noses in—into bathrooms, the cafeteria, or otherwise unoccupied classrooms—to make certain nothing untoward is going on.

This suspicion is tempered by several factors, of course. Is the student a known troublemaker? Does the teacher have a good relationship with the student? Is the offense serious? Each will shape the teacher's response.

Still, teachers relish catching students out. Some will tell the students to get going to class, others will assign detention (or send them to the office for expulsion, if the infraction is bad enough).

THE GUIDANCE COUNSELOR

In many schools, the guidance counselor's job is to track the progress of each student in their charge (many schools have a number of guidance counselors). In theory, this means all students. In actuality, they

spend most of their time dealing with the exceptional students, as well as the dregs. The exceptional students go to the guidance counselor to best shape their high school career in preparation for college applications, while the dregs, of course, simply are trying to stay in school. Average students are often overlooked while the counselor deals with these outliers.

Guidance counselors that detect a possibly uncommon student (say, a student who is exceptional at art, computers, or sports, but not at academics) might decide that the student is in need of "saving." Such students are in for a rough time, as the guidance counselor pursues them, goads them, and tracks their progress on a day-to-day basis in the hopes of getting them into a good college. In other words, counselors become an additional pair of eyes tracking the students during the day.

THE SOCIAL ORDER

All high schools have an almost unspoken social pecking order. There are the popular students; the middle-of-the-road, average students; and those that are considered "uncool." The vast majority of students are average, desperate not to fall below the waterline to the ranks of the uncool, and eager to somehow secure a seat at the popular table.

The popular kids often have been well liked their entire life, although certain ones have come into their own in high school. Some have achieved this because they went through puberty early or were naturally attractive, skilled at sports (or sometimes even at schoolwork), or just plain funny, cool, or fashion forward. They tend to police their groups in an unconscious (or sometimes viciously self-aware) manner.

The uncool students skirt the edges of the social order. These individuals interact more with one another, teachers, and other adults. Often, their world is the world of academia or other nonsocial achievements.

An important distinction for teen PCs to establish is just where their character stands in the school social order. The GM should help players to craft a believable position for their teen. Prodigy abilities (especially the ability of prodigies to see one another) will likely manifest across these social groups and complicate the established order— meaning PC groups may be composed of people from the uncool, average, and popular groups all at the same time.

GETTING INTO TROUBLE

Teens spend a large portion of their high school career getting into trouble. Most of the time, the trouble simply results in a verbal reprimand from a teacher or staff member. Other times, it can be much further-reaching and even damaging to their future. Students that cross the line can face detention or even expulsion, as well as negative comments on their permanent record.

DETENTION

Detention is the universal salve of school ills. Teachers apply it to troublesome students, using it as a stick to keep them in line. Those who misbehave, mouth off, or don't listen get detention. There are different kinds of detention (sometimes schools employ more than one method):

Study Hall: Students are sent immediately to a classroom filled with other students in detention. They are expected to read, do homework, and otherwise catch up on schoolwork while under faculty supervision. Anyone caught doing anything else will likely get more detention.

Saturday Detention: Misbehaving kills your weekend. Those who must suffer through Saturday detention find themselves sitting in a classroom at school on the weekend for several hours (usually 8 a.m. to lunchtime). They are generally not permitted to do anything at all. It is a miserable experience.

After-School Detention: This is the most common type of detention. Kids report to a room after school and must sit there—likely doing nothing—until dinnertime. Often, an infringement involves more than one after-school detention.

EXPULSION AND THE PERMANENT RECORD

Students of the 1980s lived in fear of an infraction ending up on their permanent record. This transcript tracked every point of progress or setback in a student's career, and served—for good students—as a ticket into a prestigious college. It was locked away in the school records and never readily available to be looked at, even by the student it concerned. Sometimes, it was trotted out by a guidance counselor, teacher, or principal to illustrate a point.

Those who stole, vandalized, or committed other offenses had notes put on their permanent record, which also recorded matters such as attendance, detention, and in the worst cases, expulsion. While most infringements on school rules would result in detention, expulsion was something different. Violence, threats, weapons, drugs—each of these called for expulsion. The student would be sent home from school for days (or even weeks) while the school decided what to do with them. Most of the time, the student was welcomed back within a few days. Sometimes, they were forced to perform some other service (such as painting the gym). And sometimes, in very few cases, they were asked never to return.

Students who attempt to find, read, or change their permanent record will find it very hard to do so. Even if they can somehow get past staff, unlock the security cabinets, and read the records, it will be extremely difficult to alter them enough so that it matters and for the teacher notating them not to notice. Still, it could be the basis of a very fun adventure.

PRODIGIES IN SCHOOL

Prodigies, of course, will use their masks—even in school. Clever prodigies will do what they can to conceal their activities and use their powers only when absolutely necessary. Others might behave more . . . rashly. What happens when the powers come out depends on a lot of factors: the type of school, the type of power, and where and when it was used. The next section discusses schools' possible reactions to the use of superpowers.

HOW DOES THE SCHOOL DEAL WITH HIGH WEIRDNESS?

Unmasked tells the story of teens who can transform into amazing, superpowered individuals. But those mask-forms are obsessed with keeping their teens' secret. As such, much of the game will be about sneaking around and faking out or otherwise confounding attempts to discover the identities of all these amazing, weird heroes who are turning up.

COVER IT UP

When confronted with some occurrence that breaks reality, some people will do their best to hide it. For example, a principal and janitor see a four-armed man made of shadow crawling along the ceiling of the gym. The principal claims to have seen nothing (though they know they did) and threatens the job of the janitor if the latter reveals anything.

Often, this stance is an early reaction by the subject. Only later, when they know it is not going away, do such people tend to become more inquisitive toward the phenomenon. Sometimes this inquisitiveness takes different forms, from a deep urge to disprove the phenomenon, no matter how convincing it seems, to a need to get hard evidence of the strangeness.

LOOK THE OTHER WAY

Very few normal people will believe their eyes if confronted with an absolute impossibility, such as an 8-foot-tall (2 m tall) man in a Zorro outfit leaping through a wall like it wasn't there. The first instinct of the human mind when presented with the impossible is to balk at it. Perhaps the observation was wrong, the room was dark, the witness was confused, etc. Not many people believe in themselves enough to confront reality itself with their claims. Most will simply smile nervously, shake their heads, and look the other way.

However, the more one person is exposed to the impossible, the more this reflex dies. Eventually—if they see enough—they will become believers. Those exposed in such a manner have a bad habit of becoming *true believers*. Worse than a witness, these zealots keep records, take pictures, and set traps to prove to the world they are not mad at all.

CALL THE POLICE

Many school staff members will immediately escalate any preternatural event to the police. For instance, if two students have a fistfight, the teachers will simply break that up, but if the cafeteria is under assault by a dragon man in red spandex spewing fire from his eyes, well, that's above their pay grade. You'd better bet the police (and probably the fire department) will be summoned to the school.

Sometimes, it doesn't even matter if the school's administrators don't see anything preternatural, just something unusual. An adult in red spandex wandering the halls of the school is likely enough to get them to call the police.

I QUIT! (OR WORSE)

Some people just can't take the strain and simply pack up and leave. The more amazing or life-changing the event, the more likely this outcome is, given a large enough audience. This reaction can manifest in many ways. A teacher might serve out the rest of their day, go home, and never come back. Another might quietly check into the local mental health concern. Another might do something even more self-destructive or outlandish. These people can even come back to haunt the PCs, if they somehow snap out of it and realize the phenomenon is real.

EXAMPLE HIGH SCHOOL: EMORYVILLE CONSOLIDATED

You can assemble a high school by stepping through the headings above, giving a brief thought to each, and then jotting down the results. The following is an example high school to go along with Emoryville, the example town:

Emoryville Consolidated is a large high school that serves all of Cook County.

It was completed in 1973, replacing three separate high schools scattered throughout the county and gathering all the students to one location.

Its mascot is a red hawk, and its teams are named the Emoryville Hawks.

It is a large, two-level structure with multiple playing fields, a separate indoor pool, and several parking lots.

There are two designated smoking areas in the school, one in the internal courtyard and the other behind the gym. There is also a secret area where the students gather behind the theater.

It has a student body of approximately 2,500, with a staff of 89.

Most students are bussed in from surrounding towns, but those lucky enough to live in Emoryville proper can walk there.

The school does not have security (there has been no need to date), and the teachers and some employees act as monitors.

CHAPTER 12

THE THREAT

Teacher, typical: *level 2, knowledge tasks as level 4*

Janitor, typical: *level 3*

Watchman, typical: *level 3*

Off-duty police officer, typical: *level 4*

Reporter, typical: *level 3, public speaking tasks as level 4*

What is the force that opposes the PCs? This is largely up to the GM to decide, though this book presents an array of fully formed options below, along with guidelines on how to make up your own.

MUNDANE THREATS

Most of what the prodigies face is likely to be mundane, at least at the beginning of a campaign: a police officer taking away their mask, a reporter with a videotape of them transforming into mask-form, a teacher out to discover their strange secret, and so on. Superpowers and monsters from beyond (if there are any) should be dangers that *Unmasked* builds toward, not a constant note, hit over and over again. The everyday life of being a teenager should be the focus.

SCHOOL STAFF

Teachers, security guards, lunch workers, janitors, watchmen, off-duty police officers, and others staff the school, and it's their job to make certain students do what is required of them and don't sneak about or cause any disruptions. As such, it's likely that mask-form manifestations at the school will draw the attention of school staff.

REPORTERS

The weirder the events that happen and the more people that see those weird occurrences, the more likely it is that a reporter becomes involved. Fire, violence, explosions, or just plain bizarre deeds draw journalists like moths to a flame. Some reporters—if they find a story interesting—will never let it go; they'll track down every lead they can find.

A reporter exposed to the mask-forms and their power to break reality will likely never, ever give up chasing down such a lead. (We

present a fully realized reporter to annoy and hound your players on page 146.) When the GM needs to give the PCs a kick in the pants to get them moving, or to act more carefully, sending in an inquisitive reporter might do the trick.

OTHER MEDIA

The '80s also saw the birth of tabloid television. Not *quite* reporters, the individuals employed by the tabloids worked to find strange stories, stretch (and sometimes break) the truth, and commit not-so-legal acts to get the shot. These shows were longer than the nightly news and aired less often, and they were also filled with heavily edited footage to tell each particular story.

This type of media is attracted to weirdness—the stranger the story, the better. As such, if the story is truly odd, tabloid television will spend large amounts of money and time pursuing leads, whereas a normal TV reporter might move on to the next topic.

POLICE AND FIRE DEPARTMENTS

Police and fire officials should—whenever possible—*not* be the enemy. In a town, it's likely the teen PCs know or even interact with police officers or firefighters on a daily basis (these might even be the teens' *parents*). Even if they do not, killing a police officer or firefighter is a terrible crime that few would even consider—not to mention the deaths of such officials are likely to draw the ire and attention of everyone in town until such a crime is solved. Scarier still, if the PCs (or their opponents) cause enough trouble, SWAT may be called in.

As such, a town's police or fire official's most likely function is as a force of change, movement, or goading—if an adventure slows down, send them in. Often, if other prodigies are involved, the PCs might suddenly find themselves protecting a bunch of innocent police and fire officials from superpowered hooligans.

Police officer or sheriff's deputy, typical: *level 4; Armor 1*

Firefighter, typical: *level 3, firefighting as level 4; Armor 1*

SWAT team member, typical: *level 5, combat tasks as level 6; Armor 2*

MILITARY

Soldiers and federal authorities in the 1980s were often viewed with suspicion or fear. They had motives such as national security on their minds and therefore often overstepped standard boundaries.

When the military shows up, they rarely do so in a modest manner, and this usually occurs only after some large provocation, such as a pitched battle between mask-forms in public. The GM should use the military to raise the stakes. If the game needs a new, stronger threat, the military can roll in, either in a covert capacity (black vans tooling through town and agents in suits on street corners) or in the open (tanks and troops). In both cases, the military can field weapons and vehicles likely to injure mask-forms.

PRETERNATURAL THREATS

Due to the nature of prodigy powers, preternatural threats can be nearly anything. Monsters, robots, extradimensional travelers, or aliens—all can be created wholesale by the subconscious of a prodigy. Since such threats issue from the subconscious, they may not only pose a threat to the prodigy who unconsciously creates them, but they can also be deadly. Such "created" entities are certainly real enough to kill.

OTHER PRODIGIES

The most common significant threat in an *Unmasked* campaign will be other prodigies. Not all prodigies are as kind and helpful as the PCs. Some are greedy, some hateful. Others still are justified in their actions, but they use their powers to push their wants and desires in a destructive manner.

MINIONS AND MANIFESTATIONS

Most "big bads" are served by minions. Sometimes these are non-human creatures, while other times they are simply forces that act on the world. The commonality across such matters is that—unlike most mundane threats—they operate in a power range where they can threaten and hurt the mask-forms. Sometimes, they're even more powerful than the mask-forms.

Various ideas for minion creatures and forces are presented in Chapter 15: Organizations and Creatures.

HUMAN SERVANTS

The big bad may be in control of human servants. Sometimes, these individuals have no idea they are being controlled, and other times they serve them willingly. In either case, it is unlikely such individuals represent a real threat to the PCs. Still, especially with servants who have no idea they are being controlled, it is difficult to fight them.

Prodigies are not all good guys. There are, no doubt, other prodigies in the PCs' school that are not above using their powers for violence or personal gain. Some may even serve the big bad, willingly or unwillingly. Prodigies, of course, pose a great threat to other prodigies.

THE MASTER

Selection of a big bad for your *Unmasked* campaign is very important. This is the threat behind the scenes that can match the prodigies in power or scope and perhaps is linked to their very existence. We present one such big bad in its full glory—Prester John—but it need not be the only possibility.

The master is the embodiment of the big bad threat: the person or creature behind the power that hunts, captures, consumes, or just wants the prodigies for some reason. Usually, the master stays behind the scenes, manipulating outcomes, using people and situations like a chess master plays a chess board. When the master is confronted (or confronts the PCs), the master is facing them from a position of power.

The master is usually more than a match for any one prodigy. It is only as a team that the PCs might be able to take the master down, and only then after great effort or personal cost.

Chapter 15: Organizations and Creatures, page 146

Prester John, page 151

CHAPTER 13

THE BIG PICTURE

At some point, a game or campaign for *Unmasked* will have to address the big picture: Where do the prodigies come from? Why are they here, and why now? What do they mean to the world at large? Again, in the end, this is up to the GM to decide. You'll find three fully realized "revelations" below, along with guidelines and options if you wish to make up your own instead.

EXAMPLE REVELATION 1: SCIENCE—GENETICS!

The PCs are the next wave of human development. All evolution to this point has been striving toward what the teens have become: a lens through which reality may be refocused. It is likely the teens have genetic markers indicating their otherness that science can uncover and detect through blood samples.

The prodigies' powers represent a fundamental control of classical reality

as it passes through the machine of the human consciousness. They can extrude belief to affect causality, and in fact, they do so unconsciously. Their manifestation of a "mask-form" represents a peak in such manipulations.

Because this effect is scientific in nature (even though its process is not yet understood), this means the scientific method might be readily applied to it. Scientists might contrive countermeasures to the mask-form abilities and drugs that suppress powers—or even remove them—and they might, in time, with enough subjects to study, learn how to transform someone into a prodigy.

EXAMPLE GENETICS REVELATION ARC

Below is a breakdown of an ongoing *Unmasked* campaign, with beats, revelations, NPCs, and more, spaced out

over all six tiers. A GM should feel free to use the sample arc wholesale, or simply mine it for ideas. Please note that as the PCs move up in tiers, the pace speeds up.

TIER 1 (SUMMER/FALL)

The PCs manifest their mask-forms, discover one another, and develop friendships.

The PCs begin to notice odd glowing items around town (mementos).

Other students in the high school show prodigy abilities.

The PCs trade stories of a reoccurring dream they have of a faceless man.

These dreams culminate in this figure ripping something from inside the dreamer's head.

Groups of prodigies begin assembling in the school. Cliques form.

Some prodigies form a gang called "The Future." They begin terrorizing the school.

The PCs step in and find themselves at odds with this powerful group.

TIER 2 (FALL)

An NPC prodigy who was kicked out of the Future warns the PCs that the gang is planning its revenge on the PCs.

The PCs are attacked one by one in the lead-up to Halloween night by the gang's mask-forms. The NPC prodigy who defected is somehow humiliated (for example, spray-painted, hair removed, or pelted with eggs).

The leader of the Future demands that the PCs stay out of their business.

A big fight happens on Halloween night at the school dance. Mask-forms go at it all at once for the first time. The police and fire department show up. Several normals are injured, perhaps one or more of them seriously.

The police begin investigating the incident and asking questions around the school.

The PCs all dream of the faceless man attacking and ripping something from the head of the leader of the Future, who never

EVOLUTION!

In 1984, the United States government initiated the first real push to sequence the human genome. Called the Human Genome Project, work began (on paper, at least) in the mid-1980s and truly picked up steam in the 1990s. It would not be finished until 2003. Even then, it managed to sequence only 93% of the human genome.

In the 1980s, new diseases such as AIDS and prion-based illnesses had captured the public's eye. Much time and effort went into devising genetic tests, reducing the cost of sequencing, and making the science more accessible. All in all, these public issues ignited broad interest in genetics, genetic sciences, and their application in fiction.

Television, comics, and movies were not far behind. The *X-Men, Blade Runner, The Boys From Brazil, The Fury* and other works explored the idea of genetics, cloning, and the next stage of human evolution. In 1986, such concepts were common sci-fi terms that, if not well understood by average teenagers, were at least known to most of them.

THE BRAIN CONTROLS THE WORLD, NOT THE OTHER WAY AROUND

In a genetic revelation, the world is shaped, controlled, and altered by structures and unfamiliar organs embedded in the human brain. Most humans do not possess these unusual tissues near the pituitary gland. But prodigies' brains are different. A CAT scan or a dissection will reveal bizarre, complex, unknown structures surrounding that gland at the center of the brain. It is with these organs that the prodigy reaches out and *changes* the world. It also may be why prodigies manifest in the teenage years (when the pituitary is most active).

As in other versions of the prodigy phenomenon, the genetic revelation allows the prodigies to alter reality wholesale. Somehow, the structures in their brain permit them to change atomic effects on a quantum level, allowing them to sway space-time, objects, atomic structures, and more, simply by observing them.

Since the prodigy effect is a physical, presumably biochemical process connected to an organ, in theory it can be surgically removed, perhaps controlled by some sort of implantable chip, or suppressed by the application of drugs. Secondarily, though it might take some time, scientists might be able to devise a genetic blood test to search for key genetic markers that indicate a predisposition toward prodigy abilities. They might also try to produce or develop prodigy abilities.

Once the structures surrounding the pituitary gland are discovered, the holy grail for science will of course be the removal and extended study of these new organs. The GM determines whether or not this research reveals some method to imitate, control, or exploit prodigy powers.

OTHER GENETIC OPTIONS

These weird organs in the middle of the brain are not the only option for the genetic concept, of course. The 1980s are filled with tons of cool references to unusual genetics, as well as its effect on the modern day. *Firestarter, X-Men,* and *Blade Runner* each track a world of genetic exploitation and ability, as well as the public's reaction to it. Here are some other examples of what the big reveal—in a genetic sense—might be:

The PCs are clones of former genetically advanced subjects planted with families.

The PCs' genetic structure was jump-started by experimentation, which led to accelerated evolution.

The PCs were exposed to chemicals that activated dormant structures in their brain, allowing them to access a power that everyone has, but few can use.

An accident, surgery, or violence has granted the PCs access to a portion of the brain that can manipulate reality.

The PCs have been altered by non-human creatures to be the next step in human evolution.

returns to school—they were apparently killed in a car accident.

The Future approaches the PCs and calls a truce. Something is going on. Their leader isn't dead; they were *taken*.

Investigating the accident reveals several suspicious elements.

TIER 3 (FALL/WINTER)

A doctor from the Centers for Disease Control and Prevention, Dr. Grant, arrives at the school. There are rumors that some sort of disease has infected the school. School announcements indicate it's all routine and has to do with inoculations.

All students are called to the gym to receive an inoculation.

When they enter the gym, they meet Dr. Grant one by one. A powerful, glowing memento is placed in the open on a table. If the PC reacts to it, Dr. Grant begins asking a lot of questions. He doesn't inoculate them; instead, he draws blood.

The funeral of the leader of the Future occurs. Most of the school goes. (If the PCs look, there is no body in the coffin.)

Two new, odd students appear in school, a sister and brother. They glow with prodigy power. The sister wears a wig. The brother has odd crisscross scars on his neck.

These siblings are seen following the prodigies in the school. They are also observed collecting mementos when they can.

After some time, the siblings and the PCs play a cat-and-mouse game of spying on one another. Then, the siblings vanish from the school.

On the day before the winter break starts, various reasons contrived to keep the PCs after school culminate in an attack by strange "men in black." These government personnel seem to have limited access to prodigy-like powers. Each agent, the PCs note, has a stitchlike scar on the back of their neck.

The group attempts to capture the PCs, but likely a pitched battle occurs.

TIER 4 (WINTER)

During the winter break, the NPC leader of the Future turns up, head shaved, having obviously been subjected to some sort of cranial surgery. Shortly thereafter, more agents in black suits show up, searching for them.

The NPC leader mumbles about "gods" and their powers being studied at the "Silo."

Dr. Grant appears at a PC's house and speaks to their parents at length about a special school for talented children.

Teams of agents in black scour neighborhoods and the high school searching for the NPC leader.

The PCs likely tangle with the agents in black.

The PCs capture intelligence from defeated agents. These manuals outline what is called a "GO:D"—Genetic Order: Deviant. It indicates that the teens all have a strange organ in the center of their brain that makes these powers possible.

One of the PCs attends a sibling's recital and is met by Dr. Grant, who acts very happy to see them. The doctor directly threatens their family and everyone they know. This war ends, now. They must turn in the NPC leader.

On Christmas Eve, hit teams descend on the PCs' houses. They plan to capture or kill the PCs and eliminate everyone else.

TIER 5 (WINTER/SPRING)

The government arrives in the town en masse, under the pretense of containing a Spanish flu outbreak "discovered" by the CDC.

The town population is rounded up by troops. The area is cut off from the outside world. Fake news stories circulate.

Teams of those strange, surgically altered teens show up, searching for the PCs and any other prodigies.

The PCs must team up with other town prodigies to defeat these hostile superpowered teens and the military, and to break the sham quarantine.

One of the strange, surgically altered teens defects to the side of the prodigies. He spills the beans about the GO:D project and the location of the Silo.

Several PCs or friendly prodigy NPCs are captured in the ensuing battle, but the fight causes the quarantine to drop. News begins to leak that it was a cover story for suspicious government actions.

Counterintelligence makes up a fake story about a small uranium spill from a secret cargo train crash. The government assures the town there is no risk.

TIER 6 (SPRING)

The Silo, a secret government base, is located in another state and heavily guarded by various superpowered personnel.

The PCs—along with their new ally from the GO:D project—plan a jailbreak to spring their friends from the Silo.

EXAMPLE REVELATION 2: PARANORMAL-PSYCHIC POWERS!

The PCs have the power to alter reality with their minds. There is no biological aspect to these powers; instead, they somehow exist only in consciousness. In fact, *everything* might exist only in consciousness, running like a program with the PCs capable of "reprogramming" reality on the fly.

Perhaps these powers place the PCs above other humans. Maybe they are an ancient ability coming to light. (Who built the pyramids? Prodigies!). Or maybe the PCs represent some other fundamental spiritual change in life on Earth.

As such, the prodigies are beyond science and cannot be identified through blood tests or other standard methods. In fact, although their powers are somewhat predictable, no matter what science throws at the problem, prodigy powers remain outside the realm of actual scientific understanding.

EXAMPLE PSYCHIC REVELATION ARC

Below is a breakdown of an ongoing *Unmasked* campaign, with beats, revelations, NPCs, and more, spaced out over all six tiers. A GM should feel free to use the sample arc wholesale, or simply mine it for ideas. Please note that as the game moves up in tiers, the pace speeds up.

TIER 1 (SUMMER/FALL)

The PCs manifest their mask-forms, discover one another, and develop friendships.

The PCs begin to notice odd glowing items around town (mementos).

Other students in the high school show prodigy abilities.

The PCs trade stories of a reoccurring dream they have of a faceless man.

A mask-form robs a local bank.

The local news becomes interested in the story, as do the police.

Due to clues found at the scene, suspicion falls on students from the high school. Police are searching for blue dye on the hands of the thieves.

The local police begin patrolling the school.

In their dreams about the faceless man, the PCs begin to have other visions—other places and people. They see a police officer lying dead in the road.

The PCs find a stash of mementos in the gym storage room.

A group of NPC prodigies (the "bullies") confronts the PCs for messing with their stuff. One NPC has blue dye on their hand.

A brief fight ends with the NPCs escaping before the police show up. The NPCs have planted a bag of money from the bank in the locker of one of the PCs.

The police arrest the PC, but release them when it becomes clear that the PC's fingerprints are not on the bag and that the lock to the locker had been damaged.

TIER 2 (FALL)

On Halloween night, the teens in town are throwing a huge party at the abandoned mill.

The NPC bullies confront the NPCs while they are out on Halloween night, and a big battle ensues, tearing up the mill. The PCs must protect the normal teens and, later, the police that arrive.

The NPC group escapes the scene. Several teens are injured, and the mill burns down. While it is declared an accidental fire, many reports indicate that strange powers were at work.

Back at school, the NPC group begins to antagonize friends of the PCs.

THE PSYCHIC BOOM

From the late 1960s up through the 1980s, spiritualism and the supernatural enjoyed an explosion in popularity in the United States. Jeane Dixon, Uri Geller, and others became worldwide celebrities, predicting the future, bending spoons, or stopping watches with "telekinesis." Even President Reagan and his wife employed astrologers and psychics.

More sobering, both the Soviet Union and the United States, eager to find a game-changer in the Cold War, pursued psychic research in projects such as Stargate and the Soviet remote viewing project. These secretive think tanks claimed to be able to scan enemy territory with terrifying accuracy using only the human mind. These projects persisted up until the mid-1980s and were as extensively funded as a new secret weapons system or innovative piece of military technology.

Movies, television shows, and comics all followed suit, of course, *Poltergeist*, *The Dead Zone*, *Scanners*, and *The Fury* being only a few to catch the wave of psychic interest at the time.

PROJECTIONS AND VISIONS

In a psychic revelation, creatures such as angels, demons, or other bizarre beings might *appear* to exist. In actuality, they are merely manifestations of forces that the prodigies bring to life. In this sense, the creatures can be nearly anything—dragons, aliens, or leprechauns—but in reality, they are only the mind of the prodigy shaping and controlling the world through the lens of the subconscious. As such, these beings have no real consciousness or will; they only fulfill the demands of the prodigies' subconscious. But don't let that fool you into believing these manifestations are less dangerous than the real thing; after all, the subconscious is often self-destructive, and prodigy powers are incredible.

Some prodigies can also peer into the future. Whether or not the events occur the way they are predicted and whether the prodigy power *forces* the outcome to match the vision are questions unlikely ever to be answered in a definitive manner. All that is known is that some prodigies can indeed predict the outcome of future events.

OTHER PSYCHIC OPTIONS

The egg-headed psychic is not the only option for the psychic threat behind the curtain, of course. The 1980s were filled with tons of cool references to a spiritual world beyond, as well as its effect on the modern day. *Dreamscape* and *The Sender* each described a world of secret psychic abilities and its discovery by normal people, as well as their reaction to it. Here are some other examples of what the big reveal—in a psychic sense—might be:

The spawn of an alien consciousness has infected certain people.

The development of prodigy power marks the awakening of a psychic hive-mind.

The appearance of prodigies represents the extrusion of superintelligence into our space-time.

The events herald the reappearance of the godhead.

Both groups discover that the principal's glasses are an incredibly powerful memento. The NPCs seem to want it. To prevent the bullies from stealing it, the PCs must get to it first.

The nightmare of the faceless man suddenly returns and is crippling to some PCs. He seems to have "awoken" and "broken free."

A police officer is killed on an isolated road outside of town in an unknown manner. The PC's suspect prodigy abilities.

TIER 3 (FALL/WINTER)

The funeral of the cop draws many people from town, including the NPC bullies.

One morning at school, all the PCs are summoned by the school administrators to various rooms, and there they meet representatives of the "Weimar Institute."

The representatives give them a test with a strange series of questions. The last question is, "Do you dream about a man with no face?" The representatives claim to be from a special school in a nearby state.

The NPC bullies approach the PCs and call for a truce. They do not kill people. They didn't kill the cop, but someone like them did. They too were contacted by Weimar.

The dreams now show the man without a face walking the road at night.

Poking around town, the PCs find that the Weimar Institute people never left town and instead have set up shop outside of town in a storefront.

The storefront sells crap new age paperbacks that purport to "unlock the power of the human mind."

When PC prodigies confront the Weimar Institute members, the latter use bizarre weapons to make their escape. One such device resembling a parabolic mic emits a horrible screeching that can cause even a mask-form to collapse.

The Weimar Institute members get away, but they leave behind reams of data.

The documents include maps of a strange facility, notes about "Subject 1," and dozens of photographs of teenagers—all with their heads shaven—wearing jumpsuits in some sort of institution.

There are strange photographs of a skin-colored cloth mask.

TIER 4 (WINTER)

During the winter break, an odd NPC who glows with prodigy power approaches one of the PCs at the mall. The NPC's head is shaved, and he wears a mishmash of clothes. He claims the PCs are in danger—the institute is coming for them. The NPC vanishes before the PC can ask anything more.

A strike team from the Weimar Institute shows up at a PC's house at night. Using tranquilizer guns, the team knocks the family out, and then several unfamiliar teens with shaved heads and wearing jumpsuits confront the PC. The strange teens pull on seamless masks, and they turn out to be powerful prodigies.

In the ensuing battle, the PC's home is destroyed.

The PCs all dream vividly of a group of teens gathered around the faceless man in a darkened room. There is medical equipment. They each feel a sharp pain, and then wake up in their own beds.

A police detective becomes interested in the case and begins to suspect the PC has something to do with the destruction of the house.

The teen PCs are called down to the police station for interviews. The detective asks some very leading questions about their prodigy powers.

One PC sees the faceless man in town, briefly, but then he is gone.

TIER 5 (WINTER/SPRING)

The PCs dream about the faceless man shaking and trembling in a chair.

The NPC prodigy bullies are nowhere to be found. They have vanished from school, yet people at school act as if they had never existed.

Tracking down the NPC prodigy bullies turns up nothing.

The town and the residents begin to act strangely. Some appear to have no faces.

The PCs are confronted by the townsfolk, who transform into inhuman creatures and attack them.

The PCs and their mask-forms are finally overwhelmed.

The PCs wake up in a strange facility. The teens find their heads shaved, and they are hooked to IVs in a room full of other such teens, all asleep.

At the center of the room is a teen wearing a face mask—it looks like he has no face. Blood covers the front of the mask. He is dead.

TIER 6 (SPRING)

The PCs must escape from the institute and return home. They have been missing for some time, as the institute probed their minds in an attempt to control them.

EXAMPLE REVELATION 3: SPIRITUAL— A WORLD BEYOND!

Demons and spirits have always existed on the cusp of human experience. The oracles of Delphi and Catholic, Haitian, and African ancestor possession—each of these is a real, though poorly understood phenomenon. Before that, gods, demigods, and others existed as people seized by some outside force to enact grand, unknowable plans for bizarre reasons.

Something comes through into this world, another intelligence that can cause the human body to endure and enact amazing feats that break reality.

The prodigies represent the newest stage in this phenomenon, which acts through the culture in which it is grounded. In Haiti, the mask-forms are the *Loa*, disembodied god-spirits, while in Catholicism, they are demons, and in the American teenage mind, they are superheroes from comic books. What is their ultimate goal? To experience this world and persist in it as long as possible, and perhaps to eventually replace the teens through which they manifest.

A spiritual revelation is beyond science and always will be. It can violate scientific principles six ways until Sunday, and turn a PhD into a gibbering mess, for their conclusions get continuously shattered, over and over again. As such, if the phenomenon ever breaks on a wide scale, few methods of detection and control will present themselves to the government to stop it.

THE SATANIC PANIC

Beginning in 1980, a moral craze swept the more religious areas of the United States. Now nicknamed "the satanic panic," it was the conviction held by millions—including many in law enforcement—that a secret network of devil worshippers existed throughout the United States, enacting ritual abuse on victims. "Survivors" of this phenomenon believed they had been kidnapped and tortured by an underground of Satan worshippers that had secretly infiltrated all walks of American life. These people led double lives, hiding their worship of the devil from the world at large and performing horrific rituals at night or in isolated locales.

After several high-level cases involving this weirdness came to trial, police and federal law enforcement were briefed on it as if these were real crimes. Later, the cases were dropped and the "abuse" debunked as complete fiction—coaxed from children by biased investigators. However, that doesn't mean it can't be real in *Unmasked*. In either case, such suppositions might be front and center at any investigation of prodigy abilities.

CREATURES, PORTALS, OTHER WORLDS, AND HIGH WEIRDNESS

In a spiritual revelation, creatures such as angels, demons, or other bizarre beings might exist and travel to and from this world. If such is the case, it is recommended the GM handle PC interaction with them very carefully. In the beginning, there should be no direct confrontation with such beings; instead, the PCs should uncover only evidence and hints—the smell of brimstone, a cloven hoof print, a scrawled pentagram.

Direct confrontation and confirmation of such creatures should occur only after the PCs work to locate, surprise, or trap such a being. Even then, the confrontation should be brief and terrifying. Remember, the longer and better understood a threat is, the less frightening it is. In any case, the GM should work to keep the truth from the players long enough to construct a mystery that's worth solving.

OTHER SPIRITUAL OPTIONS

Demons, angels, and spirits are not the only option for a spiritual threat behind the curtain, of course. The 1980s are filled with tons of cool references to a spiritual world beyond, as well as its effect on the modern day. *The Lost Boys*, *Highlander*, *Ghostbusters*, and *An American Werewolf in London* each illustrated a secret history and its discovery by normal people, as well as their varying reactions to it. Here are some examples of what the big reveal—in a spiritual sense—might be. The PCs could be:

Shapechangers
Immortals
Demigods
Vampires or werewolves
Fey

EXAMPLE SPIRITUAL REVELATION ARC

Below is a breakdown of an ongoing *Unmasked* campaign, with beats, revelations, NPCs, and more, spaced out over all six tiers. A GM should feel free to use the arc wholesale, or simply mine it for ideas. Please note that as the game moves up in tiers, the pace speeds up.

TIER 1 (SUMMER/FALL)

The PCs manifest their mask-forms, discover one another, and develop friendships.

The PCs begin to notice odd glowing items around town (mementos).

Other students in the high school show prodigy abilities.

The PCs trade stories of a reoccurring dream they have of a faceless man.

The PCs observe peculiar events in town, as well as weird occult graffiti and more.

The local news becomes interested in the story, as do the police.

The nightmares grow worse. When the faceless figure catches the dreamer, he embeds white-hot coins in their eyes. They wake screaming.

Rewards are offered for the "vigilantes."

A child disappears, kidnapped in broad daylight.

TIER 2 (FALL)

On Halloween, an NPC prodigy approaches the group of PCs and says a teacher knows about what's going on with the occult symbols.

The teacher is a trusted older woman who has taught social studies at the school for years. She believes some sort of cult is operating in the town, possibly even in the high school.

The teacher is a closet expert in the outré and the occult. The graffiti leads her to believe a cult may be trying to call an *Iwa* into existence—a spirit that takes over a body and can transform it. To summon it requires a young person to be murdered.

More graffiti appears in town. Now, the images show a man with no face—like in the PCs' dreams.

The PCs find and disrupt a coven performing some sort of ritual in the school gymnasium and save the kidnapped child. They are confronted by something not human that almost kills them, but vanishes in smoke. The coven escapes.

While leaving the school, the PCs are almost captured by a SWAT team, which seemed to be waiting for them.

The state police issue warrants for the PC mask-forms.

The NPC prodigy who contacted them is found murdered in his room, with a coin placed on each eye.

The local news identifies a suspect in the killing—a crazed house painter who likes heavy metal and who was found nearby with blood on his hands. He is arrested and charged. A mask is found in his possession. The PCs can tell—since it shows no power—that it is not a mask like theirs.

TIER 3 (FALL/WINTER)

A note is left on a PC's locker indicating someone knows they are a prodigy.

The PCs begin to feel like they're being watched.

Around the Thanksgiving break, the PCs begin to notice fewer mementos in town.

The trial of the innocent painter begins. Local news is all over it.

PCs who investigate find the man was living in a shack in the woods, and when authorities came looking for the NPC prodigy's murderer, he had just killed and gutted a deer—hence the blood.

Someone attacks the NPC teacher's car on a road at night and almost kills her.

A group of NPC prodigies at school begins harassing a PC.

These superbullies start making the PCs' lives miserable (for example, smashing their bikes or destroying their lockers).

This builds into a confrontation between the PC and NPC mask-forms at the school when it becomes clear that the NPC mask-forms are working with the coven. This happens at the big municipal football game, and some of it is caught on camera.

The story goes national, but no one knows what to make of it.

The NPC teacher returns to school, ready to get back to the investigation.

TIER 4 (WINTER)

During the winter break, a PC shopping at the mall with their family sees the faceless man in the crowd, but only for a split second.

The NPC prodigies attack the PC's home and destroy it. In the ruins of the house, occult evidence is found.

The house painter is found guilty of murder.

The local police become interested in the PC as a suspect.

Black vans are spotted driving around town.

The PCs notice the entire high school has taken on a strange glow.

Another PC is approached by an agent who won't say where they are from, only that they are very interested in the PC's "special abilities." They leave a nondescript card with the PC.

Later, the PC sees the agent speaking with one of the NPC prodigies in school.

TIER 5 (WINTER/SPRING)

The NPC prodigies target a PC's family.

The PC teens barely save the family.

A PC must reveal to their family that they are special, but the family does not seem overly shocked.

The police are alerted, and it looks as if the PCs will be arrested—but the agent steps in. The agent gives the PCs files on the NPC teacher.

The NPC teacher was in a cult called "ELOHAEM" in the 1960s and 1970s, attempting to "call forth" spirits.

It turns out many of the families in town once were members.

All the prodigy children are offspring of members of the cult, which fell apart in the late 1970s.

TIER 6 (SPRING)

After the spring break, the PCs find the NPC teacher has left the school. Several prodigies have not returned from spring break either.

When the PCs return home, their families are missing.

The PCs track the NPC teacher to the old cult compound on the edge of town.

There, the NPC teacher and their parents are attempting to draw forth the *Iwa*. The PC teens were an imperfect summoning gone wrong, but their deaths will bring the *Iwa*—the faceless man—to Earth.

The PCs fight the cult members, who are wielding much more powerful abilities because the ritual is near completion.

The *Iwa* comes through and must be defeated.

PART 4: WELCOME TO BOUNDARY BAY, NEW YORK
WOULDN'T IT BE GOOD

"I'm pretty sure he's dead. He must be dead." Aline was crying, and Jeremy was watching out the window of the house. The room was dark. Flickering static from the TV cast crazy, staccato shadows on the wall. The three teens were gathered near the storm door, near the bay window that looked out on the lawn.

"What happened? Tell me. Again," Michael demanded.

"The man was there," Jeremy said, almost like an afterthought.

"Shut up!" Aline shrieked. "Just shut up!"

"Okay. Calm down. Tell me."

"There were people waiting for us. Agents, in suits. And they had a machine . . ." Aline was crying again.

"Jeremy, what the hell happened?"

"They killed him, Mike. They shot Steven as he was changing. When he put on his mask—"

"Did you see the body?" Aline looked up, her face wet, eyes wide, and then she looked at Jeremy. "DID YOU SEE HIM DEAD?"

"No. Aline had already changed, and I put on my mask and went to go . . . help . . . and then I saw . . ."

"You saw Prester John," Michael finished. And just at that moment, a spray of headlights tracked across the walls of the darkened room, followed by the sounds of car doors slamming. Of people running around outside, in the dark, preparing.

Aline covered her ears.

"Jeremy, get ready. Aline, go if you have to. Change. Get out of here. Tell the others they're coming."

CHAPTER 14

THE SETTING

While the setting of *Unmasked* can be altered and changed to suit the GM's taste, this chapter presents an entirely realized style, town, high school, NPCs, a big bad, and final revelations. You can find all you need for a full *Unmasked* campaign here. You, as the GM, should of course feel free—as with all other elements presented in this book—to tweak, fold, spin, or mutilate anything found within to match your own personal vision.

Welcome to Boundary Bay, a small town on the northern shores of Long Island, New York. The kids of Boundary Bay are all right, but *different*. Today, on the first day of school at Ocean View High School in 1986, they return from summer break changed, though at this point, no one understands why. Something strange has arrived in town, and the school will never be the same.

THE SECRET OF BOUNDARY BAY OVERVIEW

As GM, you are privy to the secrets that the players must work to uncover. The secret at the heart of Boundary Bay is this: a company, hired by a division of the federal government, has accidentally released a power into the world by activating an unidentified and secret piece of technology. This effect changed everyone who happened to be asleep on August 22, 1986, at 1:55 p.m. within a radius of about seven miles around the device. Teens who were transformed by this effect became prodigies; adults and children who were asleep became conduits to some otherworldly power (called the Faceless). Everyone else who was awake at the time remained unchanged.

Few noticed the odd flash and the strange moments following the effect. But the prodigies certainly did. The major players in the mystery of Boundary Bay are the following:

Sand Point Consumer Electronics: This large electronics concern has been experimenting with an odd device (called the "key"), delivered to them by the federal government, in the hopes of reverse engineering it. This strange circuit appears to be some sort of quantum device, like one proposed the year before by Dr. David Deutsch—a "universal quantum computer." Its origin is unknown, at least to Sand Point. On August 22, 1986, at 1:55 p.m., the device was accidentally activated for the first (and last) time.

The Prodigies: Teens who were asleep or unconscious when the effect was triggered became prodigies. Soon after the event, they began creating masks and collecting mementos. There are approximately fifty prodigies in Boundary Bay, including the PCs.

The Faceless: Those adults and children who were asleep or unconscious during the August 22 event have been infected by some sort of outside force. Now, they sometimes appear to be taken over by an otherworldly power that grants them prodigy-like abilities, but that also seems to cause their faces and features to blur. They perform strange actions, steal or destroy random objects, and hunt prodigies, but only—for some reason—at night.

Prester John: The apparent leader of the Faceless. This being is incredibly powerful, and it seems to haunt the prodigies when they are alone and at their most vulnerable. It appears to want to capture them and take their masks . . .

The Circus: This tiny intelligence division in the United States Defense Intelligence Agency handles the outré, the bizarre, and the strange that turns up on the fringes of the government. If a file is weird and other divisions don't want to deal with it, it ends up with the Circus. The name of the group stems from the Polish saying, "Not my circus, not my monkeys."

OVERVIEW OF BOUNDARY BAY, NEW YORK, GAMEPLAY STYLE

The gameplay style of the *Unmasked* Boundary Bay setting is one of "realism." While the powers, mask-forms, and abilities that the prodigies can manifest uniformly shred classical reality, the teens, their teachers, their parents, and the conventional threats they face are as real, vulnerable, and mortal as normal people actually were in 1986. Violence in *Unmasked* Boundary Bay is as dangerous as it is in the real world, and if the PCs are not careful, flagrant use of their powers may lead to the deaths of innocents—something no one wants. The GM must strike a balance with the PCs where they understand and respect this fragility.

TONE

mask-forms, page 34

The tone of the *Unmasked* Boundary Bay setting is "superpowered, surreal horror." The powers and mask-forms granted to the teen prodigies are amazing and powerful, but the forces behind the powers, as well as their ultimate source, remain mysterious and frightening. The GM is encouraged to keep the players guessing and to watch for various points in gameplay where surprising twists and turns can be thrown in to keep the players on their toes. Even the final reveal presented here is a conduit to a *deeper* secret, allowing the GM to use this chapter as a jumping-off point into a much bigger game, one which might encompass the whole world. For now, this chapter deals with only Boundary Bay, Long Island, and the first outbreak of prodigies in 1986.

THE SOURCE OF THE POWERS

Unmasked Boundary Bay is a setting where the prodigy powers come from *beyond* due to the activation of a strange device. At least, the device appears to be the source of the abilities. While the PCs have no clue about this at the beginning of play, and many perceptual twists and turns are presented that might lead them to various conclusions, in the end it comes down to this: *the prodigy powers and mask-forms emanate from some other reality, and they can never be fully quantified by earthly science.*

ON SECRECY

The mask-forms of the prodigies in *Unmasked* Boundary Bay all are possessed with a single, overriding command: they must not be discovered by the rank and file of humanity. Some of the mask-forms have half-thought-out ideas as to why this is so, while others make up reasons, but none really know why they'd think such a thing. It is as fundamental as the fear of open flame.

A clear feeling of dread and horror consumes any prodigy who considers exposing their powers to a non-prodigy, one akin to a fear of death. If the Boundary Bay story ever breaks wide, the prodigies and mask-forms are certain, it will not be long before something terrible happens. Of course, this does not mean the prodigies can't tell NPCs or other nonpowered PCs about their abilities, only that such a secret must be kept and not spread widely.

A NOTE ABOUT TIMING

Unmasked Boundary Bay works best if all the PCs learned of their mask-forms recently—at the end of summer break, after the incident on August 22—and only notice others in town who glow as prodigies when they return to high school. Most of the questions they might have about the phenomenon remain unanswered, and this is the main focus of gameplay when they begin.

A NOTE ABOUT LOCATIONS AND NPCS

Unmasked Boundary Bay concentrates on locations and NPCs that are significant in the life of an average teenager: shops that a teen might go to, work at, or otherwise frequent, as well as people they might run into, run afoul of, or end up in conflict with. There are many, many, other people and locations in Boundary Bay not outlined below, because teen PCs would rarely have anything to do with them. It's up to the GM to fill those in.

HOW TO USE THIS SECTION

If you've read a Stephen King book or enjoyed shows such as *Stranger Things*, *Twin Peaks*, or *Lost*, you'll recognize this section on Boundary Bay for what it is: a grab bag filled with locations, characters, and elements with which a GM can populate their game setting. This section outlines the principal cast in a show that is Boundary Bay, Long Island, on the first day of school in 1986. From this point forward, many elements can and will change, but the secrets, interrelations, powers, and plot hooks remain here to be brought out on the table at any time. As GM, you should keep this section handy while running a game in Boundary Bay, because you never know when you'll need a plot twist or three to mix things up.

The key to making an engaging game world that players are both comfortable in and eager to explore is to have substance below the base descriptions of game elements. GMs can and should make up their own material, of course, but the sheer volume of characters, locations, and interrelationships presented here should be enough to make Boundary Bay pass the basic player test of: *do I feel like I know what my character would do here?*

During gameplay, the GM will uncover the player's preferences—what they hope Boundary Bay will be for them. Maybe they enjoy the high school aspect of the game, the horror, the interrelationships between people, the mystery, or all of it at once. Individual players often like elements to differing degrees, and it's the GM's job to tailor the game to each. Luckily, there are more than enough elements presented here to cover all those aspects for an entire campaign.

The goal, of course, is to make the players feel as if Boundary Bay were their hometown, so much so that they tell you who runs the Good and Plenty, or predict how a particular well-worn NPC might react to a particular course of action. A good hometown feels comfortable, clear, and simple, even if thousands of illicit acts are taking place under the waterline. It is only

with this level of comfort clearly established that the mysterious and horrific aspects of an *Unmasked* campaign can really sink their teeth in.

NORMAL HUMAN STATS

Boundary Bay is set in the *real* 1986. As such, the people of the town are not all that different from one another, stats-wise. Only the preternatural threats or the mask-forms have any significant power. Below is a list of the basic stats for normal humans, by type:

Teacher, typical: level 2, knowledge tasks as level 4

Janitor, typical: level 3

Watchman, typical: level 3

Professional security guard, typical: level 3

Off-duty police officer, typical: level 4

Reporter, typical: level 3, public speaking tasks as level 4

Firefighter, typical: level 3, firefighting as level 4; Armor 1

Police officer or sheriff's deputy, typical: level 4; Armor 1

SWAT team member, typical: level 5, combat tasks as level 6; Armor 2

Soldier, typical: level 5, combat tasks as level 6; access to explosives and heavy weapons grant a +2 power shift

Circus Agent: level 7, subterfuge, spying, and stealth as level 8; antiprodigy technology can grant up to a +3 power shift

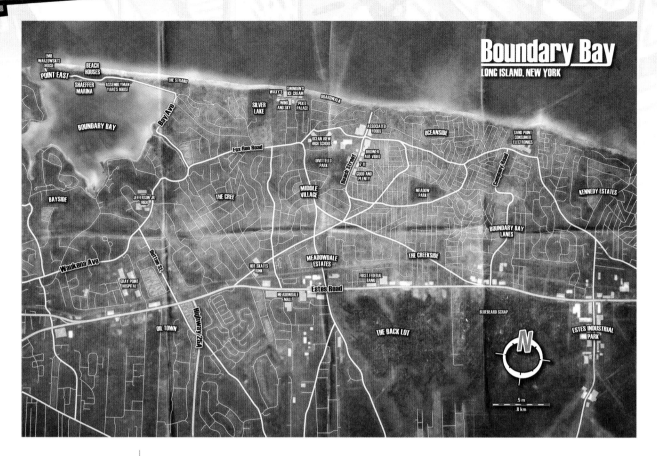

Boundary Bay
LONG ISLAND, NEW YORK

Map labels: EMIL WARZOWSKI'S HOUSE · BEACH HOUSES · POINT EAST · SHAEFFER MARINA · ASSEMBLYMAN YARO'S HOUSE · THE STRAND · BAY AVE · BOUNDARY BAY · WAXY'S · SWINDON'S ICE CREAM · BOARDWALK · SILVER LAKE · WIND AND SKY · PIXEL PALACE · ASSOCIATED FOODS · OCEAN VIEW HIGH SCHOOL · BROWER AVE VIDEO · OCEANSIDE · SAND POINT CONSUMER ELECTRONICS · Fox Run Road · DIVITIELLO PARK · BEACH STREET · 7-11 · GOOD AND PLENTY · MEADOW PARK · KENNEDY ESTATES · BAYSIDE · JEFFERSON JR. HIGH · THE CREE · MIDDLE VILLAGE · BOUNDARY BAY LANES · Waukena Ave · Butler St. · HOT SKATES RINK · MEADOWDALE ESTATES · THE CREEKSIDE · GRAY POINT HOSPITAL · FIRST FEDERAL BANK · MEADOWDALE MALL · Estes Road · Highway 25A · BLUEBEARD SCRAP · OIL TOWN · THE BACK LOT · ESTES INDUSTRIAL PARK · 5 m · .8 km

THE TOWN—BOUNDARY BAY, LONG ISLAND, NEW YORK

Boundary Bay is a beach town in Suffolk County, New York, on the shores of Long Island Sound, a huge, tidal estuary of the Atlantic Ocean that runs from New York City all the way out to Block Island Sound. Boundary Bay is approximately three hours by train from New York City (or one hour by car), located in an out-of-the-way, rural area.

Boundary Bay ends to the east at Point East, a beach area; to the west by Rockville, another small town; to the south by State Route 25A; and to the north by Long Island Sound.

In the 1930s, Boundary Bay was nothing more than a few bungalows on the ocean, occupied by families whose main income was fishing (black sea bass, bluefish, and flounder), but since the later 1950s, the place has exploded in size and importance, becoming a full-blown town, first as a commercial fishing hub (once the main local concern) and later due to the arrival of Sand Point Consumer Electronics—a large and still very successful semiconductor company founded by the town's favorite and most famous son, Emil Warzowski.

The town's total population is 24,509 people. During the summer, that number increases slightly, as several prominent homes on the sound are summer residences for the New York City elite.

There are six main areas of the town:
Point East
The Strand and Boardwalk
Beach Street
Fox Run Road
Estes Industrial Park
Meadowdale Mall

There are many smaller neighborhoods as well, each with its own character. Some of these smaller areas are noted both on the map and with a basic description, but only the major areas have deeper descriptions.

POINT EAST

This jutting peninsula of land contains large, rambling, Cape Cod–style homes belonging to some of the oldest and richest families in town. The peninsula ends in a sand beach that overlooks the inlet to Boundary Bay. Boats often pass heading into the bay to dock.

Each house on Point East occupies a select sliver of land along the stretch of road called Bay Avenue. Most of the homes were built in the 1930s, but some more recent ones are built in a geometric wood-slat style with odd oval windows. These houses border the Strand, and their backyards are usually blocked with a simple gate. Most of the houses also have a private slip for a boat on Boundary Bay.

Those that live here are the envy of the town, and many of the local families once called this neighborhood home before selling their land or beach house off to settle debts when the fishing dried up.

POINT EAST SIGNIFICANT LOCATIONS:

The Breakers: At the end of Point East, at the inlet of Boundary Bay past the end of Bay Avenue, are the Breakers. Here, huge sand dunes overgrown with reeds and high grass are interspersed around chunks of old concrete, ripped up from Beach Street in the 1930s when the sewers were installed. Several wrecked cars have been left out here, and teens (as well as some locals like David Jericho) can be found out here.

Warzowski Residence: Emil Warzowski (owner of Sand Point Consumer Electronics) and his teenage daughter Emma live in the largest house on Point East. This house is considered the "end" of the beach, though the shore does continue past the end of Bay Avenue into the Breakers. It is a friendly, old-looking house with a huge, improbable tree in the back where a tire swing still hangs. Emil's office is fully kitted out with cutting-edge electronics, multiple computer setups, and various high-tech devices. The boat slip in the back is usually occupied by the *Olyphant*, Emil's yacht.

Yaros Residence: Assemblyman Dean Yaros, his wife Eleanor, and their two teenage children, Danny and Imogen, live in a modern wood-slat house recently built in the middle of Point East. The assemblyman

can often be seen swimming early in the morning at the beach.

Smilak House: This big, three-level house on the beach is painted bright yellow with red shutters. It has a manicured yard and an inset stone pool. For much of the year the house is vacant (it is a summer home). During the school year, teens often gather here (unbeknownst to the owners, John and Alma Smilak) for parties.

Old Man Lynch's House (a.k.a. "The White House"): Walter Lynch is the only fisherman to become rich from the disintegrating fishing industry in Boundary Bay in the 1960s. He lives alone in a huge, rambling Cape Cod house that is painted white each year in June (hence the nickname). He can sometimes be spied sitting on the back patio talking on a telephone, watching the ocean. The inside of the house is a hoarder's dream. Every surface is covered in folded newspapers dating back to the 1960s, legal correspondence, or sections of books torn from old novels. A huge 1919 safe stands in the living room; inside he keeps hundreds of thousands of dollars in stocks, gold, and bills. When Walter (very rarely) leaves the house, his black 1968 Jaguar is recognized (and avoided) by all.

POINT EAST REGULARS:

David Jericho: A forty-seven-year-old local and veteran of the Vietnam War, David is often seen walking the beach with his metal detector and his dog, Doc. He lives in a rotted-out Dodge up on blocks in the dunes at the end of Point East, and he makes little or no trouble. He is well known and well liked. In fact, he often mows the lawn of the Warzowski house and does odd jobs there (he went to high school with Emil Warzowski at Ocean View High). David is a believer in the paranormal and claims to have "seen things" in the war. Teens will find a ready ally in David if they ever reveal their power to him.

Emil Warzowski: A forty-nine-year-old local self-made millionaire, Emil Warzowski made a name for himself first at Caltech working in microcomputers (some of which

David Jericho: level 3, survival and combat tasks as level 4

Emil Warzowski: level 5, science, physics, and computer tasks as level 6

Eleanor Yaros: *level 3, persuasion, deception, and social interaction as level 4*

were used in the Apollo program and other classified Air Force programs). Later, he founded Sand Point Consumer Electronics, a semiconductor production facility in his hometown that utilized a chemical bonding process he patented, bringing roughly a thousand jobs to the area and becoming a local hero. In the last two years, he has been working quietly with Director Holtz of the federal research program called the Circus, attempting to dissect a piece of unique and unknown technology referred to as "the key." Emil is talkative and easy to spot, with his horn-rimmed glasses, blond beard, and frizzy mop of curly red hair. He drives a beaten-up, light-blue Volkswagen Bug, and he knows nearly everyone in town by name, family, or reputation. His memory is legendary. Emil has little tolerance for the "supernatural" and will have a hard time wrapping his head around the concept of prodigies.

Emma Warzowski: *level 2, social interaction as level 4*

Emma Warzowski: A fourteen-year-old overachiever, Emma is insanely popular while somehow remaining kind, humble, and friendly with everyone. Despite being local royalty (many in the town owe her father their jobs), Emma fails to even notice such things, much less take advantage of them. Emma's mother, Nancy, lives in New York City and is an "actress"—that is, she lives off the monthly checks Emil sends her. Emil and Nancy never speak directly. What little conflict Emma has with her father concerns her wanting to spend more time in the city with her mom. Usually, Emma and her father are thick as thieves.

Assemblyman Dean Yaros: *level 4, politics and public speaking as level 5*

Assemblyman Dean Yaros: A sixty-one-year-old politician, Dean Yaros looks like a movie idol gone to pot. His hair is a perfect, shiny black, and each temple is touched by gray. His teeth are too straight and precise to be real, and his voice has the practiced quality of a TV host. His body is wiry and potbellied. Though he works hard at it, Dean has a difficult time with the names of those without pull in the town, though he will readily pretend to know everyone. Dean is involved in several questionable deals regarding the Meadowdale Mall and Estes

Industrial Park. It is also well known that Dean is a philanderer who sleeps with many different women in town.

Eleanor Yaros: This fifty-five-year-old matron is far more attractive than her husband and, although no one believes it, far cleverer. Eleanor plays the perfect political wife, but since discovering her husband's illicit activities in town (illegal real estate deals and philandering), she has been quietly selling household items and exchanging the cash for diamonds, gold, and jewels she keeps at her cousin's home

in Bethpage, Long Island. In addition, she's secreted away several photocopies of the deeds and titles her husband forged to establish dumping areas and construction areas in no-build zones at the mall and in the Estes Industrial Park. Once she has established enough of a nest egg to support herself, she'll drop the evidence at the offices of the Suffolk County Reporter and watch her husband's life implode.

Imogen Yaros: A nineteen-year-old drug addict, Imogen's been to rehab twice, once in high school (in 1984), and more recently when she vanished from her college dorm and turned up in jail in New Hampshire. Her drug of choice is cocaine. She is a sullen, withdrawn, bitter woman who hates her parents and most people in town, and she is eager to get the hell out of Boundary Bay. Still, she loves her little brother, and since she knows about the secret tensions between her mother and father, she is eager to protect Danny from the fallout.

Danny Yaros: This fifteen-year-old sports star plays on the junior varsity baseball team and lacrosse team at Ocean View High School. He is always sunny, genuinely happy to see everyone, and eager to get along with others. Much of this stems from the fact that he's just not very smart. He adores his sister, and the only thing anyone can do to make Danny hold a grudge is to talk unkindly about her.

Wayne Depco (Mask-Form: Swoosh): This sixteen-year-old student has mild cerebral palsy that causes him to walk with a staggering gait. Otherwise, his disease causes him no real difficulty. Wayne is popular, and despite having to deal with minor bullying, he is confident and outgoing. He is also a prodigy. His mask-form is Swoosh. Though Wayne lives in Bayside, he hides his mask (and his mementos) out in a ruined dairy truck in the sand at Point East, because his mother, Helen, is a busybody, always poking into his business. Wayne (and Swoosh) can sometimes be seen walking after school at the end of Bay Avenue, or out in the dunes.

Walter Lynch: A sixty-one-year-old miser, Walter Lynch is an old, bitter, thin man

who—no matter how well dressed he is (and he always dresses well)—appears somewhat haggard. He has a mind like an encyclopedia and a heart like an ice cube. He's well known in town, but widely avoided, as he tends to hold grudges and makes such grudges known through financial pressures. He has no family (his daughter, Yvonne, died in 1966 at the age of eighteen in an automobile accident). Most of the older folks in town believe this is when Walter "went off the rails," but in truth, he was always inclined toward the darker aspects of life. Walter operates dozens of ongoing business concerns from his office in his house in Point East, rarely leaving the property. Some of those concerns have touched on the illegal, and he is aware of many more of the business secrets in town, but he has yet to take the leap into being a full-fledged crook . . . yet.

POINT EAST HOOKS:

David Jericho sometimes picks up shifts at the Sand Point Consumer Electronics building as a janitor, since he went to high school with Emil Warzowski. Perhaps he sees something relating to prodigies there after hours, or even escapes with an important item.

John and Alma Smilak, both in their sixties, occupy their beach home only during the summer months. In the off-season, Hal Walmer, the seventeen-year-old son of the Boundary Bay police chief, "looks after it." During the fall and winter, Hal uses the Smilaks' residence as a party house, though he keeps it meticulously clean. Most kids in the high school have been to a party or two out there; they call it the "flop house."

Imogen Yaros might run off, either to look for drugs or just to escape her parents' fights. Danny, her little brother, will desperately search for her, of course. But will the PCs help?

Some kids walking the beach report being startled by a "man without a face" sitting alone at a campfire. After a brief kerfuffle in town, the news dies down. But fires on the beach at night persist.

Imogen Yaros: level 2, lying, stealing, and deception tasks as level 3

Danny Yaros: level 3, athletics, running, jumping, and climbing as level 5

Wayne Depco: level 3, positive interactions and persuasion as level 5

Swoosh: This mask-form is a lithe, superhumanly fast Mover. He always wears skintight, bright blue tights, pilot's goggles, and a yellow scarf. He looks like the Germanic ideal of a downhill skier. When he begins a run at super speed, the colors tend to blend into a vague Nike "swoosh." He claims he's from Colorado but left "before the cold fusion reactor at Millennium Springs opened in 1977." With those he doesn't know, he keeps most conversations down to two-word questions or responses, such as "Who's that?" or "Got it." He's here because of some sort of machine, but he can't recall precisely why.

Walter Lynch: level 6, business interaction, planning, and deception tasks as level 8

Some less-than-friendly prodigies declare an isolated section of Point East their own. They use mementos and their powers to scare off trespassers, including David Jericho, who becomes suspicious and witnesses the prodigy abilities in action.

Wayne Depco might recognize the PCs as fellow prodigies and enlist their help to locate a missing mask, or a stolen memento or two. Alternatively, the PCs might become suspicious of how Wayne treks out into the dunes every day and spy a transformation. Wayne, in his Swoosh mask-form, might intervene to prevent a prodigy gang from scaring people off the beach.

Walter Lynch employs out-of-town muscle to frighten the people living in two houses near the end of Point East that he hopes to get at bargain-basement prices, so he can develop his beach parking lot next to the Shaeffer Marina. Perhaps these vague threats go too far and someone gets hurt.

SHAEFFER MARINA

This social club is frequented by the richer families in town (mostly from Bayside, Bay Avenue, and Fox Run Road), who spend their weekends here during the summer season. Behind the marina in Boundary Bay itself, there are eleven docks that can comfortably moor up to twenty-two boats. In the off-season, many of these boats are taken out of the water and put up on blocks near Estes Road or next to the marina.

The large clubhouse features a tennis court, an indoor pool, the Conch Restaurant, and the Hermit Crab Cocktail Bar. Seats on a large deck overlook the beach to the north, and a dock over Boundary Bay to the south is filled with tables for dining and an outdoor bar for when the weather is nice.

The marina is run by the Shaeffer family: Seth and Gail Shaeffer and their two teenaged children, Brett and Tabitha. The whole family works at the marina in various areas, along with several other employees. In the off-season, the restaurant and cocktail bar remain open, but the staff is greatly reduced.

SHAEFFER MARINA REGULARS:

Seth Shaeffer: This balding forty-nine-year-old man with a slight paunch always wears sunglasses. He's happy, thoughtful, and outgoing, but only if he knows someone; otherwise, he's somewhat standoffish. Seth inherited the marina (which was nothing more than the moorage back then) from his great-uncle Stephen Lynch—Walter Lynch's long-dead older brother. Seth hires many busboys and waitresses during the busy season, along with a lifeguard for the pool and sometimes a tennis "pro" to give lessons. Seth keeps his business entanglements with Walter Lynch and others a strict secret from his family.

Gail Shaeffer: A slightly overweight forty-seven-year-old mother with perfectly coifed red hair, Gail is the "mom" of the marina. Many of the employees call her "Mrs. S." She takes care of what needs taking care of, and when her husband is not there, she works the desk. The two often take dinner there together with the family when "handing off." Despite her usually sunny disposition, Gail behaves like a mom to the employees in other ways, too—she doesn't put up with inappropriate behavior. Vices such as drug use, drinking, or premarital sex at the marina will show a whole new side of Gail to those subjected to her wrath. Her children know this side well. They are not cut any slack.

Brett Shaeffer: This fifteen-year-old is a slightly chunky kid with braces, freckles, a flat face, and tight, curly black hair. Despite his appearance (one might imagine a junior high school bully), he is a very quiet, well-read, and careful individual. He collects and plays roleplaying games with a small group of similarly eccentric friends. At the marina, Brett is stuck doing grunt work—mopping toilets, mooring vessels, scrubbing and treating decks, and painting boats up on blocks.

Seth Shaeffer: level 4, business administration and positive social interactions as level 5

Swoosh: level 7, Speed defense as level 10; health 50; "Mach 4 punch" inflicts 7 points of damage and ignores 1 point of Armor; regenerates 1 health per turn; can move faster than the human eye can track; power shifts: +5 to Speed

Gail Shaeffer: level 3, positive social interactions as level 4

Brett Shaeffer: level 2, science fiction and fantasy literature as level 3

Tabitha Shaeffer: This thin, spindly fourteen-year-old cheerleader is more technically proficient at dance than anyone on the Ocean View squad. Despite her severe ponytail and bulky glasses, she is considered one of the best performers in town, and she spends much of her time at the Waves Dance Studio on Beach Street, practicing. In school, she is an uninspired student who does the minimum to get by, and she has few real friends. At the marina, Tabitha usually works as a waitress or service staff, or—at the worst—she assists her brother, Brett, with menial labor. She and her brother fight. Often.

Gavin Hyk: This thirty-three-year-old cook spent eight years in the United States Army stationed in Berlin, Germany, in the late 1970s. He is a muscular, balding man with a carefully trimmed mustache and black, curly hair, and he is as fastidious in his dress as he is in his behavior. He is polite to the point of near-absurdity. He lives in a houseboat moored at the end of the "rot dock"—an old dock at the marina. His boat, the *Ulrikia*, is named after a long-vanished European girlfriend. Out of everyone in town, Gavin has noticed more than others the oddities going on. He has run into strange people out in the dunes during his morning runs, and once, he's certain, he saw a woman without a face moving through the parking lot of the marina late at night.

Patrick Villanueva: An eighteen-year-old ex-juvenile convict, Patrick lives in the Kennedy Estates with his aunt, Esther Villanueva. He is a tall, lanky man who appears older than his age—most mistake him for someone in his late twenties. Patrick grew up in Brooklyn, New York, and served seven months in a juvenile facility in upstate New York for assault. His aunt, Esther, who does the books for the marina, asked Seth Shaeffer about a job for her nephew, and Patrick came to live with her when he was released. Since he started, he has proven an exceptional employee, and he spends almost all his time at the marina—he loves it.

Dorothy "Dot" Telasco (Faceless): This attractive twenty-two-year-old works as a waitress and bartender at the Conch Restaurant. She went to Ocean View High School (class of 1982) and has worked at the marina since she was fifteen, long enough that she is almost part of the Shaeffer family. They even put her up for a summer when her father kicked her out for dropping out of college. Dot dated Rob Escadero, the full-time bartender at the marina, for two years, but they've recently broken up. So far, despite their breakup, the two have somehow managed to get along. Dot was asleep in her car on August 22, 1986, at 1:55 p.m. when the "incident" occurred. From time to time now, she forgets where she is and wakes hours later, having done things she can't recall. Like someone who suspects they might have a serious illness, she does her best to ignore it while she can . . .

Rob Escadero: This twenty-one-year-old bartender moved to Boundary Bay two years before. He has carefully feathered brown hair and a muscular build, and he is always dressed in polo shirts, jeans, and moccasins. Considered a "fox," Rob is a draw for women (and men) at the Hermit Crab Cocktail Bar. He drives a red 1977 Mustang and lives in a loft above the Waves Dance Studio on Beach Street. His recent breakup with Dot Telasco is a well-worn subject of local gossip.

Ophelia Grant (Mask-Form: Smyk): This sixteen-year-old is a wispy, quiet, blonde-haired teen who works in the marina as a waitress in the restaurant. In school, she is a nodding acquaintance with nearly everyone, but spends much of her time in the library reading (she has a deep interest in fiction). Since she was asleep on her day off during the incident on August 22, she became a prodigy. Her mask-form is Smyk. Twice, she has wandered about at night in Smyk-form, testing out her newfound powers on the cement piles in the weeds and dunes of Point East, but so far, she has barely wrapped her head around the situation.

Tabitha Shaeffer: *level 3, dancing, tumbling, and gymnastics as level 5*

Dorothy "Dot" Telasco: *level 2, positive social interactions as level 3*

Gavin Hyk: *level 4, combat, survival, and espionage as level 5*

Rob Escadero: *level 3*

Patrick Villanueva: *level 3, fighting, wrestling, and theft as level 5*

Smyk: *This mask-form is a lumbering Smasher with one withered leg and huge, overgrown, apelike arms, along with a Mr. Jekyll-like face fit with features that seem randomly selected from a dozen different ugly madmen. He claims he was created in the "London incident," and will say no more on the subject, as if everyone should know what that is. Loud and bent on intervening when he feels the odds aren't fair, Smyk loves to make a bully pay—but he's no killer. He is deeply protective of Ophelia, going out of his way to keep her from physical and emotional harm.*

Ophelia Grant: *level 3; reading as level 5*

Smyk: level 9, smashing, leaping, and jumping as level 10; health 85; Armor 3; Smash and Rend inflicts 11 points of damage (power shifted); power shifts: +1 to jumping and climbing, +2 to strength, +2 to resilience

Cassidy Geary: level 3, boating and fishing as level 5

Anthony DiGiovanni: level 4

Goop: This mask-form is an amorphous Changer with a body that runs and flows like melting wax. When it concentrates, it can focus its features and skin into a simple imitation of a person—but up close, it is obviously not human. It is surprisingly well spoken for a glob of undifferentiated matter, and claims to be an escaped experiment from the "Sino-Soviet States." Goop is less than thrilled with Anthony, whom it fears is squandering his relatively normal and comfortable life.

Goop: level 7; health 70; Engulf and Dissolve inflicts 10 points of damage (power shifted); regenerates 2 health per turn; no bones or internal organs; can slip through any nonairtight opening; power shifts: +2 to resilience, +3 to gelatinous form

SHAEFFER MARINA HOOKS:

The marina is odd; unlike everywhere else in town, it seems devoid of mementos. Have they been collected already? Is it a dead zone? What's the secret?

Seth Shaeffer has been caught up in a legal entanglement with Walter Lynch for some time. The bitter old millionaire hopes to scoop up property on the edge of the marina to create parking lots for Point East. Seth has opposed this plan and offered the owners of the properties more money than Walter (borrowed from Emil Warzowski, a high school friend)—only now, Walter has become more serious, hiring out-of-town muscle to terrorize the marina. Will the PCs step in before Seth gets hurt?

Smyk saves Brett Shaeffer from a round of bullying by local teens, and the two strike up a secret friendship. All the while, Brett has no idea Smyk is Ophelia Grant. In time, she begins to fall for Brett.

Tabitha Shaeffer is secretly in love with Rob Escadero, who doesn't think of her as anything but just another kid. She follows him everywhere, spies on his comings and goings, and does her best to make Dot Telasco—his ex-girlfriend—look bad.

People from Patrick Villanueva's past—gang members from the Yellow Royals—take the train out from Queens to settle a debt they feel Patrick owes them. If he's lucky, it'll only be a beating.

Smyk becomes a common sight around the marina at night. People begin talking about "the hunchback," so much so that the police are alerted.

Gavin Hyk recognizes the army plates on an otherwise nondescript car tooling around town. Poking around, he becomes concerned that some sort of intelligence operation is going on in Boundary Bay. He even thinks it's based out of Sand Point Consumer Electronics.

BOUNDARY BAY

This six-mile-wide (10 km wide) and five-mile-long (8 km long) natural bay is bordered to the north by the Strand and the beach houses, to the west by the marina, and to the south by the neighborhood of Bayside. In the north, it opens to Long Island Sound, and ships can often be seen navigating through the inlet there out into deeper water. The houses surrounding the bay are almost all built onto bulkheads and docks that jut out into the water. The neighborhoods surrounding it are rich and covered in lush trees, winding roads, and big houses.

Boundary Bay has several large, low-lying marsh islands that are fully visible only at low tide. Through these, several deep-water channels are marked by buoy markers. Boats that travel in the bay follow these carefully prescribed channels, or they end up beached on a sand bar.

BOUNDARY BAY REGULARS:

Cassidy Geary: A thirty-eight-year-old, out-of-shape, bleary-eyed drunk, Cassidy Geary has been the harbormaster for eight years. He patrols the bay, looking to ticket those who lay crab and eel traps, which are illegal. Cassidy docks at the marina, and can often be found there, in the restaurant, drinking. The town keeps him on because he does decent work in exchange for a small, stilted shack on one of the higher marsh islands in the bay. So far, the town has shrugged off his well-known alcohol habit.

Anthony DiGiovanni (Mask-Form: Goop): This sixteen-year-old prodigy has short brown hair, a wry smile, and a very strange, high-pitched laugh. Despite this, Anthony is headstrong and full of self-confidence, something noted by the student body; as such, he enjoys a high social status. Since the incident on August 22 and the creation of his mask, he can transform into the mask-form of Goop. Anthony's family has long maintained a shack on the low-lying marsh islands in Boundary Bay that he uses for his hideout. After school, he often makes his way out to the shack in his crabbing boat and messes with the mask.

Elizabeth Washington: Elizabeth is a sixty-one-year-old widow from Bayside. She and her late husband, Carl, called Boundary Bay home from their marriage until his death in 1982. She remains in their house, but spends much of her time walking out on the marsh islands at low tide, setting up an easel to paint landscapes when the weather suits. She is strangely foul-mouthed and has thrown her former "good matron" act to the wind since her husband's death. Many think she has lost her mind, but she promised Carl on his deathbed she would do only what made her happy from then on. She is a ready ear (and ally) for anyone on the outs with their family, although she tends to ask uncomfortable questions.

BOUNDARY BAY HOOKS:

Cassidy Geary becomes suspicious of Anthony DiGiovanni and follows him to where he stashed his mask and mementos. Cassidy takes them, but he doesn't know what to make of them. Will the PCs help Anthony get his mask back?

Elizabeth Washington runs into Goop on the marsh islands and strikes up an unusual friendship with the "creature." She invites Goop and any of its kind back to her house, if it ever needs a place to lay low.

One night, in Goop-form, Anthony DiGiovanni comes upon thugs vandalizing boats on the Boundary Bay side of the marina. There, Goop meets Smyk, and the two team up to defeat the thugs before they can torch a half dozen boats. But the question remains: who sent the criminals?

Cassidy Geary turns out to be in the pocket of Walter Lynch; he reports every strange thing he sees out on the bay to the eccentric millionaire. Late at night, Cassidy's boat can be seen moored at the "White House," where the two talk about the odd goings-on in town.

THE STRAND AND BOARDWALK

The shore is where the most coveted properties in the town are located. The rich, as well as those families whose ancestors first founded the town, live along the beach. The entirety of Boundary Bay's shoreline (called simply the "Strand") is 12 miles (19 km) long. A long wooden boardwalk—built in 1964 and expanded in 1971—covers

Elizabeth Washington: *level 3, town history and gossip as level 4*

several miles of it. Teens from town often spend their time among the piers and pylons below the boardwalk, hanging out. The following locations can be found on the Strand:

THE BOARDWALK

This winding wooden boardwalk is raised off the sand about 8 feet (2 m), and is scattered with benches, bicycle-locking stations, and occasional access to the streets heading into town. Though much of the rotten wood was replaced in 1971, there are areas of the boardwalk that have once again begun to rot through.

Below the boardwalk, a maze of wooden pylons rises to hold up the walkway. The angled, cave-like area beneath is a favorite hangout of teens and of the few homeless people found in Boundary Bay. It is covered in often garish, fluorescent graffiti.

BOARDWALK REGULARS:

Murray Greene (Faceless): Everyone calls this forty-eight-year-old homeless man "Old Murray" or "Drunk Murray." He sleeps beneath the boardwalk and begs in town. He's permitted to do so because his father

was a town assemblyman in the 1950s and everyone knows him. He spends much of his time under the boardwalk, drinking and talking to himself, or reading from a stash of paperback books he hides down there.

Timothy Buston (Mask-Form: Battlefield): This short, squat fifteen-year-old spends many nights below the boardwalk due to his volatile family life. He is unpopular at school for all the wrong reasons, and he is considered "poor" because he wears the same clothes repeatedly—but this is due more to a desire to not be at home than a lack of clothing. When Timothy wears his uncle's green beret, he manifests as Battlefield.

BOARDWALK HOOKS:

Murray sometimes spies boats coming in off the water from some of the big cargo ships at night. Twice, he's seen workers moving boxes from inflatable rafts up onto the boardwalk to Waxy's Surf Shop, but of course no one would believe him, so he keeps his mouth shut.

A grate set into a cement face beneath the boardwalk opens into a 6-foot-wide (2 m wide) pipe that carries wastewater from the

town and spills it on to the beach, where it drains into the sea. Entering these pipes can grant access to many locations in town, if the PCs know where to go . . .

Graffiti beneath the boardwalk begins to change in the fall of 1986. A stylized face of a man in a hoodie with no eyes begins to appear more and more, though the culprit painting this symbol is never seen.

Timothy warns other prodigies in high school that something bad is going down on the beach at night. Twice he's seen weird people down there, including an "ape man" and a "faceless dude." Will the PCs team up with Timothy and help him investigate?

WAXY'S SURF SHOP

Waxy's has stood on the boardwalk since 1967, when the owner, Michael Gioccino, converted his family's taffy stand into a surf shop. Many older people in town still remember the Gioccino taffy stand fondly, but Michael's parents retired long ago to Delray Beach, Florida, after running the shop for twenty years. The building is a sagging wooden structure with sun-wrecked, peeling paint and a leaky roof. While the shop is run down, it holds a strong reputation as being "authentic." During the summer, it is packed with surfers. Though it stays open year-round for "seals"—surfers who suit up in thick wet suits and hit the waves in winter—its hours are greatly diminished in the wintertime, and some days, it doesn't even open.

WAXY'S SURF SHOP REGULARS:

Ellen Paladino: A spacy, sporty, and fun sixteen-year-old, Ellen is outgoing, and somehow blind to social hierarchies, drifting effortlessly through all the groups at the school without any concern for what people think of her. She's an avid surfer. Michael Gioccino is her uncle (her mother's brother).

Michael Gioccino: This overweight, balding forty-nine-year-old surfer has a nose that's been broken many, many times. He still hits the beach every day, just like when he was a young man, but usually he can be

found riding the desk in Waxy's, listening to psychedelic rock on a cracked boom box.

WAXY'S HOOKS:

Michael Gioccino falls in with New York organized crime and agrees to store boxes in his back room in exchange for cash to settle looming bank bills. These boxes are filled with raw opium poppies smuggled from freighters at night before they reach Port Newark.

A gang of surfers from midisland who call themselves "Half-Life" squat on the beach and begin causing trouble at the store. Their leader, an ex-con named Mike Dunphy, takes an unrequited shine to Ellen Paladino. Perhaps her uncle steps in . . .

Strange fires begin breaking out near Waxy's, first in the garbage can out back, then on the roof. Who is responsible? Lewis Graham, the secret town firebug? The gang of surfers? A prodigy?

A buff soldier in a green beret thwarts an attempted break-in at Waxy's when Ellen is closing. The soldier pulverizes the thieves, karate-chopping and judo-throwing them as if they were rag dolls. Before the local police arrive, the soldier vanishes. Everyone at Waxy's—and Ellen especially—wants to know who he is.

WIND AND SKY

This building was renovated recently, though it has stood here since 1964. Owned by Betty and Marcus O'Sullivan, Wind and Sky opens on Memorial Day (near the end of May) and closes on Labor Day (the first week of September). In the off-season, it is shuttered, with most of its stock removed and stored at a storage facility two towns over. The O'Sullivans spend this time "on vacation"—though almost no one in town knows where.

When the shop is open, it sells T-shirts, gewgaws, suntan lotion, sunglasses, boogie boards, shorts, and assorted beach fare. Marcus O'Sullivan—a retired New York City accountant—is a meticulous businessman, and since the O'Sullivans took over the shop in 1977, he has turned it into a money-making powerhouse.

Ellen Paladino: level 3, surfing and swimming as level 4

Michael Gioccino: level 4, brawling, surfing, and lying as level 5

113

Marcus O'Sullivan: level 2, accounting, math, and deception as level 5

Betty O'Sullivan: level 1, positive social interactions and deception as level 3

Henry Wallaker: level 3

Lewis Graham: level 2, positive social interactions and pyromania as level 5

WIND AND SKY REGULARS:

Marcus O'Sullivan (Faceless): This stout sixty-one-year-old man is completely bald and wears suspenders, bookkeeper glasses, and garish bow ties. He is really Marcus Ford, a federal witness in a 1967 case against various Mafia-linked individuals in Kansas City, Missouri. The family has relocated twice, and in 1977 settled in Boundary Bay. O'Sullivan is a clever bookkeeper and an expert on tax law, and he has used this skill to make his shop—which began as a shoestring front provided by the government—into a success. He was ill at home on August 22 and was sleeping when the event occurred. Now, he sometimes gets strange feelings when he sees certain people in town, and twice he has woken up at night outside of his house without any memory of how he arrived there.

Betty O'Sullivan: This small, frail fifty-nine-year-old woman wears wigs and cat-eye glasses and never goes anywhere unless she is perfectly made up. She is really Betty Ford (née Gramont), and she fled Kansas City, Missouri, with her husband in 1967. Her son from a previous marriage, Peter Gramont, is in permanent care at a facility two towns over. Peter overdosed on heroin at the age of 22, and it gave him permanent brain damage. No one in town knows this.

Henry Wallaker: This tall, thin twenty-year-old man has puffy, super-fine blond hair and a wisp of a mustache. He always wears sports jerseys, sneakers, and baseball caps. Henry, who grew up on Estes Road next to the dump, is the only permanent employee of Wind and Sky not in the O'Sullivan family. He is deeply protective of the O'Sullivans, who have shown him great kindness, and he will put himself between them and harm, no matter the circumstances. The O'Sullivans let Henry drive their blue Datsun pickup truck, even in the off-season, if he looks after it.

WIND AND SKY HOOKS:

The PCs notice that one of the security doors in the back of Wind and Sky has been forced open during the off-season and then closed again to make it appear secure. Who—or what—is inside?

The shop does very well, almost too well. Is Marcus laundering money from some other group? Is he involved in some nefarious operation? Or is he simply so clever he can balance the books as no one else can?

Occasionally, a man visits Marcus at night. This is Theodore Mott, an FBI agent from Kansas City, who directs the O'Sullivan case for the witness protection program. If there's strangeness in town, especially if it seems a threat to the O'Sullivans, the agent might poke his nose in. If the Circus is in town, it may pull rank on such operations . . .

The Kansas City concern turns up in town—the criminals located Betty O'Sullivan's son Peter Gramont, and from there, they tracked his bills back to the O'Sullivans. The gangsters are here to settle some debts for the Kansas City mob.

SWINDON'S ICE CREAM SHOPPE

This ice cream parlor is owned by Lewis Graham, who inherited it from his grandfather in 1977. The Grahams have maintained the shop "as-is" since its inception. Long retired, Old Man Graham (also called "Grandpa Graham") lives with Lewis in their house on Fox Run Road.

Swindon's is a town landmark. Even in the off-season, it is a regular haunt for teens from town. Each table has a jukebox, and the interior decorations look straight out of the 1950s. Swindon's offers soft-serve ice cream, shakes, and other sweet confections. During the summer months, it also serves hot dogs and hamburgers.

SWINDON'S ICE CREAM SHOPPE REGULARS:

Lewis Graham: A strong-looking fifty-seven-year-old man, Lewis has tightly cropped gray hair, narrow eyes, and a perfect smile. He is a lifelong bachelor who usually dresses in his Swindon's uniform—

that of an old-timey piano player with a striped shirt, suspenders, and wing-tipped shoes. He is well known and well liked in town. However, Lewis is the Boundary Bay firebug; he burned down the town hall in 1947 and the library in 1955, though no one knows this. Even worse, he still dreams about lighting new fires, even all these years later. And he will kill to protect this secret.

Helen Basille: This very tall, loud, socially awkward sixteen-year-old volleyball player works the counter, scooping ice cream and wiping up after school and on weekends (volleyball allowing). She is a head taller than any other girl in her class. While she doesn't have a lot of friends, she often spends time with Brett Shaeffer at the marina; the two have been friends since second grade. Though she would never, ever admit it, she has a crush on him.

Monica Demath: This fifteen-year-old is a smart, withdrawn, bookish teen with braces and long blonde hair she always keeps braided. In Swindon's, she works tables and sometimes cooks or scoops ice cream. She needs to wear glasses, which she hates, so she can often be found squinting to keep them off her face. She lives in the Kennedy Estates with her grandmother and grandfather, and often catches a ride to school or work with Scotty Veracruz in his Dodge Dart. Despite multiple advances by Scotty, Monica remains uninterested.

Scott "Scotty" Veracruz (Mask-Form: Morrow): This big, quiet seventeen-year-old football player lives next door to Monica Demath. Scotty has long held a torch for the girl next door. He works as a busboy and general helper for cleaning up, painting, fixing things, and throwing out garbage. He's terrible at all school subjects except, surprisingly, math, which he seems to be a natural at. He often calculates and counts off the till at closing with a speed that is startling. And he's always right. In football, he is a serviceable brick wall of a player, trained to get between the ball and the opposing team. His mask-form is Morrow.

SWINDON'S ICE CREAM SHOPPE HOOKS: Swindon's is decorated with large, wooden carousel horses hung on the walls, and one glows as a powerful memento—but it is located behind the counter, in a place not readily accessible to customers. What can it do?

Hidden in the storage room at Swindon's is Lewis Graham's greatest love and shame: his scrapbook. Each page contains two black-and-white pictures of a building; in one, the building is fine, in the next, it is burned out. Graham set fire to each building. Sometimes, he comes to Swindon's late at night and pores over its pages.

One of the teens at Swindon's vanishes when closing one night. No one sees them go, and they leave the store unlocked. Only a strange symbol painted on the wall remains behind. Obviously, the police (and possibly the PCs) become involved.

PIXEL PALACE

This open-air storefront contains twenty-two video game machines, two Skee-Ball machines, a small counter that accepts tickets in exchange for cheap gewgaws, and two utilitarian toilets. The machines are all slotted with welded loops through which a security wire has been run, to prevent theft. At night, all the machines are covered in plastic tarp, to protect against the ocean air.

The arcade is owned by Margaret and Howard Jen, though their son Asa is the face most often seen here, and sometimes his little sister, Katy, as well. The arcade's business hours seem completely the inverse of high school hours. When it's open, dozens of kids are packed in under the tarp playing *Pac-Man*, *Donkey Kong*, *Frogger*, *Out Run*, *Galaga*, and even oldies such as *Space Invaders* and *Lunar Lander*.

Asa manages the counter, handles disputes, and makes change. Thanks to his "owning" an arcade, Asa is considered cool by most in the high school and gets invited to all the parties as a matter of course. On the weekends, the Pixel Palace is always packed, rain or shine.

Helen Basille: *level 2, volleyball and physical activities as level 3*

Monica Demath: *level 1, schoolwork and knowledge tasks as level 4*

Scott "Scotty" Veracruz: *level 3, mathematics as level 5*

Morrow: *This Thinker mask-form is a slight Englishman dressed in a tuxedo who carries various clocks, watches, and wristwatches all over his body. Each timepiece is tuned to a "time" when an event is going to happen—something that Morrow just seems to know. If he pulls the proper timepiece out and stops it, the event it is connected to stops as well, at least for a few seconds. He also seems to catch occasional glimpses of the future. He comes from "1555 originally, but don't hold that against me," and he is here to locate the source of some effect that has rippled through all time. He believes Scott is lazy and ill-behaved. Morrow will do his best to force Scott into situations where he has to think his way out.*

Morrow: *level 7, tasks related to time and causality as level 10 (power shifted); health 35; Armor 3 (treated as moving out of the way of attacks); can stop any action he can see before it happens (one use per power shift per engagement); power shifts: +3 to time control, +1 to time prescience, +1 to dexterity*

PIXEL PALACE REGULARS:

Howard Jen: level 1

Howard Jen (Faceless): A fifty-one-year-old drunk, Howard has short, cropped black hair, a sallow complexion, and an incredibly thin physique. He stinks of alcohol all the time, but his resistance is such that he is always clearheaded. He shuffles from place to place on the very rare occasions he leaves the Jens' apartment on Beach Street. Recently, Howard Jen has begun to go out late at night. When he comes to his senses, it is often just as he arrives back at home—he has no recollection what he does during his nightly jaunts.

Katy Jen: level 1

Margaret Jen: A fifty-five-year-old ghost of a person, Margaret has completely given up doing anything except taking care of her husband in his last extremities. At one point, the two were happy, back before the bottle got him. Now, Margaret only goes through the motions, getting groceries and liquor for her husband. She spends most of her days reading old novels. She hates her life and suffers from depression.

Margaret Jen: level 2, deception tasks as level 3

Asa Jen (Prodigy, no mask-form yet): This short, quiet fifteen-year-old kid is an exceptional artist. He's also a prodigy, but

Danny Deleo: level 3

Asa Jen: level 2

he hasn't explored making his mask yet—though he has had the urge to do so. He wears hip-hop clothing (a Run-DMC jacket, leather hat, and Adidas high-tops) and listens exclusively to rap music. He is just beginning to realize the strangeness he's experiencing goes well beyond only himself.

Katy Jen: A thirteen-year-old student at Jefferson Junior High School, Katy has a short bob haircut and big glasses, and she is usually outfitted in overalls and sneakers. She is overeager, loud, and difficult to dissuade from the "mother" role she has created for herself. She thinks she's in charge and must care for Asa. To the two teens, their parents are out of the picture.

Danny Deleo (Mask-Form: Freeze Frame): A thin, frizzy-haired seventeen-year-old redhead with big glasses, bad teeth, and blue eyes, Danny Deleo is always in the arcade when it's open, usually pumping quarters into *Berzerk*, *Robotron*, and *Stargate*. He knows Asa is "special," just like he is. His mask-form is Freeze Frame.

PIXEL PALACE HOOKS:

Asa Jen is a prodigy who has not yet made his mask, but he has collected several powerful mementos he stores on the toy display shelf. He has no idea what's going on with his weird "visions," but any day now he knows that he'll have to comply with that little voice telling him to make a mask.

Asa's mementos are displayed front and center in the toy cabinet of the Pixel Palace. He is desperate to understand the strange auras he sees on objects and people and has noticed that those who "glow" seem interested in the items in the case. Danny Deleo is one he sees all the time, glowing. Maybe Asa will approach one of the glowing PCs.

Howard Jen is slowly dying of alcoholism. He is a quiet, withdrawn drunk, however, and is rarely seen emerging from the Jens' apartment on Beach Street. His wife, Margaret, enables this self-destruction by supplying her husband with liquor. Both the adults have neglected the arcade for months now; only the children have kept it afloat.

Asa's father was asleep during the incident, and he is one of the Faceless. Soon, Asa will discover that something else woke on that day. When Asa's father is taken over by the power that hunts the prodigies, where will the teen run?

The PCs might assist Asa in collecting the mementos to make his mask. When Asa is finished creating it (from a diving mask, a bunch of puffy stickers, and some tempera paint), he becomes Orbis, a distant, scientific Thinker with orange skin, prehensile hair, and the power to control light.

BEACH STREET

The town's downtown core is built along a single strip called Beach Street that runs at a right angle to the shoreline. A few hundred yards from the beach and the boardwalk, it is a wide street with carefully maintained oak trees on either side. On weekends and in the evenings on nice days, the street is usually filled with people moving about; kids and teens often meet up here, either to go down to the beach or just to go shop to shop.

GOOD AND PLENTY

The Good and Plenty is a small candy and magazine shop right at the edge where Beach Street meets the boardwalk. It opens early and closes late, and the family that runs it, the Khalajis, are Persians who moved from Iran to the United States in late 1970 and received their citizenship in 1980. Farood—the father—most often runs the cash register, selling candy to children, newspapers and magazines and cigarettes to adults, and other various small goods like cheap baubles, toys, and kites to tourists. Sometimes his oldest son, Vahid, can be found there instead, often working with his electronic kits on the counter top, soldering components together. A tiny room in the back houses two regularly rotated video game machines that often draw groups of kids.

GOOD AND PLENTY REGULARS:

Farood Khalaji: A thirty-nine-year-old man, Farood has tightly cropped black hair and a thick beard. He is always happy and eagerly shares jokes he collects from various books with the people who come and go from the shop. He is patriotic, almost comically so, and insisted on paying for the bronze bicentennial plaque installed at the end of Beach Street in 1976. Every morning he unfurls and hangs the American flag at his store, and every night he reverentially takes it down. His English is perfect and slightly tinted with a British accent. Before he left Iran, he was a structural engineer, but he hated that job. He is infinitely happier in his new occupation as a shopkeeper, made possible with the help of a loan from an uncle in Indiana.

Vahid Khalaji: This sixteen-year-old has a huge mop of black hair, no facial hair, and wide-set, friendly features. He has a twin sister, Soraya. Despite his projected amenability, Vahid is quiet and studies new acquaintances carefully before deciding whether to open up to them. Obsessed with electronics, he builds and rips electronic kits to pieces in his spare time. He hopes to work at Sand Point Consumer Electronics in the future. In school, he is exceptional, but

Freeze Frame: *This mask-form is a young female Thinker who wears crazy, postapocalyptic-looking fashions and big, green, bug-eyed goggles. She is small and fast, but her power is to stop and allow herself to navigate among the probabilities of individual actions (for example, a single gunshot or punch). This makes her appear to "skip" the attack and end up safe and sound on the other side of it. Quiet and withdrawn, she will only say she "lost her family when we lost Omaha." Freeze Frame is secretly in love with Danny Deleo, to the point of irrational jealousy, and she will do anything to protect him. She's here for a reason, and she recalls coming here with others, but what that reason is, or who the others were, she cannot recall.*

Freeze Frame: *level 6; health 50; Armor 2; if she knows an attack is coming, she can spend 1 power shift to "sidestep" the attack (up to 5 times per engagement); power shifts: +2 to intelligence, +3 to causality control*

Farood Khalaji: *level 3, engineering and physics as level 5*

Vahid Khalaji: *level 2, electronics as level 3*

has few friends. The only person he talks to regularly is Brett Shaeffer, as the two share an interest in computers, electronics, and programming.

Soraya: level 3

Maryam Khalaji: level 2

Soraya Khalaji (Prodigy, no mask-form yet): Soraya is a sixteen-year-old with long, black hair, a winning smile, and an upfront nature. She and her twin brother were born in the United States, and she speaks perfect English with a Long Island accent. In school, she moves among the upper echelons of the popular kids, and she has dated various sports stars, including Hal Walmer, the son of the chief of police. She takes her schoolwork very seriously, and is currently all about the Scholastic Aptitude Test (SAT), which will affect her chances for college. When she is in the store, it is usually after hours, when she helps with restocking. Soraya was asleep on the morning of the incident, and she vividly

Dustin Trewes: level 2, riding dirt bikes and bike stunts as level 4

remembers a weird dream where she was holding something that went over her eyes. She's also noticed some people and objects in town appear to sparkle and shine with importance, but she has yet to pay much attention to it . . .

Maryam Khalaji: Maryam is a kind, dark-haired thirty-seven-year-old woman with a striking gray streak in the middle of her coif. Her English is limited, though she drives to Bethpage twice a month to attend English classes. She usually stays home and handles the housework while her husband, Farood, runs the store. She speaks Farsi to her children, and while they completely understand it, they don't speak it themselves.

Dustin Trewes: Dustin is a fifteen-year-old troublemaker from Dutton Street who is forever decked out in a ratty, hand-painted Van Halen jean jacket, high-tops, and ruined T-shirts. His eyes goggle beneath his huge bifocals, and his long blond hair is cut in a mullet, often tucked up under a trucker hat. He is always in the Good and Plenty, hovering around the video game machines. Dustin is the kind of kid who mouths off all the time to anyone. The only person he seems to respect is Farood. The kindly owner once caught him stealing and, instead of turning him in, had him come twice a week to mop the store for several bucks in store credit—a job which Dustin does dutifully. Dustin's Frankenstein-like bicycle, composed of a hundred different dead bikes salvaged out at Bluebeard Scrap, can usually be seen propped up outside the candy shop.

Abigail Delgreccio: Abigail is another fifteen-year-old Dutton Street kid who often turns up at the Good and Plenty for different reasons. She wants to be Madonna and spends every available penny on mesh gloves, short shorts, makeup, and hair products. She is most often at the Good and Plenty when Vahid is there, a fact that Vahid's twin, Soraya, has noticed. Abigail has tried time and again to strike up a conversation with Vahid, but so far, the boy has shown no interest—or even an

Abigail Delgreccio: level 1

indication he knows her name. In truth, Abigail spends as much time as she can away from her home on Dutton Street, because her father is a drunk and her family life is a living hell. Only Dustin Trewes knows this, though. She is often mistaken for Dustin's sister, though they are not related.

GOOD AND PLENTY HOOKS:

Vahid gets an internship at Sand Point Consumer Electronics and *sees* things while working there.

Something attacks the shop and seriously injures Farood and Dustin Trewes. The police first suspect Dustin or his family, but they later conclude that some sort of animal attacked the shop—something like a bear or large deer. The two men claim it was some sort of amorphous creature the size of a bear.

Something strange has taken a liking to Soraya. Twice, she's seen a creature shaped like an ape following her home in the dark when she leaves the shop. Who is it? A prodigy. The Faceless? Something worse?

Vahid's current electronics project—a short-wave radio—suddenly picks up a strange transmission: the voice of Lieutenant Holtz dealing with "the Circus." The signal comes and goes, becoming strongest at night.

BEACH STREET VIDEO

This tightly packed shop is relatively new to Beach Street, having recently replaced the old sewing shop, which closed in late 1984. (Before that, the building was the Aladdin Theater, which closed in 1981.) The business is usually open only after noon and closes promptly at seven-thirty every night. More and more, it has become a popular stop for those in town, as VHS players are becoming increasingly common.

It is little more than a single room filled with row after row of VHS tapes, a small laser-disc section (with a bathroom shoved in the back), and a glass counter. The owner, Delbert Stoppenhauser, is usually the one behind the register, reading an issue of *Cinefex* or a comic book.

BEACH STREET VIDEO REGULARS:

Delbert Stoppenhauser: This thirty-six-year-old retired stock trader is living out his bliss. Despite being overweight, with stringy brown hair, a receding hairline, and giant, thick glasses, Delbert is insanely comfortable in his own skin, for many reasons—the most important of which is that he's worth several million dollars. Not that anyone knows or would notice. He drives a wreck of a car (an improbably resurrected AMC Gremlin) and lives in a shamble of a house out in the Kennedy Estates. The shop is basically his own personal movie collection, and he loves nothing more than renting movies, talking movies, and buying weird VHS tapes from foreign catalogs. Stoppenhauser is an open-minded individual who has tons of resources and very little to lose. Therefore, if he becomes embroiled in the prodigy phenomenon, he will prove very, very useful.

Maria Juhasz (Mask-Form: Dead Ringer): Maria is a fifteen-year-old girl who eventually scored a job at the video store after spending a solid six months talking movies with the owner. She is slight, with long black hair (always combed straight), and she dresses in the new wave fashion (jackets, hats, lace). She can quote most movies verbatim. She lives with her overprotective father. Her mask-form is a Changer called Dead Ringer.

BEACH STREET VIDEO HOOKS:

A man wearing a thousand-dollar suit begs a filthy and half-shaven Delbert Stoppenhauser to reconsider giving his notice. In return, Delbert kicks him out of the shop. If asked, Delbert says the man is "a tick on the ass of the American investor."

Letters arrive at the shop from Isander Investments. Each contains a check to Delbert Stoppenhauser in the amount of $9,999. Dozens of these lie unopened under the counter.

Maria Juhasz begins to get a bad feeling when closing the shop one night. She sees a figure out past the lights on Beach Street, watching the shop. When she looks again, the figure is gone. Maybe she'll tell one of her new prodigy friends at school.

Delbert Stoppenhauser: *level 3, accounting, stock trading, and finance as level 6*

Maria Juhasz: *level 3*

Dead Ringer: *This mask-form is a Changer who can look like anyone from any movie or video (including their clothing). While in a specific form, Dead Ringer can say only what that actor said in the movie (stars of black-and-white movies, luckily, appear in full color). As far as is known, Dead Ringer has no real form, and when not concentrating on one particular actor, the mask-form bleeds through hundreds of forms per second in a bizarre mess of people. Dead Ringer claims to be a "memory form" from the "outer rim of thought," though what that means precisely is anyone's guess. Dead Ringer is very eager to escape the confines of Maria's mind. It doesn't dislike her and would not harm her, but at the same time it believes "anywhere is better than here."*

Dead Ringer: *level 5; health 35; can appear as a perfect replica of any character from a movie and say anything that character said on film; transformation takes one round and grants no additional new abilities (guns, weapons, and equipment are props); power shifts: +1 to intelligence, +2 to charisma, +1 to resilience*

Nearly two dozen tapes in the shop have turned up blank, most stored toward the northeast wall of the shop. Anyone with a science background can tell they were exposed to a strong magnetic force.

An odd man in a suit who says he is from the government asks a lot of questions about the week of August 22. He never gives his name. His car has a GOV license plate.

Alea Laskaris: level 3, dancing as level 4

WAVES DANCE STUDIO

This small, two-level box-front shop has a single large dance room, with bathrooms downstairs and a small office and a studio apartment upstairs. During most days, at least two classes are held here, varying from children's dance and more advanced classes such as ballet for teens to disco and flamenco classes for adults in the evening.

WAVES DANCE STUDIO REGULARS:

Alea Laskaris: This thirty-nine-year-old former dancer owns the studio. Alea is thin and lithe, with short, spiky black hair and dramatic makeup. She is always clothed in leotards and dance gear. Once, she danced in various New York productions, and she retired to Long Island in the late 1970s, opening the only dance studio in town. She is the only employee of the studio and makes at least half her money by renting out the apartment above it. She lives in a small apartment on Waukena Avenue and drives a jeep.

Rob Escadero (see Shaeffer Marina): Rob Escadero, the bartender from the Shaeffer Marina, rents the studio apartment above Waves, and his telltale red 1977 Mustang can be seen parked behind the studio at night. His apartment is accessed from the back by a rickety, rotting wooden staircase. He rarely interacts with Alea, who stays out of his business as long as the rent is on time.

WAVES DANCE STUDIO HOOKS:

While closing, Alea Laskaris is attacked by a "man without a face" and barely escapes. The story is a five-day wonder in town, and news gets around. If some of the PCs speak to her about it, she confides that the attacker wasn't visible in the many mirrors of the studio, which is how "he" surprised her.

A figure can be seen coming and going behind the Waves Dance Studio at night. It seems to be spying through the second-floor windows into the back apartment, especially when Rob Escadero has company. This is Tabitha Shaeffer, who is in love with Rob.

BOUNDARY BAY POLICE STATION

The town of Boundary Bay employs a police chief appointed by the city council. The current police chief is Chester A. Walmer, who enjoys broad support from both the politicians and the public. Chester has implemented a "zero tolerance" policy for drugs, and he has "sent up" multiple locals for stints in the county jail and elsewhere. He is tough, no-nonsense, and old fashioned. His son, Hal Walmer, is a well-known, popular high school bully who often breaks all the laws his father has sworn to protect.

The local police force has twelve police cruisers (bought in 1978) and thirty-two full-time staff. The police station, a building on Beach Street constructed in 1966, includes nine holding cells and a weapons locker with shotguns and semiautomatic rifles, as well as various emergency supplies. The town is big enough to require 24-hour policing, so the station is always occupied by some staff, even in the dead of night. Much of the local revenue is generated by traffic stops just off State Route 25A, where two Boundary Bay police cruisers are always parked with radar guns, handing out tickets as cars rush down Estes Road. Locals are well aware of this trap, and they always drop to a very slow speed when entering town from the highway.

Overall, the town has never seen much in the way of trouble (yet), but that does not mean the police are not eager to prove their worth if such a need arises. If anything, Chief Walmer and his officers will be overzealous in their pursuit of apparently "big" crimes. As Boundary Bay is still small enough to be considered a "burg," the police might cut a lot of corners, and a lot of "swearing up" might arise where it's a third party's word against the police. Still, Chester's primary concern is the safety of the town's residents. If it comes down to it, he will make the right choice.

121

BOUNDARY BAY POLICE STATION REGULARS:

Chief Chester A. Walmer: *level 3, investigation, interrogation, and police work as level 4*

Chief Chester A. Walmer: This fifty-two-year-old is slightly overweight, with thinning blond hair and blue eyes. He always wears his police hat or, when off duty, his Boundary Bay Police baseball cap. He is never without his aviator sunglasses (snagged after seeing *Top Gun* the previous May). He is friendly and goes out of his way to interact with people in the town, especially those he does not know. Some might say Chester is in everybody's business, while others say he takes a genuine interest in the lives of the people he has sworn to protect; it usually depends what he thinks of you. His son, Hal Walmer is a golden boy in town and in the high school.

Officer Dustin Wright: *level 2, running, climbing, jumping, and police work as level 3*

Officer Dustin Wright (Faceless): This twenty-nine-year-old local boy almost joined the army in 1975, but at the last minute applied for the local police. He is tall, thin, and well built, and he can often be seen running on the Strand or on the boardwalk early in the morning or late at night. Despite his athletic physique, his face is pudgy, his eyes close-set and his hairline high. Dustin Wright is a "good guy," known and well liked by nearly everyone in town. When he works the speed trap at the highway, he tends to let locals go, instead focusing his attention on out-of-towners. He is a favorite of Chief Walmer, though the police chief feels the young officer has a lot to learn. Despite all he has going for him, Dustin is withdrawn and secretive. His parents still live in town off Fox Run Road. August 22 was Dustin's day off, and he was asleep on the couch at his parents' home when the incident occurred. So far, he's suffered no ill effects from it, though recently he's been having trouble sleeping—he imagines there is someone standing in his room at night, talking to him.

Parking Enforcement Officer Henry Lopez: *level 2*

Parking Enforcement Officer Henry Lopez: Henry, a fifty-one-year-old career officer, is grossly overweight with a meticulously shaved goatee, a pate of thin black hair with a bald spot, and glasses. Lopez has suffered from problems related to smoking, diabetes, and worse, but somehow he still maintains an iron grip on his job. He keeps fastidious records (in a green notebook) and spends most of his day cruising Beach Street and nearby areas—mostly toward the beach—looking for illegal parking. He could have lost his job some time ago due to his numerous medical absences, but his uncanny ability to generate revenue from tickets makes it all but impossible for the town to get rid of him. He drives an unmarked police car that is nevertheless well known in town.

Officer Eileen Canty: This twenty-six-year-old transfer from Montauk joined the Boundary Bay police a year ago. She is young and eager to prove herself; therefore, everything she does is by the book, a practice the chief and her compatriots are attempting to get her to tone down. She is a tall, wide-shouldered woman with short, cropped black hair and an athletic build. In training, there is no contest: she is the fastest member of the BBP—and the best shot. Despite being widely liked by her fellow cops, she is loath to mix work with her personal life (such problems have caught up to her in the past), so she is somewhat lonely. She can sometimes be found on Beach Street, looking awkward in civilian clothes and walking or eating alone.

Detective Graham Arnette: This forty-nine-year-old detective is the veteran with the longest tenure on the Boundary Bay Police force. He has served since the previous police chief, so he is the only one permitted to call Chief Walmer "Chester." Graham Arnette is so thin as to be almost skeletal, his hair seems to hover around his head like some sort of poorly sized helmet, and his clothing (a normal suit) is almost always stained or wrinkled and hangs off him as if it were still on the hanger. He always wears a leather messenger bag in which he keeps a tape measure, a police crime scene kit, various notebooks and pads of graph paper, a flashlight, and a police radio. Graham spends most of his time investigating property crimes such as theft and arson, but he will of course be roped into investigations of any odd activities by the BBP that involve property destruction, violence, or disappearances.

The detective is surprisingly flexible in his beliefs, and has all manner of books on the occult, the supernatural, and alien abductions in his small apartment in the Meadowdale Estates. Out of everyone who might end up considering the prodigy phenomenon, Graham is the one who will test the weirdest possibilities without blanching.

BOUNDARY BAY POLICE STATION HOOKS:

An abandoned car is found on Estes Road near the mall. It's from out of town, and the driver and their passenger cannot be located. Those investigating it discover that Officer Wright was working the traffic stop that night. (Wright woke at home in bed, with no memory of nearly half his shift—but with dried blood on his hands.)

Officer Lopez keeps a notebook marking down the weird cars he keeps finding parked around Sand Point Consumer Electronics. All these cars have GOV on their license plates. They're all registered to the Defense Intelligence Agency.

Chief Walmer discovers his son Hal is abusing his reputation by throwing parties out at the Smilaks' house in Point East, but to cover it up, the police chief decides to blame it on another kid from the high school, one with a bad reputation. A PC? One of their friends?

A powerful memento is dead center in the middle of the main room of the Boundary Bay Police Department: the Boundary Bay Little League trophy from 1981. It glows with incredible power from behind the glass of a locked display case. What can it do?

A woman arrives from out of town and begins asking around for Officer Canty: Kelly Lifshitz, the thirty-nine-year-old wife of Lieutenant Bernard Lifshitz of the Montauk Police Department. Eileen and Bernard had a secret affair two years before that Kelly has only just discovered (by finding a hidden shoebox full of photographs), so she's here to act out her revenge on Eileen.

Officer Eileen Canty: *level 3, police work as level 4*

Detective Graham Arnette: *level 3, investigation, interrogation, and police work as level 5*

MARIO'S PIZZA

The only pizza place in Boundary Bay, Mario's is a bit of an institution. It is a grimy, grease-covered mess of a store (with a sprinkling of dried, dead flies on the window sills), but the pizza is fantastic. Two arcade games are shoved in the corner near the lone bathroom in the back. Its original founder, Mario Deseerle, established the shop in 1955 and sold it when he retired in 1979. It has remained precisely the same since its foundation, churning out and delivering no-nonsense New York-style pizza anywhere in the Boundary Bay area.

MARIO'S PIZZA REGULARS:

Winston Medina: Winston is the fifty-five-year-old owner of Mario's, and he looks the part, too. He's got a potbelly, a scrub beard, curly gray hair combed back from his forehead, and a perpetual scowl. Winston worked under the original owner in the 1960s and 1970s, and to buy the business in 1979, he took out a loan with a down payment he scrimped and saved for. He's glad he did. Mario's is an institution in town, and while other pizza shops have cropped up, none have stuck around, and his addition of a delivery driver has doubled his weekend and evening business. He owns a huge house with a swimming pool and all the amenities on Fox Run Road.

Gerald Wacter (Faceless): This seventeen-year-old delivery driver is absurdly tall, with great gawky limbs, acne, and curly brown hair. He is soft spoken and eager, but easily bullied. He has discovered he can squeeze a twenty-minute nap in on most shifts without getting caught by parking near the turnoff to Sand Point Consumer Electronics. He was asleep there on August 22 when the incident occurred. He has been having vivid dreams of wandering the town at night and meeting various people for reasons he can't recall. The last time he had this dream, he woke to find his feet and bed stained by freshly mowed grass he had apparently tracked in.

Rachel O'Hara: This seventeen-year-old pizza maker has a round face and bifocal glasses that are perpetually fogged from the stove. Her frizzy brown hair (usually under a hairnet) always looks out of control. In school, she is an eager if uninspired student, and her few friends are very close to her. But in the store, she is loud and brash and talks back all the time. She drives an improbably huge, old Ford truck and lives all the way out at the edge of town on Estes Road.

DARK DUNGEON

The Dark Dungeon, opened in 1982, is the premiere hobby and comic book shop on the north shore of Long Island in Suffolk County. It is small but packed full of product, and the walls are amateurishly painted to look like stone blocks. Half the store is dedicated to hobbies—model airplanes, Dungeons & Dragons books, miniatures, and more—while the other half is taken up by comic books.

The owner, Daniel Haas, is a huge fan of all the products he sells and is on a first-name basis with most of his customers. He puts aside "month bags" of content for various customers that contain new releases based on his near-encyclopedic knowledge of their tastes. Every month, he sells nearly a hundred of these. On Friday nights, Daniel's Dungeons & Dragons group meets and plays in the store after closing, and they can be spied in the back, rolling dice by candlelight.

Daniel Haas: This extremely tall, broad-shouldered thirty-year-old man has short blond hair, glasses, and friendly features. He speaks in perfect English and never uses contractions. Despite having a rich imagination, Daniel has a worldview dictated by absolutes. If confronted by the impossible, it's quite likely Daniel won't be able to handle it very well. He is a bachelor and owns an apartment at the Meadowdale Estates across from the mall.

Micah Geerat: This short eighteen-year-old know-it-all has poufed brown hair, large bifocal glasses, and vaguely catlike features. He is always in the store when it is open, and actively opines about anything brought to the counter (usually in the negative).

Winston Medina: level 2, business and finance as level 3

Gerald Wacter: level 2, driving as level 3

Daniel Haas: level 3

Micah Geerat: level 2, obscure sci-fi or fantasy facts as level 5

Rachel O'Hara: level 2, cooking as level 3

Geerat (called "the rat" by bullies at Ocean View), incredibly unobservant when it comes to social cues, will glom onto any conversation or group that comes his way until told to go elsewhere.

Eloise Rosemont: This seventeen-year-old new wave devotee works at the shop several days a week after school. She has short hair (dyed a different color every week) and is generally a social pariah. She doesn't put up with any monkey business in the shop and can be downright scary when she wants to be. Her uncle is Detective Graham Arnette, with whom she is very close.

DARK DUNGEON HOOKS:

Story lines from Daniel Haas's D&D game begin to play out in the town. In his campaign, the mill burns in the Hamlet—and the next week the Association Foods grocery store burns down in Boundary Bay. In the game, the constable is killed by orcs—and the police chief gets attacked and disappears on the road. What's causing this?

Prodigies seem drawn to the Dark Dungeon, perhaps because it's filled with comics that might let them piece together just what the hell is going on. PCs going there find that the place is packed with prodigies and mementos.

Eloise Rosemont was sitting on her back patio facing the Sand Point Consumer Electronics building on August 22 and saw "a huge beam of blue-white light shoot from it like a mushroom cloud," but no one believes her. She wants to know what's going on!

Micah Geerat has discovered the secret identity of one of the town's prodigies when he sees them "shift back" to their teen-form. He's following and keeping careful track of this person in hopes of becoming their sidekick.

OTHER BEACH STREET LOCATIONS:

Schwatsky's Clothing: This two-story, out-of-date fashion shop is *almost* a department store. The store sells all sorts of clothing, and most formal clothing in town comes—in one way or another—from Schwatsky's, or at least it *once* did. The owner, Yvengi Bonanni, a sixty-eight-year-old lifelong resident of town, is currently struggling to keep up

Eloise Rosemont: level 2

125

with the bank as the chain stores in the Meadowdale Mall gobble up his profits. He has already let half of his staff of eighteen go, and it's only a matter of time before the bank comes calling for the last time.

Red Badge RX: This small six-aisle pharmacy sells pills, medicine, health goods, and some simple groceries. Its owner, Adrian Schermerhorn, is a fifty-nine-year-old transplant from Baldwin, New York, who has run the Red Badge since 1976. The store is perpetually quiet and undertrafficked, as well as freezing cold (due to the air conditioner).

Association Foods: This twelve-aisle supermarket is the mainstay of the town. Its owner is Henry "Big Henry" McGill, and it is run by Henry "Little Henry" McGill Jr. Little Henry graduated from Ocean View High School in 1982, and he now lives in town with his high school sweetheart, Beth, and their four-year-old son. The supermarket is an oddity in town, as it is one of the few places that does not employ people under eighteen years of age.

Pompeii Bar & Grill: This long, thin storefront sits at the end of Beach Street. On Fridays and Saturdays, there's live music from 7 to 11 p.m., and many of the locals of age turn up. Teenagers from the high school sometimes try to get in, but the owner of Pompeii, Colleen Giordano, a fifty-five-year-old bruiser, is a stickler for checking IDs and knows almost every teen in town by sight. Most of the time, the worst that happens out at Pompeii is the occasional fight, but once or twice the police have been called out to break up something more serious.

OTHER BEACH STREET HOOKS:

Yvengi Bonanni vanishes one night, leaving Schwatsky's unlocked and the register filled with cash. The black-and-white still camera up front shows the door opening at 1:45 a.m. *on its own*, but no Bonanni. Is he somehow still inside?

A weird fellow in blue tights wearing a yellow scarf appears at the Pompeii Bar & Grill. When he's cut off after two beers, he destroys several tables, attacks a bartender, and flees so fast he shatters the mirror behind the bar. He's last seen running down Fox Run Road to the west.

Something big and scary has broken into Association Foods and is eating up the stock. It seems to come back on the full moon. What the hell can chew through plexiglass?

Tom Cruise comes into the Red Badge RX in a flight suit with the name "Maverick" on it and writes down a request for a bottle of two dozen painkillers. Since he has no prescription, he is turned away. As he leaves, he says, "Sorry to bother you on a Sunday, sir, but thank you." It is a Tuesday.

FOX RUN ROAD

This long road runs from Beach Street to Bay Avenue, further inland from the ocean. The streets here are winding and the landscape dotted with pine trees, oaks, small lakes, and parks. This area is where many influential people from the town live. The yards are large and often feature fences or natural obstructions such as stone walls and hedges, and the homes tend to be spacious.

FOX RUN ROAD LOCATIONS:

Standard Houses on Fox Run Road: There are about three hundred homes scattered in the area on or just off Fox Run Road. They are usually late 1960s split-levels or 1950s ranch houses. In general, most are well kept, and everyone in the neighborhood knows one another.

Graham House: The owners of Swindon's Ice Cream Shoppe, the Graham family has lived out on Fox Run Road since 1947. The house is a white, three-story classic with a wraparound porch and red shutters, built in 1908 and perfectly maintained. Grandpa Graham lives in the house, and can often be seen puttering about. His son Lewis's car is there in the evenings, and the two sometimes sit out on the porch.

Wright House: Officer Dustin Wright's parents, Helene and Michael Wright, live in a small one-story ranch-style home off a cul-de-sac on Fox Run Road. The young officer can often be seen visiting and, due to his father's bad back, mowing the lawn or performing other menial tasks on his days off.

Bonanni House: The Bonanni house, belonging to the owner of Schwatsky's, was once one of the most admired in town, but it has fallen a bit into disrepair. What is *not* known is that Mrs. Bonanni left her husband in late 1985, and that he has quietly put the house up on the market.

Medina House: This large, new house is built in a modern style on what was once an empty lot on Fox Run Road. The Medina family (Winston, his wife Estelle, and their junior high school–aged children, Amelia and Dianne) live here. It is huge, with three stories with over 4,000 square feet (370 square meters) and a game room, an inset stone pool with a slide, and an ample backyard. Winston is often out in front of the four-car garage, tinkering with a sports car.

FOX RUN ROAD HOOKS:

A pharmacist, Harold Beymer, is discovered after having collapsed while jogging on Fox Run Road. While recovering in the hospital, Harold describes a weird chase where a man in light-blue runner's clothing was pursuing him. He remembers nothing past their struggle, but he now dreams sometimes of losing his face.

A glowing pile of mementos, secreted by some unknown party in a culvert behind the houses on Fox Run Road, draws in nearby prodigies. But who put them there?

Grandpa Graham is being abused by his deranged son, because the old man uncovered his firebug secret. Lewis Graham has the old man locked away in the upper story of the house, where Grandpa Graham attempts to wave down the PCs during the day while his son is at work.

Yvengi Bonanni's disintegration becomes plainer and plainer to everyone in town. The once dapper man now shambles about and turns up at Pompeii more and more to drink.

SAND POINT CONSUMER ELECTRONICS

Built in the mid-1970s, this large office campus slowly expanded to engulf what was once forest and small parks in the Oceanside section of town. Many of the trees remain on the perimeter, and the winding Company Road leading to the facility cuts between them to the main building (called Building A). Almost 1,000 people work at this campus in various buildings. For the most part, they work in the assembly plants (Buildings B, C, and D), checking integrated circuit chips for defects.

The entire facility is surrounded by a stone wall topped with tightly slung (and recessed) razor wire. During regular work hours, the main gate is open, and security pays little attention to the cars that come in and fill the lot (there are *a lot* of employees). After hours, however, the gate is locked and accessed only via key card.

The specialty work goes on in the basement of Building A and is restricted by key card access. Emil Warzowski leads the team in the specially constructed subbasement investigating the bizarre, otherworldly piece of technology referred to as "the key," brought to Sand Point Consumer Electronics by the Circus in 1983.

These labs are filled with bizarre machines, videotape equipment, and dozens of specialty rooms, from a complete surgical suite to a swimming pool. There's even a full cafeteria below Building A, which is almost like a world unto itself. Many Circus agents, some regular military, and tons of scientists can be found down here at all hours. For the most part, if someone looks like they belong and they don't try to move into locked rooms, they can circulate freely without drawing attention.

The "key" is contained within a sealed vault in the center of the subbasement, which is always monitored. All the suites with thick plexiglass windows that open onto this central room are videotaped 24 hours a day, and all staff members who come and go are searched by military personnel. This room that contains the "key" is opened at set intervals and accessed through an airlock-like room with environmental suits. Various probes, monitors, and devices are moved about the room to study and test the "key" as it is flooded with various energies, chemicals, or processes. To date, only one test—that of August 22—had any effect, when an extremely low-level electromagnetic pulse was sent into the "key."

The "key" is an amorphous blob of spiky, metallic material that pulses and moves when living things or heat sources come near. It is about the size of a grapefruit. Usually, it reverts to a sphere when undisturbed, but if people interact with it or touch it, it can extend, grow, and twist into bigger, stranger geometric shapes. As far as can be determined, it is not poisonous and has no ill effect on the human body.

Emil Warzowski has his own office on this hub of rooms surrounding the "key" room. He can often be found there, poring over differential equations scrawled on wall after wall of blackboards.

MEADOWDALE MALL

Built between 1978 and 1980, this large mall off Estes Road soon found itself filled to the brim with the standard fare of shops. Its location next to State Route 25A puts it in easy travel distance of a dozen municipalities in Suffolk County, and it serves over 500,000 people annually. It is a common haunt for the kids and teenagers of Boundary Bay, particularly on the weekends.

It is a large, two-level structure with four fountains, two food courts, and dozens of shops, including large chain stores such as Sears, Brooks Pharmacy, Playworld, and more. It does brisk business, so mall leases are extremely valuable, and it is a very rare occurrence for a shop to close or suddenly change hands.

POPULAR LOCATIONS:

Wax and Stax: This is the most popular "serious" record, tape, and CD shop in town. The owner, Federico Galvani, speaks with a heavy Italian accent, but loves to talk music—all music—for hours with anyone who frequents the shop.

Ultimate Arcade: A cavernous, dark-carpeted arcade filled with every conceivable arcade machine, including oddities from Japan and Europe. Birthday parties are often held here, and high-score contests regularly take place on Friday and Saturday nights.

Meadowdale Twin Cinema: Since the closing of the Aladdin Theater on Beach Street in 1981, the Twin Cinema in the mall remains the only place to see movies in Boundary Bay. On Fridays, Saturdays, and Sundays—depending on the movie—the theater is usually packed to the gills.

The Incredible Pulp: This is a small, serious comic shop run by Ryan Cohen, who is serious about his comics. The store is simply an extension of his legendary "off-site" collection, which is in storage somewhere. Ryan has an encyclopedic memory for plots, characters, issues, and comic lines, but he only shares this knowledge with those who show comics the proper respect.

The Last Slice: This shop serves the cheapest pizza in Boundary Bay. Each slice costs twenty-five cents, and it sure tastes that way. But it's the only pizza at the mall, so the place remains popular.

HOT SKATES

This was once a heavy-equipment storage warehouse, but in 1977, it was purchased by the Lester family and converted into a skating rink franchise called Hot Skates. In the beginning, the location catered to adults interested in "roller disco," but later, after 1981, it was progressively fashioned into a place for children or teenagers. It is a common meeting place for younger teens (who go on "couple skates"), as well as for kids' birthday parties. The Hot Skates franchise died in 1982, but the Lesters kept the place open after a slight rebranding. It has enjoyed a strange popularity among the kids in Boundary Bay.

At the entrance, there is the atrium skate desk, where customers rent skates or check items. Past it are two large roller rinks separated by a food court that serves hot dogs, pizza, and soda, and finally a small arcade filled with video game machines and two small bathrooms shoved in the back. The interior is dimly lit, and all areas that are not on the rink are carpeted with an orange rug. The rinks are polished wood.

BOUNDARY BAY LANES

This somewhat dilapidated bowling alley was last updated in 1969, when it replaced the hand-set with automatic pin-set machines. Since then, it's slowly sunk into ruin—and debt. It is owned by Dee Tull (the third owner), who shoestrings *everything* in the hopes of staying afloat for just one more month.

Still, it is a popular hangout for teens, particularly because Dee is not above serving her watered-down beer to older-looking teens.

FIRST FEDERAL BANK

Once the Consolidated Bank of Boundary Bay located on Beach Street, this bank came to occupy a new building built off Estes Road in 1977, after its purchase by First Federal. This branch of First Federal is a "feature branch" for the company, and as one of its regional Suffolk County routing centers, it deals in high volumes of cash.

The location is bright, sparkling, and new-looking. It is equipped with every convenience (for example, drive-through tellers and remote night deposit boxes), as well as with silent alarms, cameras at every door and in the vault, and a time lock that can't be opened except at fixed times by multiple bank employees.

ESTES INDUSTRIAL PARK

This large area south of Estes Road was once unused grass and marshland. Now it is filled with warehouses, industrial facilities, parking lots, junkyards, and worse. It was zoned (after some contention) for industrial use in 1977 through the very vocal campaigning of Assemblyman Dean Yaros. It employs several hundred locals in various menial tasks, many of which service other nearby towns.

BLUEBEARD SCRAP

This big auto dumping yard is the final resting place for most junked cars in the area. The owner, Jose Nunez, opened it from his own backyard after buying up land in 1977. Now, it is several square miles of rusted-out car husks. Nunez has an eye for parts, and keeps a section of the yard he calls "the parts shop," where he stores pieces he feels he can sell through mail-order catalogs for collectors and mechanics. The rest he crushes in his industrial crusher and sells by the pound.

The Bluebeard in question is a 1955 Edsel up on a rotating pole that has been painted white with a royal-blue "chin"—Jose's first "real" wreck. The area surrounding the yard consists of marshland, dumps, and various undeveloped lots. Even still, Jose enclosed his property with a 12-foot (4 m) cyclone fence topped with razor wire in 1984, after some of his more select parts began to go missing.

Still, the kids get in. The yard is big and loud, and sound tends to travel, so the small groups of teens who hop the wire to hang out in the stacks can usually do so without running into anyone. When Jose catches them (as he usually does), he just kicks them out.

BLUEBEARD SCRAP REGULARS:

Jose Nunez: The thirty-one-year-old owner-operator of the yard is of medium build, with a bland face, improbably delicate half-lens glasses on a granny chain, and short black hair. The yard began as a personal collection of junkers that Jose turned into a career. Local police and firefighters know to call Jose if they need to get rid of a wreck or pull in a tow to one of the various gas stations. He is affable, quick to laugh, and eager to make long-lasting relationships— like any good businessman.

Arturo Nunez: Arturo, Jose's gray-haired fifty-six-year-old father, has been living off disability after breaking his back during the construction of the World Trade Center in 1969. He walks with a slow, dragging gait and has scars up and down his back that clearly tell the tale of how seriously he was injured. He is always smoking, and he's full of terrible, incredibly dirty jokes that he tells in mixed company. His universal defense is, "I am as God made me."

Jose Nunez: *level 3, mechanical repair as level 5*

Arturo Nunez: *level 2*

Evelyn Derecco: level 2, drug use and drug identification as level 4

Stuart Dill: level 3

Stutter: This mask-form is a lithe Mover who can tumble, leap, and flip in bizarre ways that defy physics, shooting to any wall or surface as if it were the ground, no matter the direction it's facing. He can't walk on such surfaces, but he can bounce off them, like a superball, and he often seems to flash in and out of reality as he does so. His uniform is a very odd, black skinsuit with arrows pointing in various directions. He doesn't like to talk about his past but often seems to recognize other mask-forms, and he will sometimes call them by name without introduction. Stutter can't stand Stuart, but he's not heartless—he doesn't want the kid abused either. He just can't help feeling trapped inside the teen's brain.

Stutter: level 6, tumbling, jumping, and dodging as level 10 (power shifted); health 55; can bounce, dodge, and smash a target for 6 points of damage; can climb, leap, and jump huge distances; power shifts: +5 to Acrobatics

Vahid Khalaji (see Good and Plenty): Vahid, the son of the owner of the Good and Plenty, is often found here scouring the yard (with permission) for electronic components. In return, he has wired up much of the shop for Jose.

BLUEBEARD SCRAP HOOKS:

The yard is an ideal place to safely test out mask-form abilities. Need a two-ton weight to chuck around, or an old refrigerator to disintegrate without worrying about collateral damage? There you go.

Who knows what mementos might be hiding out in the miles of junked-out cars?

Jose will readily help those who exhibit amazing powers, and he will protect their secret. He allows them to treat the yard as a hideout and keeps them safe from prying eyes. But he will also take steps, in secret, to turn such a revelation to his own personal gain. He'll copyright the mask-form's name and image, record conversations, take secret photographs, and more. When he feels like the time is right, he'll go public with his story.

BACK LOT

This large three-mile-by-four-mile (5 km by 6 km) lot of marshland off Estes Road is in the middle of being developed by various parties. Sections near the edges have been cleared, and several utility roads have been cut through the reeds, but for the most part, the core of the lot remains untouched.

This marshland is mostly soggy ground with large standing reeds that make it easy to disappear. Kids maintain a dirt bike track in the reeds by stomping paths through them. There are numerous hideouts and forts in various states of disrepair, as well as several campsites occupied by homeless people.

When teens and kids want to escape the town proper and stay away from the heavily patrolled beach, they usually come to the Back Lot. Here, they hang out, listen to music, play games, drink, and spend their time screwing around.

BACK LOT REGULARS:

Evelyn Derecco: This forty-seven-year-old homeless woman grew up in Queens. After riding out a very serious cocaine addiction, she fled east to avoid jail time and became homeless. Evelyn is rail thin, with a horrific shock of dyed blonde hair fading to black roots. She's always bundled in multiple jackets and pants, for she is always freezing—even in the summer. She's had a stern talking-to from the local police more than once, because she has a habit of building large—almost too large—fires. She's usually to be found around a small campfire, drinking cheap liquor, but her cocaine days are over. Everyone who frequents the Back Lot runs into her and knows her.

Stuart Dill (Mask-Form: Stutter): A sixteen-year-old runaway, Stuart is slight, sickly, and almost all head and brown hair. He lived in the Meadowdale Estates with his father, who regularly abused him, but once the teen discovered his powers, he fled to the Back Lot. Now, he lives in a small tar-paper shack in the reeds and cleans up by sneaking into Ocean View early and showering and changing at the school. Eventually, his father will come looking for him. His mask-form is a Mover called Stutter.

OTHER ESTES INDUSTRIAL PARK LOCATIONS:

Mill Frame Siding: This big, two-warehouse lot sells aluminum siding for construction. It is busy all day, with nearly a dozen full-time employees loading and unloading huge bundles of siding for shipping to various construction sites all over the island. At night, it is watched by a single night watchman.

Wexler Lumber Systems: This large, open lot has a single small office. Most of the property is taken up by stacks of lumber, much of it under tarps. During the day, the four full-time employees load and unload trucks with lumber. At night, the property is empty and unguarded.

Yavarro Propane and Fuel Supplies: The property consists of a storage depot for fuel oil (which most houses still use for central heating), as well as a huge propane tank. This lot employs three full-time workers and a professional car-patrol and alarm service to make certain no one siphons fuel. Trucks come and go from the site all day, especially in the fall.

OTHER NEIGHBORHOODS IN BOUNDARY BAY

Like any town, each area has its own characteristics and secrets that only locals seem to know. Below are the most significant neighborhoods in Boundary Bay not described elsewhere in this chapter.

Bayside: There are about two hundred homes on the winding, slightly hilly roads of Bayside, on the west side of Boundary Bay. This area is considered lavish, with large, multistory houses with perfectly manicured yards. Many of these streets are private, with gates and security.

Waukena Avenue: So far away from Beach Street that it's almost its own town, Waukena Avenue is still part of Boundary Bay. Waukena has cheap and run-down equivalents of almost all the shops on Beach Street. At night, the avenue tends to be a trouble spot for the police, as there are multiple liquor shops and two bars operating there. Waukena Avenue is where kids from Dutton Street go when they graduate to real crime.

Dutton Street: This is a series of streets around the once-industrial Dutton Street. The houses here are run down and in ill repair. They are low-slung ranchers (some burned out and boarded up) with cyclone fencing and occasionally razor wire. Several gangs operate out of houses in this area, including Half-Life, a surf gang; Acey Deucy, a biker gang supposedly affiliated with the New York Mafia; and the Dutton Street Kids, the local gang concern that deals in petty theft and stripping cars. There are others, and Dutton Street is widely avoided, day or night. The police leave the area to its own regulation unless things get *really* out of

hand. If some local wants to buy weapons, drugs, or a stolen car, Dutton Street is a good place to start.

The Creek and Silver Lake: This neighborhood exists in what was once a natural stream. The roads wind down into large lots with big houses spaced at such large intervals that residents can't see their neighbors. This area ends at Silver Lake—a large artificial lake that has a bicycle track, a walking path, and several playgrounds. The Creek is considered an affluent neighborhood, but the houses often have issues with flooding and a high water table.

Middle Village: With mixed two- and three-story apartments, rooming houses, and single-family residences, Middle Village is where most regular tourists stay in the summer. As such, many of the properties are rentals. During the summer, this area is filled with out-of-state cars and "toury kids"—children staying in town just for the summer break. The roads here are considered some of the worst in Boundary Bay. Poor locals think this is a rich area, but it's just average.

Meadowdale Estates: Built in the late 1960s and mid-1970s, the Meadowdale Estates are six large apartment blocks for general rental. Each has its own name (the Claremont, the DuBois, the Carter, the Maxwell, the Estate, and the Opal), and each houses at least a hundred people. This area is not generally walkable, and almost everyone here gets around by car. It's considered an area for poorer folks in town or for young people hoping to save up for a house.

Meadow Park: Meadow Park just . . . happened. When Oceanside met a natural boundary, Teralt Stream, cheaper cookie-cutter houses were put up to the south beyond it. After they sold out, the land between there and Estes Road was divided into ten house lots. One company bought half of them. Since 1981, the area has officially been infilled. Meadow Park is neutral in social standing—few care who comes out of or goes into the area.

Creekside: These last-ditch lots were stragglers from the end of Meadow Park that were never snapped up. Now, Old Man Lynch owns the area and rents cheap trailers to dozens of families, raking in money. In Boundary Bay, Creekside is considered a dead end or a place you wash up. Nothing good comes from Creekside.

Oceanside: Many locals who had family before the town's fishing crash ended up in Oceanside. The houses are generally two or three stories tall, built in the 1950s, with wraparound decks and large lots. Sand Point Consumer Electronics maintains its campus here on a slight artificial bluff that gives the upper floors of SPCE a view of the ocean. Many employees of SPCE make their home in this neighborhood so they can walk to work.

Kennedy Estates: This neighborhood is composed of cookie-cutter houses that are too small and packed too tightly together. Backyards are nearly nonexistent, and parking is always an issue. The houses all look almost identical—single-level ranch-style homes. The winding roads here are smooth and well paved, and they are an obsession with the skateboarders in town.

OCEAN VIEW HIGH SCHOOL, GO SAILORS!

Ocean View High School is the public high school for Boundary Bay. Built in 1951, it has slowly expanded along with the town. The first class it graduated was composed of fifty kids, and the latest class in 1985 had two hundred and fifty students. Its current total student count is almost eight hundred and ninety students. It is well funded by local taxes, and well maintained.

Ocean View High School is located off of Fox Run Road just west of Beach Street. It is a large campus with two big multistory buildings connected by glass-enclosed corridors and a third, smaller sports building, along with several sports fields, a full track, and a sizable parking lot.

The school teams are called "The Sailors," with a sailor mascot. The school colors are blue and white.

BUILDINGS ONE AND TWO

The remnants of the original high school, built in 1951, compose the entrance of Building One, but the rest of the structure

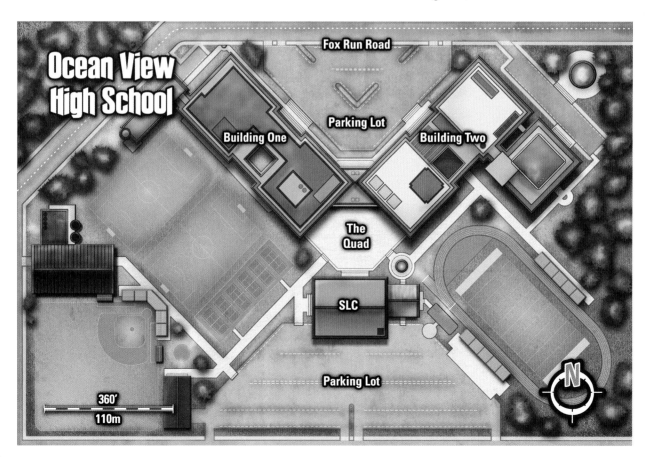

Ocean View High School

Fox Run Road

Building One

Parking Lot

Building Two

The Quad

SLC

Parking Lot

360'
110m

N

(like Building Two) is a multilevel glass-and-brick building constructed in the later 1960s. Each hallway of these two buildings (often called "Thing One" and "Thing Two" by the students) has approximately twelve fire doors, interspersed between hundreds of lockers. Each hallway usually ends in an entrance atrium, a staircase, and huge windows.

The two buildings are connected by a ground-level glass-enclosed walkway (which is always warm) with lockers on either side. Between classes, students rush through this corridor because most class schedules are split between the two buildings.

Buildings One and Two contain the office, the library, two cafeterias, dozens of classrooms and offices, as well as nearly a hundred closets and storage rooms.

BUILDING THREE

Building Three is a one-story structure with a gymnasium-sized ceiling. It is called the "sports and leisure complex," or "SLC" (pronounced "slick" by the students). It contains a large and small gym, two art studios, a music and band room, the auditorium, and a half dozen small satellite offices.

To get to Building Three from Buildings One and Two, a student must go outside and cross the "quad."

THE QUAD

The quad's grand name is wildly overblown. This semicontained courtyard has nothing more than a few picnic tables on a balding lawn strewn with cigarette butts, with views of the sports fields to the east and west.

NOTABLE OCEAN VIEW STAFF AND FACULTY

There are, of course, more teachers and staff members than the ones listed below. The following are the mainstays of the school—those who "stand out." GMs should feel free to fill in the cast of characters as needed.

Ms. Roberta Diamante (Math, AP Math). This physically perfect and brilliant thirty-nine-year-old teacher was hired in 1985. She

is the principal obsession of adolescents in the school, but beyond that, she is also known as being incredibly smart, insightful, and outgoing. Her apparent perfection is terrifying to most, and she is universally given a wide berth by her coworkers. They like her but seem to unconsciously dislike her sudden high standing among the student body. She lives in the Meadowdale Estates in a studio apartment. She was once married, but divorced her husband in 1984 and moved to Boundary Bay from Massachusetts to start a new life.

Mr. Walter Fedov (Social Studies, AP Social Studies). This tall, thin fifty-year-old man has receding brown hair, a beard, and a mustache. He's an outgoing, bubbly guy who likes to joke around with the kids and tries to get them engaged through various methods: by playing social studies *Jeopardy!*, running a model United Nations, and more. He likes his job. He lives one town over in Rockville with his wife and grade school-aged son. Mr. Fedov believes in the supernatural but will never mention this in mixed company unless he is confronted with the inexplicable.

Ms. Evelyn Hopkins (Chemistry, AP Chemistry). This forty-five-year-old has huge tinted glasses that match the artificial reddish color of her hair. She is single-minded in purpose, and that purpose is to engrain chemistry in the minds of adolescents at any cost. She is anathema to passing notes or communication in class of any kind. Students must be in their seats at the bell, and unless a student is bleeding from the eyes, it is unlikely she'll excuse them. Still, she is a good teacher that students—once they are clear of her class— look back on fondly.

Mrs. Antonia Kalakis (Home Economics, Health). This short, slim thirty-eight-year-old woman has long blond hair which she keeps up in complex hairdos that change each day. She is a no-nonsense teacher who uses her motherly appearance to cajole and guilt even the largest teens into following her instructions; somehow, she manages to control a classroom full of adolescents in a way that most other teachers cannot.

Mr. Fedov: *level 3*

Ms. Hopkins: *level 2, chemistry as level 3*

Mrs. Kalakis: *level 2*

Ms. Diamante: *level 3*

She lives in Rockville with her husband, an electrical engineer in the employ of Sand Point Consumer Electronics.

Mr. Albert Mangiapane (Principal). This tall, thin, balding sixty-one-year-old man wears the same suit on the same day each week, each only a slightly different color. When seen wandering the halls, he is usually smiling and happy, but when a student turns up in his office for an infraction, he tends to do away with this amiable persona. He is very loose with detention slips and has permanently expelled more than one student. Few people know it, but in 1948, Mr. Mangiapane played one season of professional basketball for the New York Knickerbockers.

Mr. George Saia (Earth Science, AP Physics). Mr. Saia is a fifty-nine-year-old pedant whom the kids call "Mr. Stinker" behind his back. His lack of personal hygiene is legendary in the school, and kids in his class fight for seats near the back of the room where they can open the windows. Despite this, he doesn't look filthy, he just smells bad. He is also a stickler to the smallest degree on all the subjects he teaches. His favorite saying, "Everything is equally important," torments the bad students along with the best in the school. All live in dread of ending up in his class.

Mr. Thomas Sullivan (Gym). Mr. Sullivan, a tall, potbellied fifty-one-year-old, is forever clad in Ocean View High School shorts and T-shirt, his neck hung with keys, whistles, and other crazy things. Because of the jingle that precedes him, you can always hear him coming. He is loud and brash, and he tends to shout when he wants to speak, and SHRIEK when he wants to shout. He is the coach of most of the sports teams at Ocean View (except boys' lacrosse and girls' volleyball), and he is a popular figure around town, but the other teachers tend to look down their noses at him. He is a bachelor who lives in the Kennedy Estates near the eastern edge of town. His principle obsession is his 1962 MG, which he has lovingly and obsessively restored by hand.

Mrs. Janet Wexler (English, AP English). This woman looks much older than her forty-three years. Since the death of her daughter in 1981 from ovarian cancer, her life is teaching. She is forever arriving early and staying late, and she will go out of her way to look out for kids she feels are "falling through the cracks." Those that take a shine to literature will find her an endless resource for books and knowledge on the subject. Her husband once worked for AT&T but retired early and now spends all of his time at their home off Beach Street, maintaining the house. He is clinically depressed, but Mrs. Wexler never talks about her private life at school.

COOL KIDS

Here are some of the more popular kids in the school. There are, of course, hundreds of others.

Wayne Depco (Sophomore and prodigy): Wayne is a sixteen-year-old who suffers from mild cerebral palsy, but who is outgoing and funny, making him popular. He is also a prodigy who can manifest in the mask-form Swoosh.

HOOKS:

- Wayne likes Ellen Paladino but has no idea how to talk to her. Ellen likes one of the PCs, and Wayne makes it his business to make them look bad.
- Wayne is considering using his Swoosh form to "fight crime" but has no idea where to find any "crime." Maybe he's just not looking hard enough. Then he notices the PCs all "glow"—maybe they're the supervillains?
- Wayne becomes interested in anyone and anything that "glows" and keeps a notebook of the people and objects that he's seen with the "aura." He confronts the PCs to compare notes.

Todd DeSpain (Junior): Todd is a seventeen-year-old football player who is short and stocky, with curly brown hair, freckles, and discolored teeth. He is a creature of social interactions, and he will do what he believes is required of him to be "cool." Often, this means making bad decisions.

HOOKS:

- Todd dated Ellen Paladino briefly when she was a freshman, but now the two can't stand one another, though they move in the same circles. To ruin Ellen's day, he tells one of the PCs that Ellen likes them.
- Todd's parents are divorced, and he lives with his mother in town, in the Kennedy Estates. His dad, the owner of a masonry in Rockville, buys him lavish presents (including a red Mustang for his sixteenth birthday). Todd makes an offhand offer to a PC to assist him in robbing his own dad's house and selling the loot—it's a perfect crime!
- Todd has twice gotten into shouting matches with Hal Walmer. It's only a matter of time before the two get into a fistfight. One of the PCs is present when the fight finally breaks out.

Anthony DiGiovanni (Sophomore and prodigy): Anthony is a sixteen-year-old whose outgoing nature makes him popular. He is also a prodigy who can manifest in the mask-form Goop.

HOOKS:

- Anthony has a crush on Emma Warzowski and is quite brazen about it, but so far, she just acts embarrassed by these overtures. He asks one of the PCs for advice to up his flirting abilities.

- Anthony has been trying to figure out ways to make money for his family using his Goop form; he's considered stealing from the bank ("It would be so easy!"), but he's abandoned his plans of becoming a master-thief—it just wouldn't be right. Still, he suspects one or all of the PCs might have powers and might be using them for illicit activities.
- Anthony is only three hundred dollars short of fixing up his first car, a restored 1981 Volkswagen Rabbit at Bluebeard Scrap. There are mementos all over town—maybe one can repair it? Perhaps one of the PCs has a memento or power that will do the trick?
- Twice Anthony has seen a silhouette watching him out near the beach. This figure seems to appear more often when he is carrying his mask or a memento. He recruits one of the PCs to cause a distraction so he can sneak up on the spy.

Asa Jen (Freshman and prodigy): Asa is a fifteen-year-old who is popular because his family owns the Pixel Palace arcade on the boardwalk. He is also a prodigy who has not manifested his mask yet.

HOOKS:

- Asa's father—usually a withdrawn, quiet man (and an alcoholic)—suddenly begins following one of the PCs. Why? Maybe Asa knows.

Anthony DiGiovanni, page 110

Asa Jen, page 116

Goop, page 110

- Asa's arcade seems to be a natural "sinkhole" that attracts mementos. Can the PCs figure out why?
- Asa has noticed odd guys in suits moving up and down the boardwalk with handheld electronic devices that resemble some sort of Geiger counter. Will the PCs do him a favor and help him figure out what they're up to?

Soraya Khalaji, page 118

Tabitha Shaeffer, page 109

Soraya Khalaji (Sophomore and prodigy): Soraya is a sixteen-year-old who is popular because of her up-front, friendly nature. She is also a prodigy who has yet to manifest a mask.

HOOKS:

- Soraya approaches the PCs and confronts them with the fact that they appear to glow. Will they spill the beans?
- Soraya is certain she dreamed of one of the PCs during a nightmare about the town being filled with people missing their faces. Only she and the PC were normal. She confesses this to the PC, looking for answers.
- Soraya has mentally kept count of the people who glow—as of now, she's seen more than a dozen. She asks the PCs if they will help her in her "census."

Ellen Paladino, page 113

Ellen Paladino (Sophomore): Ellen is a sixteen-year-old sports enthusiast who works at Waxy's Surf Shop.

HOOKS:

- Ellen is worried about her uncle, Michael Gioccino. He recently showed up at work with a black eye, and she's certain he's in trouble, but he won't talk about it. She asks one of the PCs to watch her back while she spies on her uncle when he meets up with a "business partner" at Pompeii.
- Ellen loves to surf and is often out off the Strand on her board at dawn, even in the winter. One day at school, she invites one of the PCs out on this usually solitary activity. But why?
- Ellen lives in the relatively rough Dutton Street neighborhood, a fact she's terrified her schoolmates might discover. Still, she knows one of the PCs knows her home address, and she asks them to keep it a secret.
- Ellen's family life is not so hot. Her father drinks too much, and her mother is always gone. She often looks after her little brothers, who are in grade school, for days at a time. One day, she turns up at a PC's house with a broken nose, asking for help.

Tabitha Shaeffer (Freshman): Tabitha is a fourteen-year-old dancer and cheerleader who is the daughter of the owner of the Shaeffer Marina and social club. Her brother is Brett Shaeffer. She is largely considered the best dancer in the area.

HOOKS:

- Tabitha can't stand her "geeky" brother, Brett and goes out of her way to humiliate him at school. She tries to rope in one of the PCs to help her.
- Tabitha is aloof when it comes to social activities. Many realize this is due to her obsession with dance, while others think she is stuck up. Many of the cool kids talk about her behind her back. She approaches a PC asking whether they've heard anyone with something bad to say about her.
- Tabitha keeps a secret journal about Rob Escadero—the bartender at her father's marina—who is *way* too old for her. She recruits a PC to talk to Rob and find out his current dating status.

Scott "Scotty" Veracruz (Junior and prodigy): Scotty is a seventeen-year-old football player who works at Swindon's Ice Cream Shoppe. He is also a prodigy who can manifest in the mask-form Morrow.

HOOKS:

- Scotty is in love with Monica Demath, his next-door neighbor. One of the PCs is friends with her, and Scotty is certain their approval is the key to her heart.
- Scotty enjoys football and thinks one of the PCs is well suited for the sport. He tries to get them to go to Coach Sullivan and try out.
- Scotty needs a tutor in social studies and English, so he approaches one of the PCs for help.
- Scotty dreams nightly of a man without eyes walking closer and closer to town. In his last dream, a PC was there with him while the faceless man chased them.

Hal Walmer (Senior): Hal is a seventeen-year-old baseball star, the son of the local police chief, and basically an all-around jerk. He often hangs out with Steven Yarborough.

Hal Walmer, page 139

Scotty Veracruz, page 115

Morrow, page 115

HOOKS:

- Hal abuses his relationship with his father, the chief of police, to get away with a lot of infractions, including petty theft, buying alcohol while under age, and vandalism. He commits some crime and then blames it on a PC.
- Coach Sullivan secretly can't stand Hal, and if he can see any way to take the kid down a few pegs without getting caught, he'll do it. He goes so far as to ask the PCs to come to him if they have any information that can help.
- Hal has an unhealthy obsession with Ms. Diamante, the math teacher, and often follows her around town in a creepy manner. He thinks he's subtle, but everyone knows. Only the PCs notice when this obsession becomes darker, however. Will they step in?

Emma Warzowski, page 106

Emma Warzowski (Freshman): Emma is the daughter of Emil Warzowski, who owns Sand Point Consumer Electronics (which employs much of the town); thus, she is local royalty.

HOOKS:

- Emma keeps crossing the lines between cool and uncool, making friends with oddballs such as Vahid Khalaji, Maria Juhasz, and Brett Shaeffer. The other cool girls are on the verge of giving her an ultimatum: stick with the clique or get kicked out. She approaches a random PC and tries to introduce them to the cool kids, even if the PC is geeky.
- Emma and Soraya Khalaji have quickly become *best friends*—a fact that their parents are quite pleased about. Soraya often spends time over at the Warzowski house in Point East. Soraya acts as emissary, telling a PC that Emma likes them or pumping them for information on a third party they think is cute.
- Vahid has fallen for Emma for reasons other than her father's profession and wealth, but he is as terrified of her as he is enamored with her. Even his sister has no knowledge of his feelings. Vahid begs the PCs to help him figure out how to confess his feelings without looking like a fool.

Steven Yarborough (Senior): Steven is a tall, well-built seventeen-year-old football star with carefully feathered blond hair and perfect teeth. He is the Sailors' premier quarterback and *knows* it. Despite this blind belief that he deserves all he has, he is not inherently a bad person.

HOOKS:

- Steven kind of likes Maria Juhasz and often finds himself in Beach Street Video coincidentally during the hours she works the counter. Due to her social standing, he will never admit this to anyone. Still, he approaches a PC and asks about her, trying to play it off as no big deal.
- Steven is a binge drinker. On the weekends or after a game, a common outcome for a night of partying is for Steven either to crash on the floor of a friend's house or to barely make it home before collapsing. It's rapidly becoming a problem. The PCs find Steven wandering the streets one weekend night, stumbling drunk, but he won't give up his car keys and insists on driving home. What do they do?
- Steven is generally unhappy. He lives in the moment. College doesn't interest him, and football—though he is good at it—isn't enough for him. He tries not to think about his future. As such, school is a very low priority in his life. He's drawn to a driven PC and looks for advice on how to change his life.

Danny Yaros (Sophomore): Danny is the fifteen-year-old son of a local assemblyman, Dean Yaros. Danny is a skilled lacrosse player and naturally popular.

HOOKS:

- Danny thinks something's up with his family. His dad, Dean, is acting weird, and his mom keeps vanishing for days on end. He's decided he's going to figure out what's going down. He needs some help, so he turns to one of the PCs.
- Danny has found drugs in his sister's room and thinks she might be getting them out at Pompeii Bar & Grill. He's looking for some loser who lives in

Rockville, and he's going to kick that guy's ass. Will the PCs help Danny find him?

- Danny is sick to death of lacrosse, and he is actually interested in music. He breaks down and confesses this to the PCs before asking just how he might escape what feels like a predetermined future.

"LOSERS"

Here are some of the least popular kids in the school. There are, of course, hundreds of others.

Helen Basille (Sophomore): Helen is a tall sixteen-year-old volleyball player who works at Swindon's Ice Cream Shoppe. There is more information on Helen Basille on page 115.

HOOKS:

- Helen gets close to a PC because *she knows* they know Brett Shaeffer—her secret crush. But it would be easy for the PC to mistake Helen's feelings for a crush on them instead.
- Helen's house is in Oceanside on Company Road, and last week she saw two big army trucks roll up to Sand Point Consumer Electronics.
- Helen's dad works at SPCE and seems preoccupied with work lately, so much so that he's there almost all day and night. These weird shifts have been in effect since the end of summer.

Timothy Buston (Sophomore and prodigy): Timothy is a fifteen-year-old sometime runaway. He is also a prodigy who can manifest in the mask-form Battlefield. There is more information on Timothy Buston on page 112 and on Battlefield on page 112.

HOOKS:

- Timothy is picked on at school because he always wears the same clothes and sometimes smells as if he's not showered in a while. A PC sees Timothy curling up to sleep under the boardwalk one evening, and his lack of hygiene makes much more sense. But will the PC do anything about it?

Steven Yarborough, page 141

Danny Yaros, page 107

- Timothy—who glows like a prodigy—pockets a mask as the PCs approach and then leaves. He seems guilty of something. But what?
- Timothy approaches the PCs. The night before, he had a dream they entered the sewer grate beneath the boardwalk together and saw something important inside.

Danny Deleo (Junior and prodigy): Danny is a seventeen-year-old obsessed with arcade games. He is also a prodigy who can manifest in the mask-form Freeze Frame. There is more information on Danny Deleo on page 116 and on Freeze Frame on page 116.

HOOKS:
- Freeze Frame is in love with Danny, and since she knows all that he knows, she realizes Danny has feelings for one of the PCs. As such, she *hates* that PC and will try to make their life miserable.
- Danny knows Asa Jen at the arcade is a prodigy but doesn't know how to help him make his mask. Can the PCs assist?
- Danny has noticed that mementos seem to turn up at or near the Pixel Palace arcade on the boardwalk. Maybe the PCs have noticed other areas in town like that. What could they mean?

Abigail Delgreccio (Sophomore): Abigail is a fifteen-year-old Madonna wannabe from Dutton Street. She's most often found at the Good and Plenty. There is more information on Abigail Delgreccio on page 118.

HOOKS:
- Abigail falls hard for one of the PCs and follows them around school all the time.
- Abigail is fairly certain the parking lot near the Good and Plenty is haunted. One night, on her way home, she saw a man with no face there.
- Abigail thinks maybe something is wrong with Soraya Khalaji—she's seen the girl collecting weird items from all over town and stashing them behind a cinder block at the back of the shop. Do the PCs know what she's up to?

Monica Demath (Freshman): Monica is a bookish fifteen-year-old girl who works at Swindon's Ice Cream Shoppe. There is more information on Monica Demath on page 115.

HOOKS:
- Despite Scotty Veracruz's obvious crush on her, Monica has taken a shine to one of the PCs. This is something Scotty—a huge football player—does not like.
- Monica often stays late at school, and three times now, she's seen strange people gathering in the courtyard after dark, talking. One of them was Asa Jen's dad, and another was a police officer.

- Monica has decided one of the PCs is her fashion icon, and she styles her looks and behavior on that PC (whether they like it or not).

Stuart Dill (Junior and prodigy): Stuart is a sixteen-year-old runaway. He is also a prodigy who can manifest in the mask-form Stutter. There is more information on Stuart Dill on page 132 and on Stutter on page 132.

HOOKS:

- Stuart's dad mistakes one of the PCs for his son and attacks him on the street. Once he figures out it's not Stuart, Mr. Dill offers them money to keep quiet and then runs off.
- The PCs have seen Stuart show up to school bruised and beaten on multiple occasions. Now, he's barely showing up to school at all—and then only in the morning before slinking off toward Estes Road.
- Stuart approaches a PC and claims to be like them—he has abilities, too. Would they like to come out to the Back Lot and test out their powers with him?

Micah Geerat (Senior): Micah is an eighteen-year-old comic enthusiast whom teens at the school call "the rat." There is more information on Micah Geerat on page 124.

HOOKS:

- Micah is certain he saw something strange having to do with one of the PCs. He's going to follow them until he can figure out what it was.
- Micah has decided one of the PCs is his greatest rival and goes out of his way to get in the PC's face.
- Micah has seen agents driving around in cars with government plates. In one car, a man on the passenger's side was holding a radio-sized device that was beeping.

Maria Juhasz (Sophomore and prodigy): Maria is a fifteen-year clerk at Beach Street Video. She is also a prodigy who can manifest in the mask-form Dead Ringer. There is more information on Maria Juhasz on page 119 and on Dead Ringer on page 119.

HOOKS:

- Maria wants the PCs to tell Steve Yarborough to piss off. He keeps bothering her, and she thinks he's a jerk, but he scares her.
- Dead Ringer wants *out* of Maria, and the mask-form thinks the key is in Sand Point Consumer Electronics—it needs the PCs' help to get inside.
- Maria falls for one of the PCs' mask-forms and does everything she can to spend time with it.

Vahid Khalaji (Sophomore): Vahid is a sixteen-year-old electronics enthusiast who works at the Good and Plenty. There is more information on Vahid Khalaji on page 117.

HOOKS:

- Vahid has long bothered the people at the front desk of Sand Point Consumer Electronics, but so far he's had no luck in getting an internship there. Still, he knows a few of the engineers and chats with them when they come into the Good and Plenty, and he thinks a PC would like to meet them.
- Brett Shaeffer and Vahid have been invited to a "game night" at the Dark Dungeon by Daniel Haas, but they need a few more to fill the table. Will the PCs go?
- Now that Emma Warzowski is suddenly his twin sister's best friend, she's always at Vahid's house. This is driving shy Vahid over the edge. He needs a PC's help to formulate a plan!

Rachel O'Hara (Junior): Rachel is a seventeen-year-old pizza chef who works at Mario's Pizza. There is more information on Rachel O'Hara on page 124.

HOOKS:

- Rachel found Gerald Wacter unconscious in the bathroom at Mario's Pizza one night. When she turned him over, thinking he was drunk or unconscious, she could swear he didn't have a face. A moment later, though, he seemed fine.
- Rachel has noticed she's making a ton more pizza and almost all the orders are coming from Sand Point Consumer Electronics. It's almost as if a bunch of new employees have started there who never leave the premises.
- Rachel has seen weird figures perched on cars at Bluebeard Scrap on Estes Road when she drives in to work. Once, a giant, deformed man with apelike arms was standing on top of the 1955 Edsel on the sign.

Eloise Rosemont (Senior): Eloise is a seventeen-year-old new wave devotee who works at the Dark Dungeon. There is more information on Eloise Rosemont on page 125.

HOOKS:

- Eloise's uncle, Detective Arnette, has asked her about one of the PCs. Does the PC know why the police might be interested in them?

- Eloise is convinced something fishy is going on at Sand Point Consumer Electronics—she is one of the few witnesses of the "light" emanating from the building on August 22. Do the PCs know anything about it?
- Eloise thinks one of the PCs is cool, and attempts to strike up a friendship with them.

Dustin Trewes (Sophomore): Dustin is a fifteen-year-old troublemaker from Dutton Street who hangs out at the Good and Plenty all the time. There is more information on Dustin Trewes on page 118.

HOOKS:

- Dustin looks dumb, but he sees everything. The whole town has been screwy since the end of August. The PCs in particular appear suspicious to him.
- Dustin has seen some really weird guys hanging out with the Acey Deucy bikers off Dutton Street. Crazy rumors abound that the gang has teamed up with a real demon.

- Dustin is desperate to become a sidekick to any prodigy that will take him. He's constantly rushing toward trouble in the hopes of being recruited.

Gerald Wacter (Junior, one of the Faceless): Gerald is a seventeen-year-old pizza delivery driver who is also a Faceless. There is more information on Gerald Wacter on page 124 and on the Faceless on page 152.

HOOKS:

- Gerald has been having weird dreams, and he seems drawn to particular students, including the PCs. He approaches one, terrified and asks for their help to figure out what's behind his fugues.
- Gerald keeps finding collections of items he's unconsciously gathered or stolen from all over town and hidden in his locker. They are mementos, though he has no idea there is anything special about them.
- Gerald has been delivering pizza to Sand Point Consumer Electronics *a lot* in the last few weeks. It's always paid for in cash by agents in dark suits. One, he saw, had a gun in a shoulder rig.

CHAPTER 15

ORGANIZATIONS AND CREATURES

Below are the details about the threats that face Boundary Bay (or that can be transplanted to nearly any *Unmasked* game).

THE MEDIA THREAT

Two major threats in the local media might impact the day-to-day lives of the mask-forms in Boundary Bay.

DAILY VIEW

Daily View is a pretaped, made-for-cable news magazine focusing on the bizarre, the violent, and the outré. It airs five days a week on various cable channels, and it is produced and filmed in New York City, with small tape crews moving around the tristate area to record local footage.

The show is all about *exploitation*. The more sensational the story (or the implied story), the more resources *Daily View* will spend on it. The reporters it employs are all second- and third-stringers—people who washed out of other, more prestigious jobs, or who couldn't get those jobs in the first place.

If *Daily View* shows up in Boundary Bay, it's because something was reported either on the police blotter or in the local news about the mask-forms or the Faceless. *Daily View* will swoop in, interview all involved on video, and then edit the story up until it sounds intriguing and weird (and in doing so, it will often embellish the truth). The one upside with *Daily View* is that unless the crews personally see something amazing, it's likely they'll forget Boundary Bay the moment their van hits the highway.

DAVID DAWKINS—NYPI REPORTER

David Dawkins is the Long Island crime reporter for New York Press Incorporated, a stringer service that sells stories to outlets all over the world. Dawkins has an eye for the unusual and loves crime stories that are

larger than life. Murders, disappearances, or strange flying people clothed in tights tend to attract his attention.

David is a thirty-three-year-old divorcee who lives out of his car, always carries a beaten tape recorder and Polaroid instant camera, and smokes like a chimney. His clothes—secondhand mostly—reek of nicotine. He tends to laugh and smile and try to take the side of the people he's interviewing, often spraying smoke in their face. When asked to put items off the record, he's not above putting them on it.

David believes that a single story can make his career. If he's drawn to Boundary Bay, it will likely be because the general public saw or recorded mask-forms. Once there, if Dawkins gets a taste of something truly odd, he won't let go until he's gotten to the bottom of it. He will break laws (within reason—he won't kill or injure anyone) and violate all the classic rules of journalism to get proof, or at least to gain deeper access.

Once on the trail, he'll be very difficult to shake.

THE MILITARY THREAT

THE CIRCUS

The "Circus" is an unofficial designation given to a desk at the Defense Intelligence Agency (DIA). The DIA is concerned with foreign intelligence "actors" in the United States, as well as other state intelligence agencies' intentions toward the United States. The Circus's mission is strangely both more and less specific.

The Circus was born in 1969, when information began coming in from foreign intelligence services about Soviet "nonconventional intelligence gathering" operations occurring on United States soil. This included reports of psychic abilities, such as remote viewing, psychometry, and other bizarre powers. Despite oddities in the report, it was deemed important by a ranking major, and these investigations were assigned to Director Damien Holtz of the DIA Directorate for Science and Technology. This opened the floodgates; soon, it became common knowledge in the Pentagon that unconventional reports should land on Desk 78 of the DIA. Since 1969, Director Holtz's desk has been the place where all odd files collected by the DIA and CIA have gone. Today, you can't even see his desk under all the dossiers.

It gained its unofficial nickname, the Circus, from Lieutenant Robert Pulaski, one of its operatives. His grandmother would often repeat a Polish saying, "Not my circus, not my monkeys," when referring to someone else's problem. The name stuck. It is almost never referred to by its official designation: DIA Desk 78, Directorate for Science and Technology, Internal.

Since 1970, the Circus has investigated fifty-four individual reports of bizarre phenomena in the United States. Most came to nothing more than conventional occurrences misreported by witnesses, or they were covert military activity. In 1981, the Circus found its first real oddity, reported by the Arizona National Guard. A strange explosion in Mesa, Arizona, caused seizures in all one hundred forty-five residents. Although the damage was light (only a single structure was destroyed), one hundred twenty-one townsfolk never woke from this fugue. Twelve died of internal brain trauma. The remaining twelve were permanently confined for their own safety, each rambling about some other world—a world like this Earth, but which had experienced another, bizarre reality. In the center of the blast radius, the Circus recovered "the key." This technology was like nothing ever before seen on Earth.

Director Holtz has worked with the civilian contractor Sand Point Consumer Electronics to discern the purpose and possible uses of the "key." In 1986, after years of experimentation, something finally happened.

PLANS AND METHODS

The agents of the Circus are experienced, no-nonsense intelligence agents. Their orders are to locate, isolate, and cover up any oddities located and reported by other federal agencies. The recovery of the "key" in Mesa, Arizona, in 1981 remains the defining moment for the Circus. That incident alone has guaranteed a budget and agent allotment that will keep the desk running well into the 2000s.

Circus operatives are used to their missions not panning out and default to believing the mundane explanation. Few in the small group believe in the supernatural, though some have seen oddities. Usually, they arrive after the fact, ask questions, and search the location. All of this is then consolidated in a classified report that is turned in to and reviewed by Director Holtz. Holtz maintains his own files, often cross-referencing various Circus operations with other classified reports from various agencies to create a "big picture."

Even with all the research into the "key" at Sand Point Consumer Electronics, Holtz has only the dimmest outlines of a theory as to what the object and explosion were that rocked Mesa, Arizona, that night in 1981. Now that a second "event" has occurred in Boundary Bay, this theory has grown more certain.

Holtz believes the "key" is some sort of connection to an alternate world, an "*almost* Earth." When it was triggered, intelligences tried to move through into this world. Twelve survived and are the rambling inmates whose every word is transcribed, talking about some other Earth.

Up until 1986, Holtz was certain the "key" had failed to operate properly, and was damaged in the attempt. Now, with the report of the "key" triggering in Boundary Bay on August 22, he is sure it has somehow reactivated. If that is so, it makes sense to expect more otherworldly intelligences and to assume that *something* is attempting to come through.

BOUNDARY BAY: PRETERNATURAL THREATS

The preternatural threat that has infected Boundary Bay seems to have arrived from an alternate Earth, though few understand this. While the mask-forms that possess the teens are (in general) "good," an opposing force—one somehow tied to the event itself—has also come through the breach. In the beginning, this force remains somewhat silent, operating behind the scenes, but as the mask-forms in Boundary Bay slowly reveal themselves, this force will expose itself and target them.

This force is led by a being known as "Prester John," an amorphous, vaguely humanoid form that seems to command an army of beings known as the "Faceless," which possess and control normal people, making them into superhuman killing machines.

In addition, there are mask-forms that are "evil" or have plans of their own that do not involve protecting the innocents of Boundary Bay from harm.

BOUNDARY BAY: DEVIANT MASK-FORM NPCS

In addition to Prester John and the Faceless, some of the mask-forms that "came through" are less-than-moral beings. These mask-forms (defined below) can be assigned to nearly any teen NPC, so only the mask-form is described. Usually, such beings want to keep their teen-form a closely guarded secret, so they can commit crimes without being ambushed in their human form. Also, keep in mind that the mask-forms these teens contain often tell them precisely what they want to hear . . .

These mask-forms have their own plans and methodologies. Out of the fifty or so mask-forms that manifested during the event, about half are either criminal or aberrant in some way. Despite their less-than-charitable attitude, each of these mask-forms lives in mortal fear of Prester John and its minions. It is likely that, if push comes to shove, they will team up with "good" mask-forms to fight against this force.

CAPTAIN MEAT

A living anatomical model, Captain Meat has no skin, for some reason, though this doesn't seem to bother him. He can fly (somehow), is bulletproof, and is always laughing and smiling—mostly at civilian reactions to his appearance. Captain Meat is all about petty comforts. He wants food, cars, and fine furniture so he can ooze blood all over them . . . He honestly doesn't care if he stays in this world or not; after all, being trapped in a teen (with skin) is kind of a godsend.

Captain Meat: *level 7, punching, lifting, wrestling, and throwing as level 11 (power shifted); health 65; Armor 4; can fly faster than sound; punch or rending attack inflicts 9 points of damage; power shifts: +4 to strength, +1 to healing*

HEADLIGHTS

The mouth and eyes of this man emit a light that blinds targets at a distance and, if close enough, can eat away at objects like a laser does. He is bitter, cruel, and used to wearing huge, bulky welding goggles and keeping his mouth shut. He is certain that if he finds the right mask-form, it will know the way back "home."

MISTERMIND

Mistermind is a fat, slovenly mask-form. It can snatch any skill and expertise from any non-prodigy it touches for 24 hours, and during that time, the target is rendered unconscious. Mistermind hunts job want ads to find its victims, showing up at interviews and stealing an electrical engineer here or a surgeon there, as needed. Mistermind is collecting mementos and working to unlock their meaning. Though it has no clear memory of the "other world" that the mask-forms come from, it's certain their arrival (and possible departure) has to do with mementos. And it wants *out.*

OOPS

Oops is a horrific being that looks like a human toddler and a praying mantis were mixed together and stretched out to stand almost 7 feet (2 m) tall. It can cause any physical activity (within a limited scale— approximately up to the size of a speeding car) to fail by pointing at the object or person in question and buzzing (this odd noise sounds vaguely like "oops," hence the name). Such an action ceases instantly, as if the energy for it had been "removed." It does not speak English, but it can scrawl it with a talon. Its plans seem to involve building a hive and creating some sort of machine inside it, but it's difficult to understand the creature. Needless to say, it does not play well with others.

THE MASTER: PRESTER JOHN (9) 27

This creature is an amalgam of human and humanlike entities from a million conterminous worlds—a chain across the multiverses that exists in and can perceive all of them at once. Its features and limbs blend and fade into odd, fractal-like averages of positions, meaning its arms—unless completely still—are blurred motion trails, and its face is averaged into a pink, seamless mass. Still, despite its hideous nature, it moves with intelligence and purpose.

It manifests in this space-time only at night, for reasons not fully understood. It seems drawn to prodigies, mementos, and mask-forms, and though its ultimate goals are unknown, it seems eager to locate and destroy the prodigies. It is attended, usually, by the Faceless—humans who were affected by the August 22 incident and who can now be "hijacked" by some sort of non-human intelligence. If this thought experiment is taken to its conclusion, it is logical to assume that, like the Faceless, Prester John is connected to one, fixed human form in town who has no knowledge of this non-human intelligence occupying their body. If that human vessel is destroyed, will Prester John perhaps cease manifesting?

It is also seemingly connected to the prodigies, as they often catch glimpses of what it is doing when they dream. The name (either given to it by itself, or through some sort of strange psychic bond with its victim) is the name of the legendary Christian king of the East—a historical being who never actually existed. Whether or not this name has a deeper meaning is unknown.

Motive: Destroy the teens occupied by mask-forms

Environment: Anywhere in Boundary Bay

Health: 99

Damage Inflicted: 12 points

Armor: 5

Movement: Short; long when flying

Combat: Prester John can cause rifts in space-time anywhere within a half mile (1 km). These fractures in causality make creatures and objects in them crack, twist, and distort in an otherworldly manner. Prester John can cause these "bubbles" of unreality to expand and engulf multiple targets, inflicting 8 points of damage to everyone within the radius.

In hand-to-hand combat, Prester John can attack all targets in melee range at once, as its limbs contort, blur, and swirl in waves of probability. This attack inflicts 6 points of damage.

It can consume a memento by touching it, instantly regaining the memento's level in health points up to its maximum health of 99. Such mementos are destroyed in the process.

Interaction: Attended by the Faceless, which defer to it, Prester John appears and strikes when a prodigy teen is most vulnerable at night, usually when they are alone. Its goal is nothing less than the absolute destruction of the teen "containing" the mask-form. It moves with a staggering gait, but sometimes it will lift and float into the air, as if carried by some invisible force.

It will attack relentlessly, and it is clearly intelligent, utilizing tricks and feints to get the prodigy or the mask-form to step into preset ambushes. When it kills a prodigy teen, it consumes their mask (in the same manner it can consume mementos), as if it were "feeding."

Use: A teen the PC knew to be a prodigy is found, smashed up and murdered. The following night, the PC sees a strange, shaking figure in the dark outside their home. Prester John has come for them.

(IN)HUMAN SERVANTS: THE FACELESS (5) 15

Adult humans affected by the August 22 event, these individuals have been infiltrated by some sort of extradimensional intelligence. During the day, these humans act normally and pursue their regular life, but at night they are subject to possession by this external force called *the Faceless*.

Some of those infected know something is wrong, but they have no clear memories of their actions while subsumed by the external intelligence. When this occurs (always at night), the subject is transformed into a horrific blend of a million slightly different timelines, causing their arms and faces to blend into a blur of probabilities. They are terrifying to see and seem to operate in perfect, unspoken concert with one another.

Motive: Locate the teens occupied by mask-forms without being discovered

Environment: Anywhere in Boundary Bay

Health: 25

Damage Inflicted: 6 points

Movement: Short

Modifications: Climbing, jumping, and dexterity-related actions as level 5.

Combat: In combat, the Faceless are horrific and relentless. They will destroy the human form they currently occupy to execute even a fleeting attack on their target. This is the greatest danger for any PC facing a Faceless—inside is an innocent person with no control over what their body is doing. Destroying a Faceless might be easy, but living with the guilt of having killed the innocent inside will be all but impossible.

Interaction: The Faceless only operate at night. During this "occupation" of the body by the external intelligence, they move around town and seem drawn to mask-forms (whether the masks are active or not), mementos, or places that mask-forms were last seen. This sense seems inconstant, as if they were searching for a particular "scent." During these searches, they steer clear of normal humans whenever possible. Usually, if confronted, they attempt to retreat and escape. Sometimes, multiple Faceless gather for a "union," where they seem to share information in the form of weird, almost subsonic moaning.

Use: A good friend of a PC is infected by the Faceless. This friend has noticed that they seem to be leaving the house at night with no knowledge of where they've gone or why. Can the PCs help them uncover the truth?

PART 5: GM'S TOOLBOX
SAVED BY ZERO

"There's Michael—he's also Friend Electric, who can jump into, like, light bulbs and stuff. There's Emily. She's, uh, Rat Pack, who is . . . uh . . . a pack . . . uh . . . of rats? Sorry. Uh—" Ian stopped talking then, and looked around at the others in the room.

"I'm Terry," Terry said, making a little wave.

They looked at him, and he could see it in them all. The Fire. They were glowing, flickering in his vision like someone was messing with the contrast—but only on them. Like God had whipped out a highlighter and covered them from head to toe in a nearly invisible color that screamed IMPORTANT. He knew they saw the same in him. It's why Ian had asked him here.

"So, what can you do?" Emily said finally, looking bored.

"If basketball is any metric, not much," Michael snorted.

Terry pulled out his mask. It was a swim cap with two rows of Mardi Gras beads sewn to it. He slid it over his face. There was a bright white flash.

"Huh," said Ian.

The man that stood before them was two heads taller than Terry, clad in blue, and . . . flat. Not thin, but flat, like a rug—but even thinner. When you looked at him side-on at the proper angle, he practically vanished.

"I am Flat Guy!" the blue man shouted, his voice sounding strangely un-echoey and slight, but the people in the room jumped anyway.

"Okay. So, Electric Dude. Rat Girl. Flat Man. Are we missing anyone?"

"Guy. Flat GUY," the man in blue said.

"Okay, so, Strangely Specific Flat Guy."

CHAPTER 16

RUNNING UNMASKED

The idea of *Unmasked*—that teens can manifest amazing abilities and become superheroes by putting on a strange mask—remains at the core of the concept. But how that premise is explored, what flavor is layered on top of the concept, how the GM mediates the PCs' powers and abilities, and how advancement and XP rewards are handled all remain up to the GM to fashion and express.

This game setting gives you, as the GM, a lot of freedom to alter and explore the setting by changing it, adding your own elements to it, and modifying the main threat that the PCs face, as well as the big reveal at the end.

Below you will find notes, mechanical ideas, tips, and tricks on how to make an *Unmasked* game or campaign your own.

FLAVORS OF UNMASKED

Unmasked can be many things to many people. The GM can fashion its "feel" in many ways, tailoring it to their group to have the most impact or to fit their favorite style of play. Below are some examples of flavors that easily fit into the world of *Unmasked*.

HORROR

The prodigies and their enemies can be terrifying. The impossible powers their mask-forms can achieve and the threats they face, which are beyond humanity, are inexplicable, mysterious, and relentless. A horror-flavored *Unmasked* campaign is a constant battle between understanding, control, and fear of the unknown.

In a horror-flavored *Unmasked,* the GM should work to keep the PCs on their toes. Just when they feel they have a good idea of what's going on, who their enemy is, and how their powers operate, it is the GM's job to mix it all up again in a surprising yet understandable way. Surprises, cliff-hangers, and unexpected twists are all hallmarks of a good horror campaign.

POWER FANTASY

A classic theme: the PCs are blessed with amazing superpowered forms. What would you do in a similar situation? Many teenagers are struck by feelings of being lost, alone, or powerless, but the prodigy powers might just give them a ticket to realizing all their hopes and dreams.

Maybe their mask-form woos the person they have a crush on, or earns cash gambling with its psychic powers so the teen can buy a Trans Am. Or perhaps the mask-form uses those powers to secretly help a friend in need, or to not-so-secretly gain the admiration of a town. In the end, a power fantasy is about focusing attention on the PCs in bright, gleaming moments and allowing them to shine. Stories tend to be big and over-the-top, and to arc toward gigantic, possibly world-ending scenarios.

TEEN COMEDY

Teen comedy is a classic genre. Now, imagine any of your favorite teen comedies with superpowers in the mix. In this kind of flavor, PCs are always struggling to get ahead of the game, and even with a secret superpowered form, it's a lot harder to look suave and attractive than might be imagined.

Maybe their mask-forms use their teleportation ability to steal beer from the QuikStop or control electrical signals to pirate pay cable. Or perhaps they're operating at the lowest common denominator: obsessing about the opposite sex. In whichever case, teen comedy is about humor (with some serious asides) and is generally upbeat, exciting, and full of broad-stroke stories.

A MIXTURE OF FLAVORS

Any of the above might be mixed into a single "flavor." Want laughs interspersed by horror? No problem. A power fantasy with humor or horror? Or all three? Easy. Just be clear to set the tone for the players when such a switch occurs.

For example, if the PCs are all trying to escape a house without getting caught, it's more than likely that it's a teen comedy thing. Let them know by making your descriptions slightly comedic. Likewise, if you want to make the tone darker, make sure to drop some hints at the sinister nature of the world.

THE AVERAGE UNMASKED SESSION

Each *Unmasked* session (in general) is composed of similar elements. Sometimes there are more or fewer examples of each type. The GM should work hard to keep a few in their pocket to drop in the game session when there's a lull, or when the adventure needs one more complication.

Most elements of an *Unmasked* session are composed of the following:

Teen Problems: The PCs deal with the standard issues of being a teenager.

Side Activities: The PCs are required to do something outside of school (such as working at a job or helping a family member).

School: The PCs need to do homework, attend classes, take tests, and so on.

Social Issues: The PC teens are caught up in endless social interactions with other teens or teachers.

Superpowered Shenanigans: The PCs have access to amazing superpowers, and being teens, they're likely to take them for a spin.

Trouble: The prodigy phenomenon attracts trouble. The teen PCs have to learn to deal with it.

Exposure: Of course, once the powers and mask-forms come out, people start asking questions. It's up to the PCs to keep it under wraps before their whole bifurcated existence becomes common knowledge.

Rewards: Every session should end with the GM awarding PCs with XP for keeping

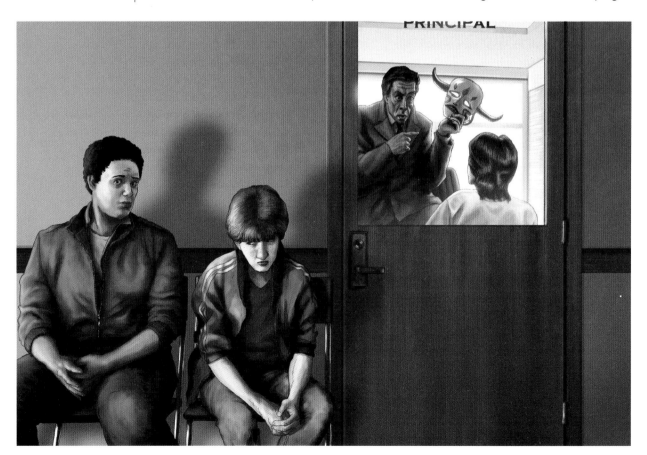

the secret of the prodigies, making progress in school or social activities, and covering up the prodigy phenomenon.

TEEN PROBLEMS

The lion's share of any *Unmasked* game concerns teen problems. Masks are usually worn only at crescendos in the action, while the rest of the game revolves around the normal lives of the teens that manifest those mask-forms. Most of a teenager's life is dealing with problems.

My friends are acting weird. My new look isn't going over very well. I need a job to pay the insurance on my used car. Mom and Dad are fighting all the time.

The list goes on and on. And, with a clever GM, it should never end. GMs should watch their PCs, note who they interact with, what their hobbies are, and what their standing in school is, and from there, keep a list per PC of hooks for their teen character to explore.

For example, an uptight, bookish teen might be flunking gym and living in fear of the gym teacher. They might be in love with a lunch worker, attempting to earn extra credit by working on the model United Nations, and more. And that's not even really getting into social entanglements. It should be easy for nearly anyone to come up with teen problems; after all, we were all teenagers once.

EXAMPLE TEEN PROBLEMS:

- A former friend stops talking to the PC
- A bully sets their sights on the PC
- An upheaval occurs at home (for example, a sibling moves out, the parents get divorced, or a family member dies)
- The PC must help with some sort of function for a hobby or a club that requires effort
- The PC must participate in a dreaded family social function

SIDE ACTIVITIES

Sometimes, distractions drag a teen PC away from their peer group, and they have some task they must achieve on their own.

I promised to mow Ms. Futterman's lawn. I need to wax my dad's car before he's back from his business trip. I agreed to help my uncle build a deck around his fire pit.

These may seem mundane, but in a world of secret superheroes, they are also *grounding*. They make the amazing, the horrific, the powerful, and the strange seem all the more incredible. They also make the life of the teen PC seem real.

These side activities also have a habit of popping up at the worst possible time.

EXAMPLE SIDE ACTIVITIES:

- Helping a family member or neighbor
- Running errands
- Working on some side project
- Practicing a hobby or sport
- Completing odd jobs for a third party

SCHOOL

Every student has to contend with school. Even exceptional students need to work to achieve what is expected of them, while malcontents must comply or face expulsion—something they may say they want, but which, they know, will really ruin their life.

Every game session that involves a normal school week should concern itself, at least a little bit, with school, attending classes, taking tests, and doing homework. No PC should feel *completely* on top of the school situation; after all, it's where they'll spend most of their day, and the demands on a teenager are pretty grueling.

EXAMPLE SCHOOL ISSUES:

- Pop quiz
- After-school requirement
- Standardized testing
- Homework deadlines
- A teacher picking on a PC
- A teacher taking an interest in a PC
- A guidance counselor taking an interest in a PC
- A school monitor or guard getting suspicious of a PC

KEEPING THE LID ON THE PRODIGY PHENOMENON

Unmasked requires the GM to be clever in a way not often required in roleplaying games. The game is predicated on the concept that the PCs have superpowered mask-forms *that don't wish to be discovered*. This is a core conceit of the mask-form. All PCs should be informed that, above all, their mask-forms (and by proxy, their teen-forms) desperately don't want to be discovered by the authorities or the world at large. The situation needs a subtle hand that both lets the players have the choice to keep or reveal secrets, but also sets up the world, circumstances, and mechanics to subtly suggest that it would be best if the PCs kept a low profile.

For the mask-forms, it's a kind of self-preservation. For the teen, it's more of a secret identity situation. Regardless, though either form might be a showboat independently, the prodigy in *both* forms will go out of their way to keep others from revealing their secret.

HOW DO PRODIGIES NOT BREAK WIDE?

Without the PCs (and other prodigies) actively working to suppress exposure of the prodigy phenomenon, the story will soon break into the public consciousness. It will appear on the news and in government reports, and it will quickly become the focus of scientific study.

Luckily, all prodigies are naturally secretive with their abilities and almost instinctually want to keep their teen identities a closely guarded secret. It is because of this prodigy "shyness," as well as the mask-forms' habit of actively removing evidence or diverting the stories, that the news does not usually go much further than a small blurb in the local paper.

Combine the above with the fact that prodigy abilities are just plain *impossible*. I mean, they still occur, but no one in their right mind would ever believe in such powers without seeing them in action first. Lastly, information in 1986 travels slowly. Compared to today's ever-connected, always-on, television-station-in-your-pocket world, news in 1986 circulates at a positively *glacial* pace.

DE-ESCALATION

Sometimes, all a story needs to drop out of the public eye is *time*. If a giant plant man keeps turning up in the news, it might be enough for the teen behind that mask-form manifestation to lay off transforming for a while.

A good rule of thumb is this: the bigger and more public the superpowered incident, the longer a prodigy has to stay below the radar to effectively de-escalate the situation. Likewise, the more evidence (for example, photographs, videotape, film, or other records) exists, the longer the story tends to linger. Removing such evidence (in a manner that doesn't make the issue bigger) is also a great way to mitigate the situation.

SHELL GAMES

Clever PCs or allies will think outside the box to come up with new methods of removing suspicion and obfuscating the truth. For example, if the police are hot on the trail of a teen they believe to *somehow* be the Red Rider, the PCs might go out of their way to plant a facsimile of a Red Rider suit in the home of a known bad guy or even set up an incident that makes it seem as if the Red Rider were killed.

Remember, most normal people will do *anything* to explain away the impossible. Such bizarre occurrences don't fit well into everyday life. All most people need is even a *shred* of evidence to suggest some other explanation, and almost all of them will run with it. The alternative—that something *beyond* reality is happening—is just too difficult for most to process.

SOCIAL ISSUES

Teen PCs are, of course, obsessed with their social standing. Dating. Friends. Bullies. Every day is another adventure in discovering just what it means to (eventually) be a grown-up. Every day is filled with more questions. *Why is no one talking to me? Will Tara, like, ever see how I feel about her? Will I ever date anyone? Does Timothy like me? Who will I take to the dance?*

Social obligations also have a wonderful habit of coming up at the worst possible time. Do you have to deal with a nasty superpowered threat? Of course, that's the moment that your girlfriend calls you.

The GM should track the ups and downs of each PC's social life. Sometimes, a PC enjoys an unbroken chain of popularity, and sometimes they are social pariahs. In any case, due to the nature of the game, though the PCs' relationships with NPCs might change dramatically, their relationships with the other PCs should remain at least cordial. After all, the PCs all share the secret of being prodigies—they may be the only ones who understand what it is to be truly different.

EXAMPLE SOCIAL ISSUES:

- An NPC has a crush on the PC
- A PC is obsessed with an NPC.
- A dance is coming up and the PC needs a date
- A peer group has ceased interacting with the PC
- The PC's social standing drops or jumps due to some event

SUPERPOWERED SHENANIGANS

All the PCs have access to mementos (which grant one-off powers), as well as to their mask-forms, which open a whole suite of superpowers. It is unlikely teenagers could resist using such abilities for long. Still, a central precept of *Unmasked* is that the teen and mask-forms *both* do not wish to be discovered.

This means that, above all, teen prodigies will do what they can to cover up their true identities, hide their powers, and use them only when they feel like they can do so without compromising the secret.

EXAMPLE SUPERPOWERED SHENANIGANS:

- Using a prodigy ability to gain an advantage in school
- Using a prodigy ability to gain a social advantage
- Using a prodigy ability to get more information on the prodigy phenomenon
- Using a prodigy ability to help a loved one or friend

TROUBLE

Prodigies attract one another and are drawn to mementos, so it's no surprise they end up in proximity to other prodigies. This often results in conflict. Not all prodigies are as forthright as the PCs, and some are straight-up superpowered juvenile delinquents. Sometimes this leads to fights. And when the fights occur between mask-forms, people might uncover the teen PCs' secret. Even worse, people might get hurt or killed.

Secondarily, there are elements of the prodigy phenomenon initially unknown to the PCs: Why they are prodigies. Where the powers come from. Who is behind it all. These questions must be identified and contended with, and often (depending on the big reveal) these are not simply static concepts, but individuals and organizations out to destroy, capture, or dissect the teen PCs.

EXAMPLE TROUBLE:

- A prodigy NPC decides a PC is their new enemy
- A new, super powerful memento turns up at school, and all the prodigies are after it
- An unknown mask-form keeps manifesting and causing trouble
- A prodigy NPC is on a crime spree in town, and conventional forces can't stop them
- Strange people begin poking around the school with odd electronics, and they seem drawn to mementos
- People in dark suits pull up in government vehicles and set up shop in an old AV room on the second floor

EXPOSURE

Manifesting prodigy abilities on any real scale will lead to questions. When school security, the police, or even the military shows up, those questions don't go away too easily. Often, PCs need to clean up their own mess. They can do this by collecting and destroying evidence, creating distractions, or fabricating other plausible explanations to inexplicable incidents.

EXAMPLE EXPOSURE EVENTS:

- The PCs must stage or create a plausible explanation to cover up prodigy abilities
- The PCs must use their prodigy powers to locate or destroy evidence of the prodigy phenomenon
- The PCs must orchestrate another incident to draw the attention of law enforcement or the authorities elsewhere
- The PCs must plant evidence to throw law enforcement or the authorities off the trail.

REMEMBER, PLAYERS PORTRAY TEENS AND THEIR PSYCHES

Killing another person—even one who is evil—is *extremely* difficult for the human mind. People are hardwired to abhor violence, and seriously injuring or killing another person can ruin them emotionally. In *Unmasked*, death and killing should *always* be a big deal. In the lives of teens, who feel immortal to begin with (and especially teens with superpowers!), mortality is often hard to imagine—at least until they see their own fragility demonstrated.

A good GM should keep on hammering these points. Do not allow a teen PC to haul off and break an NPC's arm (or worse) without some emotional impact. Take a moment to describe the horrific reality of the way the arm dangles, the shrieking of the victim, and the fear in their eyes. No act of conscious violence by the teen PCs should be without consequence: emotional, legal, or worse. It is the GM's job to center the world the PCs occupy in *reality*, even as their mask-forms exist just a bit outside of it.

KEEPING BYSTANDERS AND LAW ENFORCEMENT ALIVE

While the PCs are upstanding people with consciences, this doesn't mean *all* prodigies are. Some are delinquents—prone to violence just like normal criminals, but with access to superpowers. Others are misunderstood, backed into a corner, or otherwise deluded into believing something that puts them at odds with the status quo. This doesn't even begin to account for other non-human threats that can manifest.

When the superpowers come out, often it is the number one job of the PCs to protect and save those normal people who happen to be present. If Lord Ember chucks a jeep with two people in it, you bet the mask-form PC had better try to save them. If killing is hard, standing by and failing to save someone from certain death is equally so. GMs should make sure to set this tone. When engagements occur, take your time to explain the danger the PC sees in the superpowered tussle. Make suggestions: *There are a dozen people in the food court staring at Lord Ember as he rips up the huge statue. They're frozen in place. Innocents are going to get killed unless someone steps in.* Once this tone is set, reward those players who pick up that slack naturally.

REWARDS

In the Cypher System, XP is used to advance your characters. In *Unmasked*, though, your teen doesn't advance—only your mask-form. Both forms *earn* XP, but only the mask-form can spend it to increase tier abilities, skills, and so on. Therefore, each session you play offers the following rewards:

1 XP for not revealing your teen's connection to the mask-form it manifests to any non-prodigy

1 XP for doing homework, attempting to fit in at school, or engaging in some social activity

1 XP for investigating and removing evidence about the prodigy phenomenon so it remains a secret (this includes collecting mementos)

DESCRIBING MASK-FORMS AND SUPERPOWERS

When mask-form abilities are used, they routinely break the laws of physics. Impossible things can and do occur. To most normal people unexposed to the phenomenon, seeing such a wonder for the first time is exceedingly difficult. For others (especially those who have seen it before), it awakens a need to get to the bottom of the mystery.

When powers are activated, the GM should take a few moments to illustrate what occurs, to describe witnesses' reactions to it, as well as state its effect on the world. Of course, if it's a power a PC uses all the time, one need not become tedious in the description. Still, the GM should work to make mask-forms and the superpowers they wield *feel* weird and amazing. They are, quite literally, magic. They should never feel mundane.

HOW NORMALS REACT

Most normal people confronted by prodigy powers will either freeze in place or flee the scene. Luckily, eyewitnesses tend to be awful at recalling details. The more extreme the incident, the less likely it is that a bystander will have anything useful to say about it. And the bizarre nature of prodigy powers means that those that *do* describe the incident will likely be dismissed as crazy.

Many people will have trouble even believing themselves. If a reptilian man with an "A" on his chest emerges from the woods and says, "Excuse me," before vanishing in a puff of smoke, it's highly unlikely Ms. Futterman is going to go on and on about it. More likely, she'll stay quiet and eventually convince herself she must have seen something else.

HOW LAW ENFORCEMENT REACTS

Police are trained to arrive at a chaotic scene and establish control. This will not go well when they're trying to get mask-forms to stand down. More often than not, police will end up as a target or in the middle of a superpowered scuffle. Needless to say, this is an awful place to be.

When police officers are exposed to the bizarre, they try to center those events in their established worldview. After all, many police face nothing but call after call of oddities all day, every day. Still, there are some phenomena that are beyond such centering. If police officers are confronted by something truly inexplicable, their reactions vary from person to person.

It is likely that the more outrageous the story of the confrontation, the less likely it is that the law enforcement official will report it as it happened. If a cop runs into a mask-form that's a 9-foot-tall (3 m tall) robot with glowing green eyes, the official report might read "unknown animal" or, in a more severe case, there might not be a report filed at all.

Even worse, there are some law enforcement officials who will view such oddities as their "white whale." They'll keep a normal demeanor while focusing all their effort on uncovering, identifying, capturing, or killing the prodigy in question. Such officers know they'll get pulled from duty if they tell the truth; hence, they'll smile and lie, and who knows what other rules they may break to get the job done and prove to themselves they haven't lost their mind.

HOW THE MILITARY REACTS

The military is much less forgiving than law enforcement. If exposed to a combat situation while armed, the military will likely respond with force in an attempt to squelch the threat and then, only later, uncover what it is.

Exposure to prodigy powers might be enough to throw even experienced military off their guard, at least at first. Whether or not they report the oddities of such encounters depends on the individual. The higher the rank or the more focused on career the soldier is, the more likely that reports filed on prodigy powers will be heavily edited (at best) or fully redacted. Low-rank military personnel will likely agree with whatever their superior officer says.

MAKING MUNDANE THREATS FUN

The real fun in *Unmasked* is making the PCs devise interesting solutions to their problems (with and without superpowers) without exposing their secrets. Facing mundane threats, such as police, school security, first responders, and more without the PCs revealing their true identities and their powers should be the centerpiece of the game.

When a PC with power shifts can achieve difficulty 10+ tasks, what hope does a mundane threat have of affecting them? Directly? Not much. But such threats can cause other kinds of damage. First and foremost, the PC can get into trouble. Second, the threats can affect other people—loved ones, significant others, other innocents—that the PC might not want involved. Third, every use of such abilities leaves behind witnesses and evidence. Only the most careful, clever, and forward-thinking PCs will keep ahead of the curve of discovery.

FIELDING PRODIGY-LEVEL THREATS

NPC prodigies and any creatures that might exist in your particular version of *Unmasked* should be unleashed on the PCs only at fixed points during a game session. If the PCs are constantly facing superpowered baddies or power-shifted threats, these will become boring. The GM should work hard to keep such moments spaced out to maintain the tone of the game. After all, *Unmasked* is about teen PCs who happen to do incredible things in the real world of 1986. It's not just about superpowers.

When a threat that can truly harm a teen PC is introduced, this should entail a big event, or at least a surprising one. It should never, ever be predictable.

KEEPING THE PLAYERS ON THEIR TOES

It is the GM's job to make certain the game never falls into a boring routine. Part of this involves paying attention to what the players are doing in-game and keeping notes or at least coming up with ideas on how to continue such threads. The other part is noticing what excites the players. Did they really have fun sneaking beer from the local 7-Eleven? Maybe throw in some more teen activities like that! Or did they really enjoy spying on the strange federal agents that have set up shop on the edge of town?

CHAPTER 17
RULE OPTIONS, ORIGINS, AND BIG SECRETS

An earlier section of this book explored three distinct options for the source of prodigy powers: genetic, psychic, and spiritual. Here, we'll dig down a bit into specific high-level concepts for the origins and big secrets in your *Unmasked* campaign.

RULE OPTIONS

Do you want your *Unmasked* game to resemble comic books and be less rreality-based? Do you want it to be crazily over the top? Or incredibly gritty and deadly? As a GM, consider the following options to make the *feel* of the game more or less "realistic."

COMIC BOOK FEEL: ONCE-PER-SESSION BONUS POWER SHIFT

A GM who wishes to reward a player for a dramatic, in-character, or otherwise awesome in-game action can grant them a one-use, assignable power shift for that game session only.

This power shift can be applied to any power or ability of their mask-form and can be used *once* before it vanishes. The player can either assign it to an ability immediately or wait and assign it on the fly before an action (in either case, the GM must agree that the assignment makes sense).

If it is unused or unassigned when the session ends, it is lost. Only one assignable power shift should be given to a player at any given time. GMs might make this a permanent rule—a goal for players to shoot for, always available during a game session for those who go above and beyond.

Example: Harrison's mask-form, Ugarte, manages to sweet-talk his way past a clot of military personnel just through roleplaying. The GM thinks he was amazing, so they give him an assignable power shift. But he doesn't want to put it in anything right at the moment. Then, later, in the middle of a super battle where Ugarte is certain to be smashed, he places the power shift in his Speed defense. It saves him, but right after, the assignable power shift vanishes.

COMIC BOOK FEEL: BULLETS ARE AN ANNOYANCE

In many comic books, heroes wade through bullets like they weren't even there. If you want your *Unmasked* game to feel more like this, there's a simple solution: against prodigies (both their teen-form and mask-form), all firearm damage is cut in half, to a minimum of 1. Or, you could make it so all mask-forms possess Armor 1 or even 2 by default, but only against bullets.

MORE OVER THE TOP: UNCOVERING NEW POWERS

Exploring the edges of powers and pushing them to shift and change, or even trying to discover *new* powers, *are* common tropes in comic books. For example, a mask-form might be able to destroy an object with a bolt of flame, but can that same power light a stove top at a distance? Brand a picture in burned wood on a wall? Extinguish a fire? All seem like they might be possible.

This requires negotiation with the GM. A good player will push their abilities to their limit— and look for what is just a little bit beyond. They should then bring it up with their GM. Attempting such an action is always one step more difficult than usual and costs 1 XP per tier of the power or ability it is based on. On a failure, the XP is lost and the new power fails to work (whether this means the PC can never do it is up to the GM), while on a success, the player's mask-form gains that new ability.

Example: Mica's mask-form, Starchild, can focus light like a human prism and attack with it as if it were a laser. What if, she asks, she could also use the beam to light a fire? The GM says this is possible. Starchild spends 2 XP (it is a tier 2 ability) and makes a roll on her ability to light a fire with it. She succeeds, and she now has access to a "firestarter" power. She and the GM work out the details as they continue to play.

GRITTIER: MEMENTOS FUEL MASKS

To make your *Unmasked* campaign grittier, and to make mask-forms more difficult to use, you can establish that each time the mask is worn, the prodigy in question must "replenish" their ability by sacrificing a memento (or mementos) of a level equal to the tier of their mask-form. This is treated as the prodigy holding and draining the memento of its power without activating its normal power effect.

Example: Louisa's mask-form, Alabaster, is tier 3. She used the mask once, and she now wants to put it on again, but it needs "fuel." She could consume three level 1 mementos, one level 3 memento, or one level 1 and one level 2 memento to give her enough power to activate it. When that mask comes off again, she'll have to replenish this power again.

Likewise, this ability might be able to move damaged mask-forms up the damage track. Each step up the damage track requires the sacrifice of a memento of a level equivalent to the tier of the mask-form.

Example: Alabaster (tier 3) is at debilitated on the damage track. She could sacrifice one level 3 memento (or any number adding up to 3 levels) to move up the damage track to impaired, or one level 6 memento (or any number adding up to 6 levels) to move up the damage track to hale.

GRITTIER: NORMALS ARE FRAGILE

To make your *Unmasked* campaign grittier and deadlier, you can treat normal non-prodigies as very fragile. An easy way to do this is to say any attack that inflicts 4 or more points of damage to health in a single hit effectively incapacitates the target—usually by sending them into shock, knocking them out, or causing so much trauma that they're out of action.

GMs who hope to be even *more* realistic can state that targets hit by weapons that pierce and cut continue to bleed out 1 point of health per minute until treated by a skilled doctor, surgeon, or someone trained in first aid.

It is not recommended that this option be used for prodigy teens, since they are supposed to be somewhat exceptional compared to normals. Making a prodigy this weak would have serious repercussions on gameplay.

ORIGIN

Players will naturally push to discover the origin of their prodigy abilities. This doesn't mean a GM must necessarily have one in mind from the start. Sometimes, seeing how the game sessions play out, where the PCs go, and who they interact with can give the GM a good idea of what kind of resolution they are looking for. Other times, the GM has a clear idea from the get-go as to what the ultimate origin of prodigy abilities will be.

There are an infinite number of origins possible. The list below is by no means exhaustive:

ARTIFACT

The PCs were all exposed to an artifact that altered them permanently, making them prodigies. This exposure might have occurred in such an unremarkable manner that the PCs failed to even recognize where and when it occurred. Even scarier, the artifact might still be around and could still grant prodigy abilities to any teenager exposed to it.

Example: Since you found the strange carved stone at Lake Point Park, it's become the main hangout for the school. You all gather out there, drinking, partying, and just plain fooling around. However, for you and a select few of your friends, the mysterious carving seems a powerful draw that speaks to you. But why is it there? And how has it imparted such powers?

CONNECTION TO AN ALTERNATE REALITY

The mask-forms of the prodigies are superheroes from another, alternate 1986 that is real, though inaccessible. When prodigies wear their mask, they are pulled through a dimensional rift into this world and persist here for some time before being swept back to their world. As such, the stories the mask-forms tell—of having adventures and an identity separate from the teen prodigy—are true.

Example: You dream of a world where superpowered people are an everyday occurrence. More and more, your dreams are dominated by thoughts and memories of an alternate world where you possess incredible abilities that defy science. And then, one day, your alternate form comes back with you from your dream . . .

CURSE

Some sort of spiritual power has infected the PCs, granting them prodigy powers. This force is not based on science and most likely comes from a non-human intelligence. Whether this ability can be removed, changed, or detected is something for the GM to determine—and for the PCs to puzzle out.

Example: You and your friends were all present at the Witches' Burn celebration. This party is thrown every year at the old stone circle to celebrate the lynching and burning of Abigail Ezrah, thought to be a witch. Then, at midnight, you saw the old crone and the strangeness began . . .

DRUGS

Some sort of chemical unlocked the prodigy abilities in the teens. Perhaps they were purposely injected (a school vaccination, perhaps?) or unknowingly exposed (they swam in a river ripe with chemical runoff). Either way, the chemicals either woke latent abilities or created those abilities wholesale. Perhaps their prodigy powers will lose potency after a time and require a new "dose" of the chemical, or maybe they're permanent.

Example: PolymerDyne Inc. settled out of court with the subdivision of homes that housed you and your friends. For nearly a decade, the company illegally dumped an undisclosed chemical into the ground in the area. Now, you and your friends are teenagers, and the case is long forgotten. But this year, something is different . . .

EVOLUTION

The teen PCs represent the next step in human evolution. They appear normal, but their bodies contain unique structures that allow them to manipulate reality. Their parents or other people in the town presumably also have such genetics (if there are other prodigies). Why the genetics manifested here and now remains a key mystery for the PCs to solve.

Example: Your uncle was a mind reader, or so he claimed. He had a power he called the "look" that could open up other people's minds. He said you had it, too, only you were much, much more powerful. The headaches began during the summer, and now that they've grown worse, you're starting to see what your uncle meant about the power . . .

INFECTION

The teen PCs are infected by some sort of disease that caused changes in their body and brain, allowing them to see and manipulate reality on the atomic level. Perhaps this disease is debilitating, degenerative, or, at worst, terminal. How the PCs discover the truth without being exposed to the medical community is great fodder for adventures.

Example: You and your friends found the man in his car on the side of the road while riding down to the beach. It was a military car with United States Army plates, and it looked like he'd been living in it for a long time. The man was sick, and then he died. The army showed up and took the body and car. Now you and your friends are sick, and you are beginning to think it's more than just some cold . . .

POSSESSION

Non-human consciousnesses possess the teen PCs, allowing them to access incredible powers. The purposes of such immaterial beings are up to the GM to devise, and while they are in general beneficial to the teen they take over, their methods and end goal may be in direct conflict with the PCs' wishes. They might ultimately be the enemy the PCs face!

Example: The voice tells you things. Secrets. Facts that on your own you could never know. It says that if you let it in, it can make you powerful. It can give you abilities unimaginable in the everyday world.

TRAUMA, SURGERY, OR VIOLENCE

A car accident. A bump on the head. Treatment for a particularly dangerous disease. Physical trauma can awaken powers in the PCs. Perhaps all the PCs suffered life-threatening events, had seizures, or fell into comas. Maybe they flatlined suddenly, or they were all struck by lightning during the same thunderstorm.

Example: At 3:57 p.m. on July 22, you all dropped to the ground like puppets whose strings had been suddenly clipped. It was only later, when you and the other teens compared notes, that you figured this out, of course. Is that what gave you the power to make the mask?

CHAPTER 18

MEMENTOS

Mementos are mundane items somehow imbued with a one-off superpowered effect that prodigies can sense and activate. These are, in Cypher System parlance, *cyphers*. In *Unmasked*, they take the form of everyday items (such as a toothbrush, car keys, or a typewriter) that—to prodigies—seem to glow with a powerful internal fire and somehow possess the ability to do the impossible.

When they are used, each memento releases a *feeling* (hence their name). This feeling is clear to the prodigy activating the memento, but not overwhelming. For example, tapping a memento contained within a troll doll might make the prodigy feel—for a moment—the hopeful expectance and excitement of Christmas morning, but this is more of a side effect than something central to the power of the item. Still, this odd runoff of emotion might hint at the memento's origins.

WHERE MEMENTOS ARE FOUND

At the beginning of an *Unmasked* campaign, mementos begin *everywhere* in the wild. Prodigies can walk the streets of their town and see a lawn sprinkler memento, an evergreen car freshener memento, and a bird house memento, all on the same street. But as time goes on and prodigies begin sorting and collecting them, the mementos rapidly vanish and are gathered in stashes. Sometimes, they even seem to move on their own.

Mementos also seem to repel one another. Over time, a pile of mementos will naturally become scattered by normal people and improbable events. For example, a stash of mementos placed in a garden shed might be collected by the fire department after they are called to the shed to control a weird, brief fire there. Those same mementos might be split up

over time, some ending up on the shelf of the fire chief, others in a garage sale after sitting in a rubbish pile, and others still in the back seat of a gardener's car. In any case, they seem to push away from one another in ways that go unnoticed by the everyday world. It's very rare for a handful of mementos to remain in one place together for very long. The more mementos, the faster the scattering effect seems to happen.

APPEARANCE AND POWER LEVEL

All prodigies (in teen and mask-form) can see mementos. To a prodigy, a memento is a mundane object that appears lit with a halo of power, fire, or energy, or emits an "aura." Prodigies have a difficult time explaining this phenomenon to non-prodigies; it's instinctual for them. To the rank and file of humanity, mementos are mundane—even boring—objects that normal people simply overlook.

Seeing a memento is enough to tell the

prodigy how powerful it is. The higher the level of the memento, the brighter the effect is. In gameplay, this means a prodigy PC can glance at a memento and know its level, even if they can't touch it.

COLLECTION AND USE

When a prodigy PC touches a memento, they instantly know what it can do. This is innate, unconscious knowledge, but it requires touch. For example, at a glance, a prodigy PC would know a memento consisting of a pair of keys was level 6, but only after touching it would they know it allowed the user to teleport. A PC need not activate a memento to understand its function.

Both the teen and mask-form of a prodigy can pick up and use mementos. They do so as a normal action during a turn. All mementos in *Unmasked* are one use.

MEMENTOS INTERFERING WITH PRODIGY SIGHT

Prodigies can see one another in much the same way they can see mementos: the objects and prodigies appear as if they are illuminated by a supernatural fire. Because of this "light," any area with a large number of mementos in it may interfere with prodigy sight, in much the same way a room full of bright lights might make it difficult to see.

Any enclosed area with six or more mementos in proximity to one another, or any open area with ten or more mementos in proximity to one another, makes prodigy sight difficult. An attempt to see or gauge a prodigy or memento under these conditions requires a difficulty 4 Intellect roll.

MEMENTO ORIGINS

Why do mementos exist? As for the prodigy phenomenon, the GM doesn't have to begin the game with the answer to this question all figured out. Instead, they can wait for gameplay, PC action, or some other cool inciting event to give them an idea on just how to sell it to the players.

Why mementos exist, how they replenish, and what their ultimate purpose is remains up to the GM to establish. In the beginning of any *Unmasked* campaign, mementos are just amazing "one-use superpowers in a can" for the PCs to use to even out the playing field as needed. As gameplay develops and mementos begin to move around, get depleted, and somehow replenish, the PCs might start asking questions about them.

Sometimes, the GM might decide they are beyond explanation, while other GMs will have a very careful explanation for their origin. In either case, the GM should have an idea of where mementos come from and how they replenish before it becomes an issue for the PCs. Below are some secrets about mementos (but these are not the only possibilities, of course) that the GM can sprinkle throughout the game:

Mementos contain prodigy power, and when enough is released, new prodigies manifest.

Mementos slowly suck up ambient power over time until they become "live."

Mementos are created by prodigies transforming into their mask-form nearby.

Mementos are constant in number. Using one up creates another.

Mementos multiply. When enough are placed in proximity to one another for a sufficient period, others are created nearby.

When gathered together, mementos cause bad luck. When carefully spaced, however, they may produce the opposite effect for a short time.

Mementos are runoff from whatever force makes the prodigies' powers work, and their beginning location marks an important conduit to this other, unseen world.

CREATING YOUR OWN MEMENTOS

Creating your own mementos is incredibly easy. Select a boring object in 1986, add a cypher ability from the *Cypher System Rulebook*, set a level, come up with some sort of emotion associated with its activation, and you're done.

Good GMs will keep mementos in steady supply. As they are used up, more should turn up in the world, so they can serve their purpose as a way for players to level the playing field just a little bit when things become too difficult.

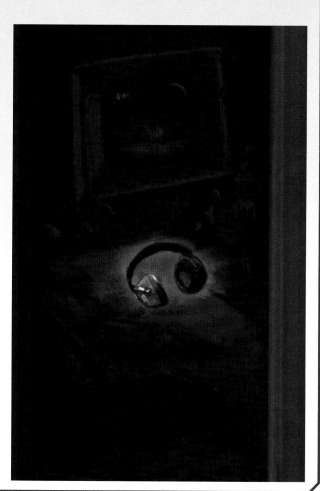

MEMENTO LIMIT AND "SLIPPERINESS"

Prodigies can only carry so many mementos. The cypher limits presented in the *Cypher System Rulebook* also apply to mementos, but in *Unmasked*, excess mementos carried above that limit *do not disappear*. Instead, every memento above the memento limit makes all actions for the character one step more difficult as long as the PC holds the excess mementos. This is reflected as a certain slipperiness in probability—what a lay person might call a run of bad luck.

The GM should portray this as extraordinarily dramatic bad luck for the affected party. For example, if the mask-form (or the teen) were carrying two extra mementos over their limit, all of their actions would be two steps more difficult. A bad outcome might just be a normal failure, but it might also involve slipping and falling on their face on level ground, a ladder coming apart in their hands as they scale a building, or a soft drink exploding in their face while they're trying to look suave. Often, such disasters cause the character to drop several of their mementos. Whatever the negative outcome, if it's caused by exceeding the memento limit, it should be something striking.

In this manner, carrying more than one or two mementos over the memento limit is a recipe for disaster, and only characters with power shifts to offset the effect should attempt it for long.

MEMENTO LIST

Below are a bunch of options for mementos the prodigies can find. This is by no means an exhaustive list. The GM should feel free to make up their own mementos or select them from the cypher list in the *Cypher System Rulebook*.

ALIEN DOLL

Level: 1d6

Effect: If the doll (of a famous movie alien) is kissed, the user is overcome with the feeling of lying down on clean sheets, and they can emit light from any portion of their body at any intensity up to that of a normal flashlight for six hours. The user can turn this effect completely off or on at will.

FLOPPY DISK

Level: 1d6

Effect: If the disk is destroyed (ripped or cut, for example), the user is overcome with the nervous feeling of going to school for the first time, and they can select an inanimate object of up to 2 tons (2 t), which then floats a few inches off the ground for two hours. The object can be easily pushed in any direction, but will remain close to the ground. When the effect ends, the object drops to the ground.

FRUIT ROLL

Level: 1d6

Effect: If the fruit roll is eaten, the user is overcome with a momentary feeling of having food poisoning, and gains the ability to burn any memento they are holding to restore a number of points equal to the memento's level to any of their Pools.

GOOGLY EYES

Level: 1d6 + 3

Effect: When the googly eyes are affixed to a surface, the user is overcome by a feeling of vertigo, as if they were climbing a great height, and for the next 24 hours, they can see through the googly eyes as if these were a regular pair of eyes. At the end of that time, the googly eyes' adhesive fails.

GUITAR PICK

Level: 1d6

Effect: If the pick is placed beneath the tongue, the user feels the bell ring on the last day of school and immediately increases their Might, Intellect, or Speed Edge (user's choice) by 1 for one hour.

HALL PASS

Level: 1d6

Effect: If the hall pass is folded up and stepped on, the user feels as if they had leaped from a swing at the top of its arc, and they gain the ability to be effectively invisible to all normals for one hour. Only prodigies can see them or their actions. All others ignore them, no matter how outrageous or violent their actions.

Cypher Limits, page 341

A Listing of Various Cyphers, page 345

JUNK COMPUTER PRINTOUT

Level: 1d6 + 2

Effect: If the printout is ripped up, the user feels the fear of seriously injuring themselves for the first time and gains the ability to see the positive and negative intentions of all people within sight (even prodigies). This is portrayed as a black or white "aura" on the target. Those with evil intentions have a black aura. Those with neutral or positive intentions have a white one.

LP RECORD

Level: 1d6 + 2

Effect: If the LP is broken, the user feels as if they're getting ready to surprise someone for their birthday, and their aura becomes invisible to prodigy sight for two hours. Other prodigies looking at them see only a normal person. Mementos the user carries glow normally.

METAL TOY CAR

Level: 1d6 + 1

Effect: If the car is filled with dirt, the user is overcome with the feeling of accomplishment one gets from building a snow fort and gains the ability to instantly transport one handheld object they are grasping anywhere they have been in the last 24 hours. The object blinks into existence at that location outside of visual range of anyone present and seems to have simply "appeared."

NAIL CLIPPERS

Level: 1d6

Effect: When this pair of travel nail clippers is put in the mouth, the memento emits the feeling of accidentally dropping fresh food on the ground on a summer's day. It immediately either restores 5 points to two stat Pools or moves the subject up one step on the damage track (user's choice). The user can use this effect on others as well.

NEON SHOELACES

Level: 1d6 + 2

Effect: If the shoelaces are cut in half, the user feels the satisfaction of eating ice cream on a hot summer day and can then read the intentions of every normal (that is, every non-prodigy) in sight for 24 hours. Such indications are expressed in a single word—worried, working, hurried, scared, etc.— appearing over the subject's head. As intentions change, so does the word.

PLASTIC HINGED TOY BLOCK

Level: 1d6

Effect: If the hinge is pulled into two pieces and reconnected, the user is overcome with the exhilaration of getting their driver's license and it allows them to send a ten-word message telepathically to anyone they have spoken to in the last 24 hours, regardless of the distance. The subject receives this message whether they want to or not.

PLASTIC PARACHUTE MAN

Level: 1d6

Effect: When this toy is thrown in the air and begins to parachute, the user is overcome by an intense need to eat pizza and all damage inflicted within a 20-foot (6 m) radius is automatically reduced from any amount to 1 point for three rounds. This affects enemies as well as allies.

PUZZLE CUBE

Level: 1d6 + 2

Effect: When this spinning multicolored puzzle cube is solved by a prodigy, the user is overcome by the feeling of being terribly embarrassed, and the cube becomes a bomb that explodes in an immediate radius, inflicting damage equal to the memento's level.

ROTARY PHONE

Level: 1d6

Effect: If the handset is smashed, the user feels the thrill of a first kiss and is granted the ability to sound convincing to any non-prodigy for one hour, no matter what they say. This is treated as reducing the difficulty of all non-prodigy interaction tasks by two steps. Even if such a task fails, the affected party assumes it is an honest mistake.

RUINED EIGHT-TRACK TAPE

Level: 1d6 + 2

Effect: If the dried-out tape is pulled out and eaten, the user feels drunk on a moonlit winter's night and can understand anything anyone says, regardless of language, obstruction, or other restrictive effects. For example, a prodigy using this memento could understand someone speaking in Mandarin, French, code, or binary, or even make out the words of someone who is trying to speak with a gag in their mouth or who is mute.

STOP SIGN

Level: 1d6 + 3

Effect: If the stop sign is tapped with the forefinger, the user feels as if they've been caught cheating at a test, and all projectiles in flight in a 50-foot (15 m) radius stop moving and drop to the ground, instantly spent. This does not affect flying people, energy blasts, or other nonphysical projectiles.

STRONGMAN ACTION FIGURE

Level: 1d6

Effect: If the arm is removed from the figure, the user feels like they're sneaking out late at night after curfew, and they can spend points from any Pool, converting them to an additional point of damage for a single attack.

TWIRLY PENCIL

Level: 1d6 + 2

Effect: If the pencil is snapped in two, the user is overcome with the feeling of losing a pet to old age, and the memento transforms their skin into a strange, metallic form of organic tissue, granting them a +2 bonus to Armor for twenty minutes.

VELCRO-SEALED NOTEBOOK

Level: 1d6

Effect: If the only page in the notebook is torn out, the user feels the joy of their favorite song coming on the radio and can store any inanimate object up to 10 tons (9 t) in the notebook for up to 24 hours. While the object is stored in the notebook, it is only a notebook. Anyone can carry it, but only a prodigy can see and release the object inside, which reappears in the nearest unoccupied open space that can accommodate it.

CHAPTER 19

MASKS

It's possible that during play, the GM will need to come up with some masks or mask forms on the fly. Alternatively, players may want some inspiration for devising a mask for their character. Use the following masks and mask-forms as needed to trigger ideas, add depth, or otherwise enhance your game.

KITSUNE

The Mask: This is a carefully fashioned and painted traditional Japanese Kitsune (fox) mask, the kind used in several festival and kabuki plays. It's white, with some red and black lines representing the eyebrows and whiskers. As a distinct feature, it has a few red threads hanging from one of the eye sockets, as if it were crying tears of blood.

Mask-Form: The Kitsune appears sometimes as a conventional fox, sometimes as a normal person of Japanese descent, and sometimes as a mixture of both (a "fox person"). This Thinker can see through, change, and project illusions of all sorts, but it always carefully allows its opponent a chance to discover it—otherwise, where is the fun in it? The Kitsune is wise, nimble, and mischievous.

Kitsune: level 7, stealth, trickery, and illusion as level 9 (power shifted); health 65; can inflict 7 points of damage from a bite, or as much as 9 points of damage (if it spends power shifts) from a surprise attack; power shifts: +2 to stealth, +2 to resilience, +1 to intelligence

SHAMANISTIC

The Mask: The mask is fashioned from a turn-of-the-century anatomical skull, which has been cut and shaved down so that a rawhide band can be tied about the head to hold it up in front of the face. The skull is adorned with various torn and ruined stickers from pharmacy bottles.

Mask-Form: The mask-form of Shamanistic is a small, somber Thinker whose powers involve the creation and spread of disease. When Shamanistic wishes, it can spray a target with a debilitating sickness, speed up their metabolism with a bizarre, never-before-seen infection, or give them specific hallucinations. The biological processes of the body are Shamanistic's playground.

Shamanistic: level 6, disease, health, and biology as level 10 (power shifted); health 60; can infect any target in short range for 6 points of disease damage; power shifts: +2 to resilience, +3 can be assigned to hinder or help others through strange infections

SHADOW LINK

The Mask: The mask that manifests Link is fashioned from an old T-shirt showing Boris Karloff as Frankenstein's Monster that is bound with a wallet chain and locked in place by a padlock. When worn, the prodigy is transformed into a living shadow known as Link.

Mask-Form: This mask-form is an indistinct Changer composed of liquid shadow. The darkness spreads, congeals, and expands around it in the air like squid ink in the water. The main form of the Shadow Link is never clearly visible, though sometimes the shadow liquid retreats to reveal the vague outline of an imposing human figure. These tentacles of shadow can focus into solid tentacles of unlight that can grab, throw, and pull in the unwitting.

Shadow Link: level 7, grabbing, throwing, and stealth as level 10 (power shifted); health 65; can smash a target for 10 points of damage; can use its shadow tentacles to climb and traverse large distances; power shifts: +2 to strength

VORTEX

The Mask: The mask that manifests Vortex is an extremely smooth oval shape that covers the entire face and is a deep black color with a mirror sheen, made of meticulously placed pieces of a smashed mirror glued onto the surface of a fencing mask. When it is worn and activated, a continually swirling vortex filled with stars appears in front of the mask-form.

Mask-Form: The mask-form of Vortex is a thin, tall Changer that can mime movements which then play out in the world as a swirling mass of reflective mirrors. These powers include telekinesis, regeneration, and the ability to absorb the life force of others while temporarily stealing any powers they might possess so the wearer can use them.

Vortex: level 8, telekinesis and smashing as level 9 (power shifted); health 65; telekinesis attack inflicts 9 points of damage; regenerates 2 points per round when living targets are in short range; power shifts: +1 to resilience, +2 can be assigned by the wearer of the mask to imitate any power present within short range, although the power vanishes when the source of power leaves short range

STORMCHASER

The Mask: This mask is a ruin of storm-destroyed debris from Long Island's latest hurricane: a portion of a bent street sign, cloth from a ripped parachute, and torn straps from a ruined backpack all bound together to form a strange hood.

Mask-Form: The mask-form of Stormchaser is a stout, strong Changer whose powers include the ability to "absorb, amplify, store, and redirect weather." When the teen-form or the mask-form is exposed to a weather type, it can produce that weather effect locally for up to an hour per minute of exposure. This effect is stored for 24 hours, whereupon it vanishes if not used. Stormchaser can also compress this effect, doubling what was "stored" for one round—for example if it was exposed to 60 mph winds, it could project 120 mph winds for a single round.

Stormchaser: level 9, weather manipulation and flight as level 10 (power shifted); health 85; can batter a target with winds for 9 points of damage or with a single lightning strike for 12 points; can fly short distances by riding the winds; power shifts: +2 to resilience, +3 to weather manipulation

PATCHWORK

The Mask: The mask appears to be a patchwork of red, blue, green, yellow, orange, and purple puzzle pieces in no discernible pattern or order, bound together with packing tape, and backed with a bandana, to which it is fastened with thread.

Mask-Form: The mask-form of Patchwork is a small but muscular Smasher whose powers involve seeing *through* conventional reality to identify the "focal points" on people and objects that can be controlled. To this being, the world is an odd array of shapes and colors which it can "read" and—at the proper time—manipulate. When Patchwork wishes, it can push or pull on one of these focal points, spending a power shift. It can spend any number of power shifts in this manner, but once all 5 are spent, it cannot do so again until it rests (at the GM's discretion).

Patchwork: level 9, lifting, stopping, or throwing as level 11 (power shifted); health 99; can inflict 9 points of damage from a punch or as much as 12 points of damage (if it spends power shifts); power shifts: +5 to be assigned to individual "focal points"

CHAPTER 20

QUICK ADVENTURE GENERATOR

FINDING THE RIGHT TEEN-TO-SUPERS RATIO

Some GMs will want to lean heavily on the superpowered action and tread lightly on the teen drama. Sometimes this is okay, but it should not be sustained.

It's essential for *Unmasked* to remain a game about teens who can manifest superhero forms, not a game about superheroes trapped inside teenagers. This is a hugely important distinction to make for many reasons, but most of all, because the life of a teenager is something everyone can relate to.

We've all experienced those years, and we can easily imagine what it is like to be uncertain, young, and ready to enter adulthood. It is through this lens that the amazing powers of the prodigy mask-forms are introduced, making them seem more "real." Add in the need to control, hide, and conceal these powers to keep the teen's secret, and you have a rich backdrop for the teens to act in, with occasional moments of heightened tension, fear, and power when they use their mask-forms.

In playtesting, players spent most of the time in an average *Unmasked* adventure in teen-form, working on teen problems, trying to cover up and explore prodigy problems, and dealing with everyday affairs. Just a short amount of time each session was spent in mask-form (usually at the climax of some story arc or when the teen was ambushed or surprised).

An average adventure breaks down like this:

Teen problems—school work, home life, friends, and relationships (70%)

Prodigy problems—mementos, finding other prodigies, searching for clues (20%)

Mask-form manifestation—fights, using powers, etc. (10%)

WHERE TO MINE IDEAS?

There is a marvelous resource for devising the basics of the teen sections of an *Unmasked* adventure: tens of thousands of hours of teen movies and TV shows. Need a central emotional conflict or arc for one of your teen PCs? Watch an episode of *Degrassi Junior High, Freaks and Geeks,* or *My So-Called Life.*

Reduce the episode to elements you can steal or mix and match: *An unrequited crush. A friend who begins experimenting with drugs. A PC's parent who begins dating a strange person who may be dangerous.* You'll soon find most of these elements can be easily slotted in and just as quickly resolved to give your game the feeling of depth needed to make the superhero elements more fantastic. A good GM will keep a running list that they can pick from when the game feels like it needs more oomph.

For the mask-forms, comic books are a ready resource for story ideas. The mask-forms are larger than life, and their motivations, hopes, and dreams are about as divorced from reality as their powers and yet, to them, just as real. Again, grab the larger story lines and render them down to their core elements: *The big theft. The secret plan. The brainwashing. The loved ones in danger.* Again, keeping a list of ideas like this on a sheet to throw into the game when it needs a kick in the pants is a good practice.

Sometimes, in a pinch, a GM needs to make up something on the fly for their PCs. To that end, this section provides an adventure generator; roll 3d10 and consider the WHO, WHY, and WHAT. It is likely the GM will have to finesse the results, but overall the outcome should be relatively straightforward.

WHO

1	Preternatural threat
2	Teen
3	Townsperson
4	Classmate
5	Teacher
6	Bully
7	Authority figure
8	Parent
9	College kid
10	Prodigy

WHY

1	Wants
2	Hates
3	Loves
4	Follows
5	Steals
6	Loses
7	Discovers
8	Sees
9	Hides
10	Hurts or destroys

WHAT

1	Memento
2	Mask
3	Records
4	Property
5	Classmate
6	Valuables (burglary)
7	Media (film, pictures, audio)
8	Drugs
9	Car
10	Money

SPECIAL

(If you roll two or more of the same number, roll on this chart and take this result instead.)

1	Murder
2	Runaway
3	Fire
4	Vehicle crash
5	Kidnapping
6	Drugs
7	Explosion
8	Natural disaster (tornado, earthquake, etc.)
9	Corruption
10	Hostage situation

Example: The GM rolls a 2, 1, and 3 and gets: Who: Teen. Why: Wants. What: Records. The PCs are approached by some overachieving students and asked to remove a particular portion of paperwork from their permanent record. Will the PCs help? Or report them?

Example: The GM rolls a 5, 3, and 1 and gets: Who: Teacher. Why: Loves. What: Memento. A teacher is never without a coffee mug with "GREAT ESCAPES PARK" on it, one which thrums with incredible power. What other prodigies might be after it?

Example: The GM rolls an 8, 3, and 5 and gets: Who: Parent. Why: Loves. What: Classmate. A parent has inappropriate feelings for their kid's classmate, and drama ensues.

Example: The GM rolls a 7, 7, and 1. The duplicate 7s means the GM rolls another d10 and considers the SPECIAL chart. The GM rolls a 5. A kidnapping occurs in the town, perhaps of a child the PCs know. Will they become involved?

CHAPTER 21

MISTER MONSTER

Like the PCs, Arnie Desedero made his mask but told no one. However, unlike the PCs, he never even put it on. The voice that came from it scared him too deeply. It said awful things. But due to the torment he suffers every day, he finds himself listening to it more and more—about how it could make people pay for making his life hell. The mask, which calls itself Mister Monster, wants to get revenge on all the popular students who have picked on Arnie since the seventh grade. It's only fair, Mister Monster says, after all the pain they have caused Arnie.

All Arnie has to do is put on the mask, and Mister Monster will do the rest. Now, the voice talks to Arnie at night, and Arnie feels increasingly like the mask is his only friend. Soon, he will succumb to the voice. Will the PCs be able to intervene and prevent a possible tragedy?

ARNOLD DESEDERO

Arnie is a frail, withdrawn sixteen-year-old who is an incredibly polite and upstanding member of the school's sophomore class. Arnie volunteers to pick up trash at the Strand on the weekend, helps out at the senior center (where he is well liked), and is the apple of every teacher's eye. Even the gym teacher, Mr. Sullivan, lets Arnie—due to his asthma—ride the bleachers and do homework instead of run laps.

Arnie is an avid Boy Scout, and he has a great relationship with his family and even a girlfriend, Patty Boyd, who lives in New Jersey and whom he met at computer camp in Piscataway the year before.

It is also well known (at least among the students) that Arnie somehow raised the ire of Steven Yarborough, the school's star quarterback, sometime in the past. Steven and his team do everything they can to make Arnie's life absolutely miserable. Of course, no one says anything about this to the school staff.

Steven is too clever to just go ahead and beat Arnie up—least not in a situation where they might be caught doing so. Instead, the athletes have played various awful pranks on Arnie. They've dumped chocolate shakes through the slots of Arnie's locker, destroying all of his schoolwork and books and leaving Arnie surrounded constantly with the faint scent of rotten milkshake. They've tripped him multiple times in the cafeteria, so much so that Arnie sits down directly when he gets his meal and often eats propped up against one of the tiled walls. Worse, and most recently, they pinned him to the ground off campus and Krazy-Glued the fingers of his right hand together. Arnie ran home and used an X-Acto knife to cut thin layers of skin away to free them. It hurt—a lot.

Arnie lives in constant fear of the football team and does everything he can to avoid them. His mask, Mister Monster, realizing its direct assault on Arnie's psyche is not working, has instead slowly goaded him into getting revenge on the football team in other ways: through mementos. The mask-form doesn't want to hurt Arnie, of course (it *is* trapped in Arnie), and it *does* want revenge on the football players, but it is also not averse to putting Arnie in situations where becoming Mister Monster might be Arnie's only viable choice.

STEVEN'S PLAN

The problem with Arnie's plan is that Steven has discovered that Arnie will be attending the fall formal with his out-of-town girlfriend. Steven plans to jump Arnie and humiliate him (or worse) outside the dance, in front of his girlfriend. This will all take place before the big game but after the team spirit rally.

Unfortunately, Arnie now carries the mask with him everywhere, and if hurt badly enough, he will likely put it on, releasing Mister Monster for the first time.

TIMELINE OF EVENTS

The following events will occur one after another, and the GM should be ready to reorient the adventure as needed due to unexpected player solutions, changes in pacing, and other factors that might shift due to PC (or NPC) action.

FRIDAY, OCTOBER 24— THE INCITING INCIDENT

The PCs find themselves front and center for a bullying incident. The GM can set it up to occur in many different ways; the teens may turn a corner and find the incident going on, it can happen in the cafeteria in front of the whole school, or it can happen somewhere in Boundary Bay.

Arnie is being pushed around by the football players Todd DeSpain and Steven Yarborough, when he falls in front of the PCs, dropping a troll doll toy that glows with significant memento power. Arnie himself does not glow as a prodigy, but he snatches up the troll doll.

Arnie keeps attempting to leave, but the football players keep blocking and shoving him. If the PCs step in, the football players begin threatening *them*. While this exchange goes on, Arnie sneaks off. If a fight breaks out, it's likely to end in a stalemate of pushing. A good way to end it is to have Ms. Hopkins, the chemistry teacher, show up and break it up. (Or, if the scene takes place outside of school, an adult or cop can do so instead.)

MONDAY, OCTOBER 27— A NORMAL SCHOOL DAY

On the Monday following the Krazy Glue attack, Arnie plans to destroy Todd DeSpain's new Mustang using a memento Mister Monster showed him. The memento looks like a single Nike shoe, but any prodigy observing it can clearly see it for what it is. Those that can touch it can tell it is a powerful destructive force that will implode all nearby matter.

But before he can enact his plan, something unforeseen happens—Steven Yarborough's locker explodes.

STEVEN'S LOCKER EXPLODES

Yasmine Blumenthal shows up a few seconds after the crowd gathers, present on the periphery, looking at the destroyed locker. She glows with the inner light of a prodigy. The locker has been reduced to a near-molten slag, as if someone had subjected it to a smelter. Everything in it is on fire or cooling from molten metal. A few seconds after the explosion, the fire alarm is tripped, the water sprinklers turn on, and everyone runs outside.

ARNIE'S BIG SECRET

Though he is a prodigy and he's made a mask, Arnie has never worn it, because he fears it. For some reason, he does not "glow" as other prodigies do—at least not yet. If he puts the mask on and becomes Mister Monster, from that point on he will "glow" normally in Prodigy Sight, but as far as the PCs are concerned, at first glance Arnie appears mundane (except, perhaps, for the memento in his possession, although this in and of itself is not unusual in Boundary Bay).

Arnie has access to a hoard of mementos he has gathered and hidden in a field near Ocean View High School. He plans to resist Mister Monster (who scares him) and use the amazing powers of the mementos to enact his revenge against Steven Yarborough and the rest of the football team.

First, he will destroy Todd DeSpain's new Mustang in the parking lot with a memento.

Then, he will ruin the team's uniforms with another memento at the team spirit rally.

Finally, he plans to confront and disable Steve Yarborough using another memento before the big game and then to set him up to become the laughingstock of the school.

THE OTHER PRODIGY

Another prodigy hovers at the periphery of this relationship: Yasmine Blumenthal, who has a terrible crush on Arnold Desedero and follows him around. She has noticed Steven Yarborough's abuse, and she has decided her mask-form—a creature that calls itself "Suomi"—can do something about it. She has no idea Arnie is a prodigy as well (though, at a glance, she'll be able to tell that the PCs are).

Suomi: level 7; health 70; Armor 2; can burn or freeze any target it can touch, inflicting 7 points of damage that ignores 2 points of Armor; claws or horns inflict 5 points of damage; power shifts: +2 to dexterity, +1 to healing, and +2 to strength

Yasmine is an outgoing yet bookish seventeen-year-old girl who is much taller than her classmates. She is always eager to help and make things better. Having a strong sense of self-esteem, she cares little about what others think of her (a rare trait in a high school student). She goes out of her way to appear aloof, especially around Arnie, though she is deeply in love with him.

When Yasmine is confronted by Arnie or with questions about Arnie, her normal confident demeanor vanishes; she is replaced by a stuttering, blushing girl who does anything she can to disengage. It is a striking transformation.

Her mask-form, Suomi, is an 8-foot-tall (2 m tall), almost satyr-like creature. It looks *mostly* human, except for its legs, which have reversed knees like a horse's and which end in hooves. It has stubby bone-ivory horns on its head and empty yellow eyes. Its skin blends into a thick, short white fur. It is big, fast, and strong, and it can somehow focus and control heat—concentrating it or dispersing it. Suomi speaks broken English, interspersed with words in an unrecognizable foreign tongue.

WHY STEVEN HATES ARNIE

When he was in sixth and seventh grade, Arnie tutored Steven's youngest sister, Clementine, before she was forced to switch schools. Clementine suffers from severe learning disabilities. She fell for Arnie, but after a brief puppy-love phase and first kiss, Arnie made it clear that he didn't feel the same for her. Clementine goes to a special education program in Rockville now, but she's never forgotten about Arnie or the hurt he caused her. And Steven—who adores his little sister—has not forgotten either. He's going to make Arnie *pay*.

Arnie will never admit to this episode without somehow being coerced, and Steven will never bring it up, because he promised Clementine he would say nothing about it, particularly in front of Arnie. Still, this bad blood hovers between them, and both know precisely the cause. Remember, in the "real" world, no one thinks they're the villain.

Steven's friends commiserate with the football player in the parking lot until someone points out that Arnie is laughing. Those present will note that Steven drags his finger across his throat while looking at Arnie indicating, "You're dead." Arnie stops smiling and vanishes into the crowd. However, it's Yasmine—and more specifically Suomi—who is responsible.

TUESDAY, OCTOBER 28— A NORMAL SCHOOL DAY

On Tuesday, Arnie is getting ready to exact revenge during the team spirit rally when he is set upon and pushed by some football players. But since Steven is not with the group, the athletes let him off after a few shoves, and it doesn't escalate into a manifestation of Mister Monster—yet.

THE PUSHING INCIDENT

Arnie is caught by four members of the football team near the back exit of the school, which leads to a few picnic tables in the back. The group drags him outside and begins to push him from person to person, antagonizing him and asking whether he was behind the slagging of Steven's locker.

Arnie is terrified but says nothing; he only cries silently. Twice he's thrown to the ground, and the second time he tears his pants. Then, just before things escalate, the home economics teacher, Mrs. Kalakis, steps in and stops the melee, threatening the team. She says if she ever hears of them picking on Arnie again, she'll go directly to Coach Sullivan.

Grumbling, the athletes disperse, and Mrs. Kalakis helps Arnie inside. Before she can take him to the nurse's office, Arnie begs off and disappears. He claims he is fine.

THE IMPLODED CAR

Todd DeSpain received his new red 1985 Mustang from his father for his birthday in August. It is his pride and joy. He always parks it close to the school and visits it several times a day (often with friends in tow). Around 2 p.m., a car alarm begins to bray in the parking lot. It goes off for a short time, makes some weird noises, and then

falls silent. This happens in the middle of class. The alarm sounds familiar to Todd, but the teacher—who can't stand him—won't allow him to leave until the end of the period.

Todd rushes out at the bell and finds his red Mustang in its parking space—but it has been crushed into a 3-foot (1 m) sphere of ruined metal. Liquid from inside the vehicle (gasoline, oil, wiper fluid, and water) has sprayed everywhere.

The car is utterly destroyed. It is so round you can push it around as a solid, 3,500-pound metal ball. As Todd weeps and swears and circles the wreck, many students gather. People whisper and some laugh, but Todd is incensed.

The scene ends with Todd screaming, "Who did this!? WHO!?" No one answers. A teacher—Mr. Fedov—begins to talk with Todd about the incident, and the school calls the police. As Mr. Fedov takes Todd inside to the office, the students disperse, and school goes on.

THE SCHOOL PERKS UP

Those asking around soon find some juicy gossip: Steven Yarborough's talking about hurting Arnie. There are also rumors that Todd's car was destroyed by the football team from the next county over, the Rockville

WHERE WAS ARNIE?

PCs that poke around can discover that Arnie slipped out of Mrs. Wexler's AP English class at 1:34 p.m., shortly before the car alarm triggered. Yasmine Blumenthal had a "skip period" with no class, but persistent PCs can find out that she was seen near the back of the building at about that time, on the other side of the building from the parking lot. The witnesses say she was watching someone cross the soccer field into the woods back there, though they can't say who that person was (it was Arnie, retrieving the memento to destroy the car).

Corsairs. Many on the team are discussing whether to gather up a group and drive over there to exact revenge after school.

THE POLICE

Two policemen from the Boundary Bay police department, Detective Graham Arnette and Officer Dustin Wright, arrive. After examining the "car" and being suitably impressed by the level of the "prank," they decide they are going to question the teachers about who was out of class during fifth period, which coincided with the alarm being triggered.

This goes on for the rest of the school day, with the two police officers walking around the school and stopping passersby—seemingly at random—to ask them questions. *Where were you when the car alarm went off? Do you know Todd DeSpain? Do you know of anyone who held a grudge against DeSpain?*

The police are all bark and no bite. They may try to intimidate students by implying they possess inside knowledge of what's gone on or have access to a witness who saw the PC being questioned near the wreck. This is, of course, all false.

The GM should use the police as a tool to push or pull the PCs (or Arnie) in particular directions. Need to speed the story up? Have the police become interested in one PC as a suspect in the destruction of the car.

WEDNESDAY, OCTOBER 29— THE TEAM SPIRIT RALLY

Arnie plans to use another memento shown to him by Mister Monster to change the color of the football team's clothing to bright pink in the middle of the team spirit rally. The memento, which looks like a multicolored click pen (with six colors), is clearly visible as a powered item to any prodigy. He recovers it from the field and brings it to the rally in his backpack.

THE UNIFORM CHANGE

The team spirit rally occurs at 3:30 p.m. after school in the gym. Almost the entire school gathers there, as well as the teachers and staff. This rally is run twice a year to usher in and close out the football season.

First, the marching band plays some songs: "Louie Louie," the theme to *Star Wars,* and a few others. This is followed by a cheerleading display. Finally, it's time to introduce the football team.

When the team runs out into the gym, all appears normal—at first. The players trot out to the fight song booming from the band, and then, a few seconds into them circling and gathering in a group, the color on their uniforms, helmets, and shoes begins to change. A ripple of "oohs" and "ahhs" travels through the crowd as this shift becomes evident. It happens on all players at once, spreading from the middle of the uniform outward, replacing the blue and gray of Ocean View with a bright, sickly pink. The players cease clapping and goggle at one another. The music stops midtrack. The talking in the stands stops, and the gym falls completely silent.

After a minute, someone in the crowd shouts, "AWESOME!" and everyone begins clapping, shouting, and screaming. It is the most amazing thing they've ever seen! The team is confused at first, but it soon embraces the adulation. What else are the football players going to do?

BEHIND THE SCENES AT THE RALLY

Those watching for prodigy powers or mementos at work (perhaps those on guard after Steven's locker was destroyed) see several glowing individuals and objects in the crowd. Yasmine Blumenthal glows as a prodigy, as does the stapler she takes from her backpack and then quickly puts away as the crowd begins to react to the uniform change. It's difficult to see whether the memento was used up when it disappears into her bag.

Arnie is there as well. He doesn't glow, but those watching him carefully see something flash in his hand briefly just as the team enters the gym, and just as suddenly, Arnie is lost in the standing, shouting crowd of people.

TALKING TO ARNIE OR YASMINE AFTERWARD

Arnie seems upset and leaves rapidly after the cheering dies down. Teen PCs can easily intercept him and talk to him in the hall, but he seems distant. He's mad his prank didn't make Steven look like an idiot; if anything, it made him more popular. But it's easy to misread Arnie's furtiveness as his hurry to escape running into Steven. Searching his pack (something he will protest) reveals a normal-looking notebook and a six-color pen (drained of its memento power). Arnie keeps his Mister Monster mask in his front pants pocket, but its glow is not visible through the jeans.

Yasmine leaves shortly after Arnie but hangs back. If she's confronted, she seems guilty. She is obviously a prodigy of some power. Her face turns bright pink, and she denies everything and does her best to flee the scene. If she is asked about Arnie, she blushes crimson red. If the questions persist, she runs off, making up some excuse. In her backpack is a stapler that is a powerful memento, as well as her mask (an odd ski mask with television cable wrapped around it), which also glows.

ESCALATION

PCs who become too zealous in interacting with Arnie may end up facing Mister Monster. Anyone attacking Arnie or trying to seize his mask will be met with Arnie putting it on and letting Mister Monster out for the first time.

Such a manifestation will be striking. Arnie suddenly transforms into a giant, hulking shadow that emits thousands of moans, roars, and mutterings. Its face has a dozen red eyes in a sea of perfect black. Its teeth are yellowed fangs that seem to drift around its body as needed. It is HUGE.

It attacks the source of the threat to Arnie and then vanishes into a nearby shadow. From this point on, Arnie glows as a prodigy, and his attitude seems to change. He becomes more brash and demanding, and he pushes back when picked on.

TALKING TO THE TEAM

The team has *no idea* what's happened to their clothing and gear, now somehow all a uniform pink that will remain so—shoes shoelaces, their helmets, everything. Some of the boys think it was the coach. Others, the school. Still others, some other teammate who has yet to come forward.

Talking to Steven Yarborough about it gives a very similar response. He's confused, but he also thinks it's kind of funny, and it turned out to be cool, so . . .

THURSDAY, OCTOBER 30— THE FALL FORMAL

Arnie intends simply to go to the dance with his out-of-town girlfriend, Patty Boyd, who knows nothing of his troubles. But Steven Yarborough has other plans: he will ambush and beat up Arnie in front of his date outside the dance.

Clever PCs might find out about this plan in many ways:

- Talking to Steven as if the PCs *also* hated Arnie.
- Talking to one of the dumber teammates as if Steven had already told the PCs the plan, tricking them into spilling the beans.
- Searching Steven's backpack, which might reveal a note outlining the plan, or a list of people going to the formal with Arnie and Patty's names circled, along with a stick figure with Xs for eyes next to them.

If Arnie has previously manifested as Mister Monster, he now glows as a prodigy. This change has caught the attention of his unrequited (and unknown) admirer Yasmine. She now thinks they are *destined* to be with one another—they are the same!

PATTY BOYD

Arnie's out-of-town girlfriend is a loud, funny sixteen-year-old who is very, very much into computers. Patty and Arnie met at computer camp the year before, and while there, their relationship developed into something a bit more than friendship. Since that time, Arnie and Patty have traded letters as well as postcards with funny, short BASIC programs that do goofy things.

Patty arrives in town on Wednesday, October 29, with her mom. The two are staying at a small motel in Rockville. Though her parents trust her and want to make her happy, and though they like Arnie, they of course do not want her staying by herself with a *boy*. They plan to let the couple go to the dance, Patty and her mom will stay in the motel until Halloween morning, and then they'll drive back to New Jersey.

THE AMBUSH AND PUNCH

Patty and Arnie are dropped off at the fall formal at 7:30 p.m. She wears a blue dress, and Arnie a powder-blue tuxedo. As they walk toward the gym, where the dance is being held, the football players fall in around them and begin harassing Arnie. Patty tells them to shut up and leave them alone. Other students drift by but don't stop.

If Arnie has previously manifested as Mister Monster, he glows as a prodigy here and is much more confrontational with the football players. It also means Yasmine is present, following Arnie and *her* (Patty). If a fight begins and Arnie takes out a mask, Yasmine intercedes and gets in the football players' faces. Patty is confused, Steven begins swearing at Yasmine, and, if the PCs are lucky and can manage to talk him into it, they get Arnie and Patty to go inside.

If Arnie has not yet manifested as Mister Monster, he does not glow, and he's much more withdrawn when he is attacked by the football players. Patty shouts at them, but they don't seem to listen. If the PCs step in, Steven threatens *them*. Steven's group will antagonize both Arnie and the PCs, with a focus on Arnie. If the PCs can somehow manage to get Arnie to go inside (perhaps

MISTER MONSTER APPEARS
If Mister Monster manifests because of Steven Yarborough hitting Arnie outside the dance, the creature will run rampant. Its target will be Steven, followed by any member of the football team, as well as anyone who gets in its way. See Fighting Mister Monster for more details.

by playing up how much Patty needs to get out of here), it can de-escalate the situation.

If they can't and Steven Yarborough lands a good punch on Arnie, it's likely Mister Monster will make an appearance outside the dance.

THE FALL FORMAL DANCE
The fall formal dance has a vague Halloween theme. Students are dressed in formal wear, but some have masks, fake cobwebs on their clothing, or vampire teeth in their mouths. Even some of the teacher chaperones have gotten in on the fun, with one (Mr. Saia, an earth science teacher) in a full Victorian tuxedo with tails and a top hat.

If the PCs managed to break up the earlier incident and get Arnie inside without Mister Monster manifesting, he continues to enjoy the dance with Patty, occasionally casting worried glances at the football players, who watch him.

FRIDAY, OCTOBER 31— THE BIG GAME
One of the big sporting events for the Sailors, the Ocean View High School football team, takes place on Halloween. They are playing rivals, the Tambrook Musketeers, in their second match of the season. Steven and the team are looking to even out their record by defeating Tambrook. But Arnie has other ideas—he hopes to use a memento on Steven as he arrives at the game and then humiliate him in front of everyone.

However, Steven has outthought Arnie once more. Todd DeSpain—wound up by Steven Yarborough and convinced that the geek ruined his Mustang with some sort of science—follows Arnie before the big game. He finds Arnie with an umbrella (under a clear sky) waiting near the parking lot outside the football field. He drags Arnie behind the locker rooms, and the other football team members gather and begin to terrorize him.

In truth, the umbrella is a powerful memento, but Arnie is quickly disarmed. As the team begins to land hits on him, the voice of Mister Monster grows more and more powerful in his mind.

FIGHTING MISTER MONSTER
At some point, Arnie will put on his mask and become the demonic Mister Monster. This creature is the opposite of Arnie in nearly every way. It is selfish, destructive, cruel, and powerful. It has a huge, shadowy form with glowing red eyes composed of living shadow, with yellowed teeth that seem to move around its form as needed. It can vanish and reappear in shadows, teleporting between them. This means it can likely get ahead of anyone at the game looking to escape. It will cause a disruption on the football field and force the crowd to scatter—although, due to the amazing display, many will stay nearby to witness the events.

Mister Monster is all about *revenge*. It will seek out and torture the football players, picking them out of the screaming crowd one by one. It isn't out to simply kill them—it wants them to suffer. But it will attempt to injure or possibly kill anyone who tries to get in its way. If it encounters a mask-form, it will open up and lash out at full power—something which might prove deadly to any normals present. It will also do its best to prevent people from escaping.

Worse, it will use innocents as distractions, hostages, or even shields to prevent other prodigies from attacking it.

REMOVING THE MASK
Only prodigies can see and attempt to wrest the mask off Mister Monster. A prodigy struggling to take off *another* prodigy's

Mister Monster: *level 9 (+1 every time Mister Monster is injured, up to level 12); health 90; Armor 5; throwing debris at long range inflicts 9 points of damage and ignores Armor from power shifts; punch and claw swipe inflict 6 points of damage; regenerates 3 health per turn; can teleport and emerge from any shadow anywhere in sight range; power shifts: +4 to strength, +1 to resilience*

mask must succeed at a difficulty 10 task to do so. If it is pulled off, Arnie collapses in his normal form, weeping. Anyone who attempts to take off Mister Monster's mask and fails becomes the creature's primary target.

KNOCKING MISTER MONSTER OUT

Mister Monster is extremely resilient. Knocking out or "killing" the mask-form will be an outcome that PCs will be hard pressed to pull off. Those that manage to land hits on Mister Monster that somehow breach its significant armor become its prime target for a few rounds.

If a PC manages to really hurt it, Mister Monster—which has all of Arnie's knowledge—will do anything it can to make that person suffer. It will terrorize and injure the PC's friends, girlfriend or boyfriend, favorite teacher, or more, all the while telling the PC it is their fault.

SURPRISES

Other prodigy mask-forms might suddenly show up to save the PCs (or vice versa) if it is clear to the GM that the PCs are losing the fight against Mister Monster. Yasmine Blumenthal, in the form of Suomi, is an obvious candidate for a last-minute assist or designated target.

ENDING THE ADVENTURE

Mister Monster is unmasked: Prodigies that manage to unmask Arnie can hang onto and possibly destroy his mask. Outside the influence of the mask, Arnie will even *encourage them to do so*. He's afraid of it and of the power it contains.

Mister Monster is knocked out or "killed": Prodigies that manage to defeat Mister Monster with brute force will likely unmask Arnie at that point as well.

In either case, a huge superpowered fight in front of more than two hundred people is likely to have far-reaching repercussions. Will it make the news? Will the police become involved? Did anyone see the PCs change or change back?

PART 6: BACK MATTER

KICKSTARTER PLAYTESTERS AND CONTRIBUTORS

A huge thanks to every one of our Kickstarter playtesters, who helped us make this game so much better:

Aaron Mortensen
Arturo Caissut
Carlos Ovalle
Charles Myers
Chris Malone
Chris Piazzo
Chris Wine
Christian Taylor
Cory Bonifay
Dave Hanlon
Dave Moyer
Dwayne C Schueller
Eric M Jackson
George H. Trace Webster II
J Aaron Farr
James a.k.a. uber
James Gray
James McKendrew
Jeff Scifert
Jeff Wheeler
Jenifer Doll
Jessie Beasley
Jim Sharples
John Kender
Jon Schreife
Jonathon Smith
Joseph A Noll

Karl Apsel (CidCalypso)
Kurt Blanco
Lars Lauridsen
Lee Sims
Lord Deron Creag Mhor
Luc Teunen
Marc Plourde
Mark Craddock
Mark Parish
Massimo Cranchi
Matthew Sercely
Michael Goldrich
Mike Greszler
Paul Huey Hubbard
Paul Wocken
retnuH Kelly
Robert Beck
Rod Holdsworth
Ryan Dukacz
Ryan Hyde (Num'bokwei)
Shawn Lamb
Tekfactory
Teófilo Hurtado Navarro
Tim Watkins
Troy Pichelman
Zanth

With extra special thanks to our in-person playtesters:

Chris Piazzo
Troy Pichelman
Dave Hanlon
Marc Plourde
Kurt Blanco
Brett Gann
Jake Linford
Matt Jensen
Michael Parker
Tracy Gosell
Jeromy French

And triple-special thanks to our Unmasked Patrons:

Chris Piazzo
Cory Bonifay
John Smith
Michael Greszler
Ryan Williams Hyde

UNMASKED
by Dennis Detwiller

MASK FORM

NAME _____ WHO _____

IS A _____

DESCRIPTOR _____ TYPE _____

FOCUS _____

TIER	EFFORT	XP	ARMOR

MIGHT
POOL	EDGE

SPEED
POOL	EDGE

INTELLECT
POOL	EDGE

ATTACKS

MOD DAM

SKILLS

Pool | T | S | I

T = trained, S = specialized, I = inability

CYPHERS

SPECIAL ABILITIES

ADVANCEMENT

INCREASE CAPABILITIES
+4 points into stat Pools

MOVE TOWARD PERFECTION
+1 to the Edge of your choice

EXTRA EFFORT
+1 into Effort

SKILL TRAINING
Train in a skill or specialize in a trained skill

OTHER
Refer to the Cypher System Rulebook

RECOVERY ROLLS
`1d6+`

1 ACTION
10 MINS
1 HOUR
10 HOURS

DAMAGE TRACK

IMPAIRED
+1 Effort per level
Ignore minor and major effect results on rolls
Combat roll of 17-20 deals only +1 damage

DEBILITATED
Can move only an immediate distance
Cannot move if Speed Pool is 0

LIMIT _____

TEEN FORM

NAME _____

IS _____

DESCRIPTOR _____

MIGHT
POOL	EDGE

SPEED
POOL	EDGE

INTELLECT
POOL	EDGE

SKILLS

Pool | T | S | I

T = trained, S = specialized, I = inability

EQUIPMENT

CASH _____

RECOVERY ROLLS
`1d6+`

1 ACTION
10 MINS
1 HOUR
10 HOURS

DAMAGE TRACK

IMPAIRED
+1 Effort per level
Ignore minor and major effect results on rolls
Combat roll of 17-20 deals only +1 damage

DEBILITATED
Can move only an immediate distance
Cannot move if Speed Pool is 0

INDEX